A Hobbyist's Guide to THEA500 Mini

Holger Weßling

Published in 2022 by
Acorn Books
acornbooks.uk

Copyright © 2022 Holger Weßling

The right of Holger Weßling to be identified as the author of this work has been asserted in accordance with the Copyright, Designs and Patents Act 1988.

All rights reserved. No reproduction, copy or transmission of this publication may be made without express prior written permission. No paragraph of this publication may be reproduced, copied or transmitted except with express prior written permission or in accordance with the provisions of the Copyright Act 1956 (as amended). Any person who commits any unauthorised act in relation to this publication may be liable to criminal prosecution and civil claims for damage.

The views and opinions expressed herein belong to the author and do not necessarily reflect those of Acorn Books.

All attempts have been made to contact the owners of any copyrighted material and permissions sought for use in this book. If you believe any information within infringes a copyright you own, please do not hesitate to contact the publisher.

Contents

1: THEPreface 2
   1.1: THEA500 Mini 3

2: THEInterviews 5
   2.1: THEIdea 6
   2.2: Paul Andrews 7
   2.3: Darren Melbourne 16
   2.4: Dimitris Panokostas (THEDeveloper of AmiBerry) . . 17

3: THEPartners 20
   3.1: CLOANTO 21
   3.2: Koch Media 24

4: THEA500 26
   4.1: THEHardware 27
      4.1.1: THECase & Connectors 33
         4.1.1.2: USB-C power connector 34
         4.1.1.3: USB 34
         4.1.1.4: HDMI & Audio 35
         4.1.1.4.1: TV-Out 36
         4.1.1.5: LEDs & Blink codes 36
      4.1.2: THECPU (Main Processor) 36
      4.1.3: THERAM (Memory) 39
      4.1.4: THEGraphics 42
      4.1.5: LAG & Latency 44
         4.1.5.1: Display-Lag Database 45
   4.2: THEEmulator 49
   4.3: THEPeripherals 51
      4.3.1: THEGamepad 51
      4.3.2: THEMouse 57
      4.3.3: THEJoysticks (THEC64 joystick) fire buttons . . 62
      4.3.4: THEKeyboards 64
      4.3.5: Virtual Keyboard 67
      4.3.6: Using third party devices 68
   4.4: THEMaking of THEA500 Mini 70
      4.4.1: Introduction 70
      4.4.3: Production Update 71
      4.4.4: Prototypes 71
   4.5: Troubleshooting 76

5: THEUpdates & Firmware 79
   5.1: Formatting a USB-Drive 82

6: THEStart & THEOptions 85
   6.1: Starting a carousel game 92
   6.2: ADF File support 95

    6.3: Game Settings 101
    6.4: Help for a game 116
    6.5: Exiting, resuming and suspending a game. 118
    6.6: Save & load suspended games 120

7: THEGames 122
    7.1: Built-In 123
        7.1.1: Alien Breed 3D 123
        7.1.2: Alien Breed: Special Edition '92 131
        7.1.3: Another World 138
        7.1.4: Arcade Pool 145
        7.1.5: ATR: All Terrain Racing 149
        7.1.6: Battle Chess. 153
        7.1.7: Cadaver 157
        7.1.8: California Games 161
        7.1.9: The Chaos Engine. 165
        7.1.10: Dragons Breath 170
        7.1.11: F-16 Combat Pilot. 174
        7.1.12: Kick Off 2. 180
        7.1.13: The Lost Patrol 184
        7.1.14: Paradroid 90 188
        7.1.15: Pinball Dreams 193
        7.1.16: Project-X: Special Edition 93 197
        7.1.17: Qwak. 201
        7.1.18: The Sentinel 205
        7.1.19: Simon the Sorcerer 211
        7.1.20: Speedball 2: Brutal Deluxe 215
        7.1.21: Stunt Car Racer 219
        7.1.22: Super Cars II 224
        7.1.23: Titus The Fox: To Marrakech and Back 228
        7.1.24: Worms: The Director's Cut 233
        7.1.25: Zool: Ninja Of The "Nth" Dimension. 241
    7.2: Bonus USB Games: Citadel 246
    7.3: Adding games & WHDLoad 251
        7.3.1: Install and Update WHDLoad 256
        7.3.2: Making a WHDLoad archive 257
    7.4: Transfer original Amiga disks 258
        7.4.1: Transfer by Nullmodem cable 258
        7.4.2: Greaseweazle 261
        7.4.3: External drives 263

8: Rebuild to a Maxi .264
    8.1: Keyboard 267
    8.2: New Amiga 500 Cases 272

9: Amiga Operation System 273
    9.1: Kickstart 278
    9.2: Operation Systems & Workbench 279

  9.2.1: The Command Line Interface – CLI 295
  9.2.2: Startup Sequence. .300
 9.3: BASIC 302
  9.3.1: What is Amiga Basic?. 302
  9.3.2: Beginners guide to Amiga Basic 305
 9.4: Disk Images & File Formats 306
 9.5: Archive Files 308
 9.6: Picture Files 309
 9.7: Animation Files. 311
 9.8: Amiga Filesystems 312
 9.9: Amiga DOS – The Disk Operation System 315
 9.10: Guru Meditation 320
 9.11: Open-Source Amiga Operation Systems 321
10: THEDemoscene & Demos 322
11: THESources & Acknowledgments 338

A Hobbyist's Guide to THEA500 Mini

1: THEPreface

"AMIGAAAAAAAAAAAAAAAAAAAAA" is what we use to shout in a crowded demoscene party all the time.

If you do not know what demos are, read the chapter "10: THEDemoscene & Demos" on page 322 :)

It is still one of the most popular retro Computers on which demos are programmed. And what demos.

Just as there are always amazing things that were tickled out of the Commdore 64 with an 8Bit processor and around 1 Megahertz clock speed, it's still amazing what can be calculated on an Amiga in real time, which triggers a storm of enthusiasm from fans, nerds, geeks, gamers and users of all ages.

The Amiga was, and still is, a marvel of the technology of its time and many, very many beautiful hours I have experienced have been with it, together with my friends.

We played games, made and printed greeting cards, created 2D and 3D animations and much more.

I have taken all my Amigas apart, upgraded them again and again, and installed them in other cases.

THEA500 is more than just a revival of old times and memories of my youth, for me it is new a retro feeling for hours of old & yet new fun.

I wish you a lot of fun with this book and hope it gives you as much pleasure to read it as I had to make it.

Holger Weßling

1.1: THEA500 Mini

This is not just an emulator that represents the capabilities of an Amiga 500 as the name may suggest.

In fact, it's much much more.

In order to run all Amiga games THEA500 Mini emulates the original Amiga 500s' OCS chipset, as well as the Enhanced Chip Set (ECS) and the Advanced Graphics Architecture (AGA) that came with the Amiga 2000, 600, and 1200.

The motive of this 3-System strategy is that users should be able to experience the pre installed games as well as many other titles as possible. To make this work THEA500 Mini supports WHDLoad, allowing importing games via USB stick. The device is thus an all-in-one Amiga emulator with all sorts of practical additional functions, incluing display modes.

For example, the CRT filter simulates an old analog screen. The image smoothing provides a less pixelated look, and with three scaling modes, the image is zoomed in, displayed in a fixed size, or formatted for optimal use of the available screen space via "Screen fit". The picture output is always 720p at a refresh rate of 50Hz or 60Hz. As with the THEC64, the firmware and WHDLoad can be upgraded via USB stick.

In addition, game saves can be saved at any time. This not only allows to pause a game at any point, but you can also save high scores with programs that originally couldn't.

THEA500 Mini runs a Linux operating system to which there is no direct access. After extensive testing, I unfortunately found that with the first firmware and every attempt, with different settings and versions, neither the Workbench 1.3 nor 3.1 is running.

Since I strongly believe it will soon be possible, either through a firmware update or some users' resourcefulness, I have compiled some information for you in the following chapters in this book.

Some Reviews:

"So I give "THEA500 Mini" Retro Recipes' first ever score of 5 chips out of 5. It does everything you'd hope, but the production quality, speed, and optimisation options exceed expectations. Recommended for all nostalgia seekers."

Perifractic

Retro Recipes

Watch the full review https://bit.ly/retrorecipies_r1

"If that isn't the cutest thing I've ever seen, I don't know what is. The attention to detail here is really impressive. I'm impressed with the build quality, especially the thought that went into the design. And you get a fully functional Mouse and Controller you can use on your Computer."

The 8-Bit Guy

Watch the full review https://bit.ly/8bitGuyRV1

2: THEInterviews

In the following chapter you are about to read insights and thoughts, funny and interesting things all about Amiga, THEA500 Mini and more.

Here are some short notes:

One question that came up after the annoucement of the THEA500 Mini was, if there'd be a maxi version with a fully funtional keyboard.

And Darren said on sceneworld interview https://sceneworld.org/blog/2021/12/18/podcast-episode-130-the-a500-mini-with-darren-melbourne-and-chris-smith/, that for some upcoming anniversaries, we should always look up retro games for new announcements :)

Paul Andrews

To be clear, we would like to do a full sized THEA500 but it does depend on how well the mini sells first in total volume (not just batch one), and even if we do eventually do a full sized one we cannot confirm any timelines at all obviously.

Also as it's very likely with the combination of preorders and stock timelines, it's quite unlikely retailers will lower their prices/margins, nor can we confirm or guarantee future production runs/further stock timelines in 2022, for so many reasons from global chip shortages, shipping issues, and so many other things beyond our control, so users should presume if they don't preorder or get one soon after launch they potentially will not get one this year as we just can't guarantee that currently.

Again to be clear we hope we will do the full sized in due course but no one should presume at this point for all the reasons above it will be in the immediate future and by default they then miss out on the mini and regret that while others are enjoying theirs!

"Retro Games have created a truly unique product," said Debbie Bestwick MBE, CEO of Team 17, "and I am delighted that our classic games are being showcased in all their original glory."

"With this first mini version of THEA500®, we've created something that we think game fans will love and consider the evolution of mini game consoles," said Paul Andrews, CEO of Retro Games.

2.1: THEIdea

Question to RGL: WHY Amiga 500 besides that he was the most sold Amiga, and not any other model? Or are there plans?

Answer RGL: We modeled THEA500 on the Amiga 500 because it is the most iconic. However, THEA500 reproduces many Amiga models such as the Amiga 500, 600, 1200 because it supports the OCS, ECS and AGA chipsets, along with various memory configurations and CPU options.

Paul Andrews and Darren Melbourne have worked together on and off since around 2004. I Paul was working on a spectrum version of the C64DTV but it didn't happen due to licensing issues. Paul's former company later worked on the C64 games for the Nintendo Wii. So Paul and Darren been doing things together for a long time. Paul also works on many media and tech projects, and also some government backed schemes for SEMLEP as well as a lot of experience in media and retail sales since about 2000. Darren has been in the games industry most of his adult life. Paul bought Chris into the original ZX Spectrum Vega, and also then into Retro Games LTD, Chis made the firmware for ZX Spectrum Vega too.

Darren Melbourne and Paul Gouge was from Ironstone Partners that designed the C64 DTV in 2004, that's where the design of THEC64 Joystick came from and why some of the games are the same.

Chris Smith built and designed the Carousel and the C64 emulator, if you look at the source code C64OSS you see it says "Copyright 2017 Chris Smith", any update that is made for THEC64 Mini/Maxi and THEVIC20 is built by him, he is a experienced technical architect, software and hardware engineer, product designer.

Chris wrote a book about the inner workings of The ZX Spectrum "The ZX Spectrum Ula": https://www.amazon.co.uk/ZX-Spectrum-Ula-MicroComputer-Computer/dp/0956507107

2.2: Paul Andrews

He is the Co-Creator of several games-based consoles. His prior games company was also responsible for many PC-based retro games and the Nintendo Wii's Virtual Console C64 games. Paul has extensive experience in digital content publishing and management across many formats.

A Short Interview with Paul

Tell us something about your youth – how did you get into Computers, which one was your first, how did it go on and when was there an Amiga?

The first Computer I owned very briefly was the Sinclair ZX81, then I had the Sinclair ZX Spectrum 48k, plus the interface 1, and microdrive's, and Kempston Joystick interface. Later I had an Atari ST as well, picking that at the time over the Amiga as I used it for music, as I was in a band once upon a time ago. Darren is the real Amiga aficionado!

What fascinated you about Computers and especially about the Amiga.

I've been involved with retro Computers more since I created RetroTrader the website which was around the year 2000, which lead me to sponsor the original first two CGE-UK retro game shows in Croydon London, it was how I meet a lot of people originally, and then lead me into a path of creating my own first games development and publishing company company, and then other media companies down the line, plus of course my involvement with Retro Games Ltd. I have also gone on to own hundreds of original games from back in the day, including some Amiga ones, one of which is on THEA500 Mini, a classic game called Lost Patrol.

Who from the Computer history do you know personally and why or how did it happen?

I know and have known a lot of very key figures some of them sadly dead now, such as Sir Clive Sinclair who I was actually in business with as most people know, the amazing designer Rick Dickinson, but also many others from artists to designers to coders, many of whom have become good friends.

Is there a really funny incident related to retro games that you would like to tell us?

I could tell you about the time I was a guest of Nintendo in Germany some years ago for an event they organised, for some retro themed games for the Nintendo Wii, and a strange but funny incident which happened, but I literally cant!

How did the idea to develop THEA500 Mini come about?

It was always on our development road map since almost day one of the company.

What particular hurdles did you have to overcome?

Licenses are always the most hardest part of doing these sort of consoles, plus obviously the technical changes, and logistical ones.

What was the most fun part of the development?

n/a

What kind of expectations do you have for sales and user behavior, considering everything that happened with the THEC64?

We have no final expectation of overall sales figures, if people like what we do we hope they will buy it and support us, and if they do we hope to make more and more different products as the years go by!

If you wanted to give to the readers a statement, what would that be?

I would just like to thank all the many hundreds of thousands of people who have supported us over the last few years, and who have loved our products enough to buy them we genially wouldn't be here without you and I and the rest of the team thank you all for your support. You make it all worthwhile, and we love it when we see messages from people saying how it has bought back happy memories for them, or for a relative, or even of a long gone loved one, those are the messages and stories which make it really worthwhile.

Thanks goes to Blitterwolf for this interview held on the 24th of December in 2021.

1: Hello and welcome from us at Blitterwolf, again, for this second interview. For our new readers could you tell us your name, country and occupation please?

A: Hi my name is Paul Andrews, and from the UK, and I'm the managing director of Retro Games Ltd, plus also director of several other tech and media companies.

2: We know of your first experience with Computers, Spectrum and other 8-bit machines, could you expand and tell us where you went from there, 16-bit onwards?

A: Both myself and Chris Smith had ZX Spectrums, and then Atari ST Computers, our colleague Darren Melbourne started with a ZX Spectrum, then moved onto a C and then Amiga I believe!

3: What drew you to the Commodore brand and specifically the development of the AMini?

A: Much as myself and Chris started with ZX Spectrums, obviously the Commodore brand was globally much bigger than Sinclair plus I've known Mike at Cloanto since the early 2000s, in fact my wife and myself had a memorable lunch many years ago with both **Mike of Cloanto and Trevor Dickinson** at the Radisson Blue at Stansted airport I recall, so I've known these guys a long time now.

4: How long has it taken from initial idea, through research and development to the release date of March 31st 20in UK?

A: We did include the rights to do this console when we did the original paperwork with Cloanto for THECso we always had the option, so once the various THECmodels and commitments were complete, obviously we cracked on, but having said that some licensing and other work had started in parallel with the last parts of THECPast that Covid has of course has had multiple knock on effects in terms of timelines for manufacturing.

5: Could you give some of the specifications of The AMini and are there any that couldn't be added?

A: THEAMini has primarily been made similar to THECmini in that it's more aimed at people who wish to play games, put it down, come back and play more etc. We hope to do the a full sized THEAif the mini sells well, in a similar manner to the pattern of THECwhich would have more extensive features of course.

6: We have said it before but it's worth mentioning all the models we make (THECTHEVICand if we do THEAin a full sized version) are 1NOT called 'maxi' that was just what some retailers started calling them, the minis are called minis, and the full sized versions the model name.

7: Does the AMini run using recreated classic hardware or through emulation?

A: Emulation, the cost of doing it all in hardware just is not practical for mass market mini consoles sadly.

8: Who decided the number of games and which games to be included on The AMini?

A: Darren Melbourne is the licensing director and he has been doing this for his whole adult working life. We have to work within a budget and the honest answer is Amiga games generally cost more to license than Cones, for obvious reasons, plus some companies either do not wish to license their games or the costs asked for some games are just too prohibitively high to be possible. We do not have huge margins on consoles, or the huge economies of scale such as Sony, Nintendo or Microsoft. We have sold good volumes for such a small company, but obviously not the millions of units the big games companies do, so we have to be realistic in these matters. But people can of course add and plus their own owned games via USB-Drive.

9: Can additional hardware be connected to the AMini such as flash drives, external hard drives and CD Rom drives?

A: Not out of the box, but we are looking at some options working with third parties.

10: Will the AMini be a purely gaming system or can applications be installed?

A: Day one it's mostly games/whd compatible software, but never say never.

11: Will the AMini be able to emulate any other OSs?

A: No.

12: Are there any planned updates for The AMini in the near future?

A: Let's release it first, but potentially, we have tried to do what is possible and practical with THECrange, we don't earn any extra revenue at all, in fact lose money and time doing extra firmware updates but we have tried to support the users as best we can like they have us.

13: Do you have a favourite Computer magazine, online or printed, past or present?

A: Popular Computing! It's why we have done as an early venture Popular Retro, as a sort of tribute!

14: What are your thoughts on other recreated retro platforms such as the many mini consoles available?

A: They are all pretty cool, and we love doing our part of that bigger picture, obviously we try to make ours the best of course!

15: Have you noticed an increase in demand for your products as each of your new products is released?

A: We hope we now have a good reputation we hope for quality, usability and so on. So we are a more known factor now I guess for users, so people know what we do is real, exists, or will, not vapour wear, and you will get a quality product out of the box, plus retailers now have confidence in us as well.

16: We know of your fondness for gaming but are there any Amiga applications that you enjoy using?

A: I am biased of course, but I love the morals of Lost Patrol in that there are no winners in war, so that's a good moral lesson from a great game.

17: What other hardware do you have in the pipeline?

A: Now that would be telling, but 2we are just getting going, so be prepared to see and hear from us (and hopefully buy from us) many things for many years to come!

18: You told us that you had a lot of plans after the CMini which we now know was the full size Ccan you tell us if there are further plans after the AMini?

A: Yes many! Obviously we hope to do the full sized THEA500 if the mini version sells well, but as I mentioned before we have many other products in our pipeline!

19: 18. I'd like to close the interview by asking if you have any further comments, thought or general musings?

A: I'd like to thank the hundreds of thousands of people who have bought one or more of THEC64 range we have done so far, and for those fans, I'd like to say a huge thank you, and also we have not finished with that range yet, so we hope we can bring a few more dreams to life for those people yet. Also we would like to thank the fans and press for the great reaction to THEA500 already, and we can't wait to get it into all your hands!

Thank you readers for taking the time to read this interview, most will notice that it is the second interview with Paul Andrews but greatly needed due to recent news items.

The interview will begin with the usual questions as an introduction for our new readers.

FUN TIME, AMIGA TIME!

1. Hello and welcome from us at Blitterwolf, again, for this second interview. For our new readers could you tell us your name, country and occupation please?

A: Hi my name is Paul Andrews, and from the UK, and I'm the managing director of Retro Games Ltd, plus also director of several other tech and media companies.

2. We know of your first experience with Computers, 48K Spectrum and other 8-bit machines, could you expand and tell us where you went from there, 16-bit onwards?

A: Both myself and Chris Smith had ZX Spectrums, and then Atari ST Computers, our colleague Darren Melbourne started with a ZX Spectrum, then moved onto a C64 and then Amiga I believe!

3. What drew you to the Commodore brand and specifically the development of the A500 Mini?

A: Much as myself and Chris started with ZX Spectrums, obviously the Commodore brand was globally much bigger than Sinclair plus I've known Mike at Cloanto since the early 2000s, in fact my wife and myself had a memorable lunch many years ago with both Mike of Cloanto and

Trevor Dickinson at the Radisson Blue at Stansted airport I recall, so I've known these guys a long time now.

4. How long has it taken from initial idea, through research and development to the release date of March 31st 2022, in UK?

A: We did include the rights to do this console when we did the original paperwork with Cloanto for THEC64, so we always had the option, so once the various THEC64 models and commitments were complete, obviously we cracked on, but having said that some licensing and other work had started in parallel with the last parts of THECPast that Covid has of course has had multiple knock on effects in terms of timelines for manufacturing.

5. Could you give some of the specifications of The A500 Mini and are there any that couldn't be added?

A: THEA500 Mini has primarily been made similar to THEC64 mini in that it's more aimed at people who wish to play games, put it down, come back and play more etc. We hope to do the a full sized THEA500 if the mini sells well, in a similar manner to the pattern of THEC64 which would have more extensive features of course.

6. We have said it before but it's worth mentioning all the models we make (THEC64, THEVIC20 and if we do THEA500 in a full sized version) are 100% NOT called 'maxi' that was just what some retailers started calling them, the minis are called minis, and the full sized versions the model name.

7. Does the A500 Mini run using recreated classic hardware or through emulation?

A: Emulation, the cost of doing it all in hardware just is not practical for mass market mini consoles sadly.

8. Who decided the number of games and which games to be included on The A500 Mini?

A: Darren Melbourne is the licensing director and he has been doing this for his whole adult working life. We have to work within a budget and the honest answer is Amiga games generally cost more to license than C64 ones, for obvious reasons, plus some companies either do not wish to license their games or the costs asked for some games are just too prohibitively high to be possible. We do not have huge margins on consoles, or the huge economies of scale such as Sony, Nintendo or Microsoft. We have sold good volumes for such a small company, but obviously not the millions of units the big games companies do, so we have to be realistic in these matters. But people can of course add and plus their own owned games via USB stick.

9. Can additional hardware be connected to the A500 Mini such as flash drives, external hard drives and CD Rom drives?

A: Not out of the box, but we are looking at some options working with third parties.

10. Will the A500 Mini be a purely gaming system or can applications be installed?

A: Day one it's mostly games/whd compatible software, but never say never.

11. Will the A500 Mini be able to emulate any other OSs?

A: No.

12. Are there any planned updates for The A500 Mini in the near future?

A: Let's release it first, but potentially, we have tried to do what is possible and practical with THEC64 range, we don't earn any extra revenue at all, in fact lose money and time doing extra firmware updates but we have tried to support the users as best we can like they have us.

13. Do you have a favourite Computer magazine, online or printed, past or present?

A: Popular Computing! It's why we have done as an early venture Popular Retro, as a sort of tribute!

14. What are your thoughts on other recreated retro platforms such as the many mini consoles available?

A: They are all pretty cool, and we love doing our part of that bigger picture, obviously we try to make ours the best of course!

15. Have you noticed an increase in demand for your products as each of your new products is released?

A: We hope we now have a good reputation we hope for quality, usability and so on. So we are a more known factor now I guess for users, so people know what we do is real, exists, or will, not vapour wear, and you will get a quality product out of the box, plus retailers now have confidence in us as well.

16. We know of your fondness for gaming but are there any Amiga applications that you enjoy using?

A: I am biased of course, but I love the morals of Lost Patrol in that there are no winners in war, so that's a good moral lesson from a great game.

17. What other hardware do you have in the pipeline?

A: Now that would be telling, but 200% we are just getting going, so be prepared to see and hear from us (and hopefully buy from us) many things for many years to come!

18. You told us that you had a lot of plans after the C64 Mini which we now know was the full size C64, can you tell us if there are further plans after the A500 Mini?

A: Yes many! Obviously we hope to do the full sized THEA500 if the mini version sells well, but as I mentioned before we have many other products in our pipeline!

19. I'd like to close the interview by asking if you have any further comments, thought or general musings?

A: I'd like to thank the hundreds of thousands of people who have bought one or more of THEC64 range we have done so far, and for those fans, I'd like to say a huge thank you, and also we have not finished with that range yet, so we hope we can bring a few more dreams to life for those people yet. Also we would like to thank the fans and press for the great reaction to THEA500 already, and we can't wait to get it into all your hands!

Thank you for your time and I sincerely look forward to testing and reviewing the A500 Mini.

2.3: Darren Melbourne

Darren Melbourne – Co-creator of the C64DTV direct to TV C64 games console, and has held senior positions in many game development and publishing companies such as Square Enix and many more. Darren has extensive knowledge in game licensing and production.

He started in the games industry in 1984, working on a contract basis with companies such as Firebird and Anco. In 1987 in conjunction with Mark Greenshields and Ned Langman he set up a small development company called Paranoid Software that created games such as Hades Nebula and Blazer for the C64, Spectrum, Amstrad and Atari ST. All Paranoid games were published by Nexus.

During 1988 he became the first employee of the newly formed SCi and was it's acting head of development. During his time there he worked on titles such as Shinobi, Ninja Warriors and Gemini Wing. Towards the end of that year he produced Speedball on the C64 with a small development company called Pantheon Software.

Darren Melbourne has been in the games industry continuously since 1984 and has worked on literally dozens of titles in the role of Producer or Game Designer. A cross section of these titles follows: Populous: Gameboy & NES, Porky Pig's Haunted Holiday SNES, Super Kick Off: Gameboy, NES, SNES, Sensible Soccer: Gameboy, The Lion King: Gameboy & NES, Kick Off 3: Game Gear, Megadrive, PC, Player Manager: SNES, PC, Splitz: Gameboy, Casper the Friendly Ghost: Gameboy Colour, Addams Family: Gameboy & NES, ToCA & Colin McRae: Gameboy colour, Mia Hamm & Michael Owens Soccer: N64, Micro Machines 1 & 2 Twin Turbo: Gameboy Colour, Micro Machines V3, Gameboy colour

In 1998 Darren Melbourne assumed the role of European Development Director for THQ overseeing all of their development in Europe. He left THQ with it's UK Managing Director to assume a similar role at Ubisoft. Darren is still in the industry today 04.2022.

Darren Melbourne also designed and produced Tiny Troops a resource and management game on the Amiga that was years ahead of it's time. Published by Vulcan Software in 1997 and written by Al Dukes, with Graphics by Paul McKee and Chris Edwards. Music and Sound effects by Jez Taylor.

2.4: Dimitris Panokostas (THEDeveloper of AmiBerry)

See also: "4.2: THEEmulator" on page 49

The Story of Amiberry

When the Raspberry Pi came out in 2012, I thought it was great. It had a low price tag, and was easy to customize and use for various projects – if a bit underpowered. I didn't imagine it could handle emulation well, not to mention that all the known Amiga emulators back then were for the x86 platform only.

The Raspberry Pi 2 came out in 2015, which made things more interesting. I was thinking to myself that this little board would make a great new way to cheaply emulate an Amiga. Ideally, it would make a great board to port AmigaOS to and run things natively, but that project stumbles upon the license hell that is Amiga-Land, not to mention the development time. The next best thing would be to have an Amithlon-like environment, where you could use a minimal Linux part to get the low-level stuff running and run an Amiga emulator optimized for this board on it. Since the hardware was standard, you wouldn't have to worry about supporting multiple different platforms. Just optimize the hell out of it for this specific one, and you'd have a very accessible new hardware platform which you could turn into a cheap Amiga.

Obviously, other people thought of the same thing, and shortly after I discovered that some had already started working on similar ideas. I came across a Facebook group bringing people with similar ideas together, and lots of them were working on their own project. I was very happy to see that I wasn't alone, and I started looking into what people were doing and offering. The best such project I saw, was named "Amibian", by Gunnar Kristjánsson. It fit the description exactly: Minimal Linux system, booting directly into emulation, much like Amithlon did in the past with the x86 platform. And, if needed, you could still drop back to Linux and use it for other tasks, like copying files over or having SSH access. The emulator used was "uae4arm-rpi" by ChipsFr, a port for the Raspberry Pi based on "uae4arm" by TomB, who made the original port for the Pandora platform.

The first versions were a little buggy and unstable. For example, if you tried to upgrade the Linux system, things would stop working. I decided to see if I can help improve it a bit and contribute towards the common goal. I reached out to Gunnar, and we collaborated on this, but since I didn't want to mess up his process of doing things, I started working on a separate automated script that would strip down a Linux system and put things in place so that it could run the emulator directly. I needed a separate name for my project, and my girlfriend suggested the name "Amiberry", so that was it. Amiberry v1 was basically a collection of shell scripts, and nothing more. Which led to a lot of confusion later...

After I finished working on the scripts and published them on Github, it became obvious that the next thing that needed work was the emulator itself. There were a lot of things that I wanted to improve there, so I started by reaching out to the author of "uae4arm-rpi" and suggesting a few things. When it became clear that I would probably need to implement any improvements or changes myself, I forked the project and worked with the intention of sending changes back as Pull Requests.

My pull requests remained unanswered for longer than I would like, and I wanted to keep working on it in the meantime. So I had to decide whether to wait until something happens with what I sent upstream, or break off from "uae4arm", name my project differently and keep moving. I decided on the latter, and on 11th August 2016, the first Amiberry commit was made. The rest, as they say, is history.

I knew I couldn't afford to spend time in both a distro or scripts to create it and the emulator, so I had to focus on the emulator. Using the name Amiberry for this was confusing to a lot of people, since they originally thought that the name represented another distro (like Amibian was), not another emulator. It took a lot of effort to clear that up, but I still come across some people that confuse distro and emulator names.

My aim for Amiberry was always to get it closer to WinUAE, where most of the code comes from, but carefully stripping away features that are not very useful on the platform or that impact performance a lot. We won't be emulating PPC on the Raspberry Pi anytime soon, I'm afraid.

The GUI was redesigned to match WinUAE closer, the colors were from the AmigaOS 3.x palette, the font used is the Amiga Topaz's. But most of the changes are under the hood, where countless hours have been spent fixing bugs, optimizing performance, improving behavior and implementing new and unique features, based on community feedback. Some from that community have also contributed code and hours of help with feedback, troubleshooting and discussions. The community in general is a core ingredient of projects like this.

Amiberry has grown over the years since it started and is now running on more platforms that just the Raspberry Pi – just recently a member of the community (SigurbjornL) helped port it to Apple M1 hardware! It's also included in multiple distros, including Amibian, which was the inspiration for this project in the first place.

Additionally, there are more new features implemented, to improve the experience. The WHDLoad booter was one such feature, but recently there was support for real floppy drives added (thanks to Rob Smith), more features from WinUAE implemented (DiskSwapper, Input Recording, Sampler support, AHI and more) and some completely new ideas based on community feedback (e.g. being able to launch a Linux application or command from inside AmigaOS).

I believe that as a project, Amiberry helps achieving the goal I set out for: Give the people a cheap, easy way to relive the Amiga nostalgia. I hope you have fun with it!

Amiberry is an open-source project under the GPL-3.0 license, and can be found on Github: https://github.com/midwan/amiberry

There are numerous online sources to get help, but there's also a wiki page we have set up, which gets updated with new information: https://github.com/midwan/amiberry/wiki

Besides the Wiki, you can use the Discussions page to ask questions or discuss ideas: https://github.com/midwan/amiberry/discussions

And of course, you can use the Issues page to report any bugs or request new features: https://github.com/midwan/amiberry/issues

There is a Facebook page, where announcements are made (e.g. for new releases): https://www.facebook.com/amiberry.emulator

And if you'd like to financially support the project, we have a few alternatives:

- OpenCollective: https://opencollective.com/amiberry
- Patreon: https://www.patreon.com/amiberry
- PayPal: https://paypal.me/midwan

3: THEPartners

Retro Games Ltd is made up of people with over 100 years of combined games industry experience, having successfully produced and released many games across many formats, such the C64, Spectrum, GBA, and Wii. Members of the team also successfully brought to market the C64DTV direct to TV C64 games console, and Nintendo Wii Virtual Console C64 games. Based in the UK but operating on a global basis.

3.1: CLOANTO

See also: "9.1: Kickstart" on page 278

CLOANTO is the licence holder of the Amiga Kickstarter.

Cloanto held Commodore/Amiga copyrights and started distributing Amiga System Software. Traditionally the publisher refers to it as "Workbench" instead of "AmigaOS". The disribution is on CF cards, Floppy Disks and as a downloadable Workbench Disk Image Pack. Approached by Amiga-News, Cloanto's Michael Battilana confirmed that the company owns the copyrights for all works created by the Commodore/Amiga companies up to 1993.

The deal was finished in 2012, as Battilana states: "We already had licenses from some older agreements with various parties, including Gateway and Amiga Inc., which in part were exclusive. The transfer of these copyrights to Cloanto was then completed with new agreements a few years ago."

The combination of the multiple agreements makes Cloanto the rights holder of not just any Amiga related products and media, but also the system software, documentation, Commodore-owned publications, videos and advertisements for Commodore's various product lines.

As it turns out, ESCOM had assigned all former Commodore/Amiga copyrights to Gateway in 1997 – not just the Amiga-related ones – and they were handed over to every new IP owner since then. Only the "Commodore" trademarks (but not any patents, nor any copyrights) were sold to Tulip Computers in 1997.

A look at the database of the US Copyright Office confirms Battilana's statements: The items in the list of titles are now assigned to Cloanto.

Note from the editor: While Cloanto's agreements, according to Battilana, cover everything created by Commodore/Amiga up to 1993, not all of the copyrighted works are listed in the public database. Like most publishers, Commodore did not deposit everything with every new release. As the US Copyright Office explains, registration is voluntary, and not required for protection. Advantages that come with registration include the availability to copyright owners of statutory damages and attorney's fees in case of court actions.

CLOANTO®

https://cloanto.com/amiga/roms/

Cloanto: The Name

Long before it became commonplace to use machines as an aid in researching possible company and product names, "CLOANTO" appeared on top of a list of several thousand names generated by an 8-bit Computer. The system had been programmed with consideration to issues such as originality and ease of pronunciation in different languages. It did not know, however, that "Cloanto" also was a rarely-used transliteration of the name of a friendly hero which first appeared in Greek mythology more than 4000 years earlier. We are not sure if that's the way the Hellenic gods intended it to be, but our official pronunciation is clo-'an-to.

Retrocomputing and Classic Gaming

These are the dreams of our youth and a sign of our passion for excellence and commitment to long-term support. As a developer since the 1980s, Cloanto has had a constructive relationship with all Commodore/Amiga companies. Since 2019 we have been supporting the efforts of Amiga Corporation to consolidate the Amiga IP as well as the copyrights for all Commodore/Amiga works (software, ROMs, manuals, videos, etc.) that had previously been assigned to Cloanto.

RetroPlatform Infrastructure and Player

Building on more than 10 years of experience with Amiga Forever (version 1.0 was released in 1997), the Amiga Forever team started in 2007 to lay down the foundation for a modular and platform-neutral "RetroPlatform" architecture. RetroPlatform includes a skinnable player that can use multiple emulation engines, and the infrastructure to catalog, sell, buy, download, play and organize thousands of games, including both free and commercial titles, and non-game content. Products based on this technology include Amiga Forever and C64 Forever.

Amiga Forever

Amiga Forever is the official Amiga preservation, emulation and support package which allows Amiga software to run on non-Amiga hardware legally and without complex configuration. All versions of Amiga Forever include everything you need to run different "Classic" Amiga emulation and OS environments in simple one-click steps. This makes it possible to run thousands of Amiga games and demoscene productions which are available for free download from software publishers and Amiga history sites alike.

Amiga Explorer

Connect an Amiga with one or more PCs, and access Amiga resources (including virtual floppy, hard disk and ROM image files) from the Windows Desktop. Now with a revolutionary self-install technology that requires no additional Amiga software (PC file system, terminal software, etc.) Supports serial and TCP/IP connections. Available in a stand-alone package or as part of Amiga Forever.

C64 Forever

C64 Forever employs the same RetroPlatform infrastructure and player used by Amiga Forever, revealing a powerful end-to-end content management ecosystem already supporting over 20,000 games.

3.2: Koch Media

The Koch Media Group is a global developer, publisher and distributor of video games, VR games, gaming hardware and merchandise.

KOCH MEDIA

The group's publishing activities, marketing and distribution extend throughout Europe, America, Australia and Asia. Koch Media has over 25 years of experience in the digital media business and has risen to become a leading global publishing partner. The Koch Media Group runs a multi-label strategy with fully owned publishing units such as Prime Matter, Deep Silver, Milestone, Vertigo Games and Ravenscourt, publishing games for consoles, PC and VR platforms across all physical and digital channels.

Additionally, as global publishing partner Koch Media has formed long-term multi-national publishing collaborations with numerous game publishers including Activision Blizzard, Bethesda, Capcom, CI Games, Giants Software, Kalypso, Koei Tecmo, Konami, Paradox, Sega, SNK, Square Enix, Techland, Tripwire, Warner Bros, and many others.

With its parent company in Höfen, Austria, and the Publishing HQ in Munich, Germany, Koch Media owns local publishing companies in Germany, UK, France, Spain, Italy, Sweden, the Netherlands, Austria, Switzerland, Poland, Australia, the United States as well as Japan and Hong Kong.

The Koch Media Group owns ten game development studios: Deep Silver Volition (Champaign, IL/USA), Deep Silver Dambuster Studios (Nottingham/UK), Deep Silver Fishlabs (Hamburg/Germany), Warhorse Studios (Prague/Czech Republic), Milestone (Milan/Italy), Voxler (Paris/France) , Flying Wild Hog (Warsaw, Kraków, Rzeszów/Poland), Free Radical Design (Nottingham/UK) and Vertigo Games (Rotterdam /The Netherlands), DigixArt (Montpellier, France). Additionally, the Koch Media Group collaborates with numerous independent development studios around the world.

Part of the Koch Media Group is also Koch Films, a leading European independent film distributor with business primarily in Germany, Switzerland, Austria and Italy as a cinema, TV, online and Home Entertainment distributor.

The Koch Media Group also owns Gaya Entertainment, a leading video game merchandise company in Munich, Germany, and the Quality Assurance Facility in Olomouc, Czech Republic.

Koch Media is an Embracer Group company.

4: THEA500

See also: "9: Amiga Operation System" on page 273

The start animation of THEA500 Mini is a reference and homage to the very famous Amiga Boing Ball. This was the first demo that showed the capabilities of the first Amiga 100, shown on the ECS the 1984 Consumer Electronics Show. It was groundbreaking.

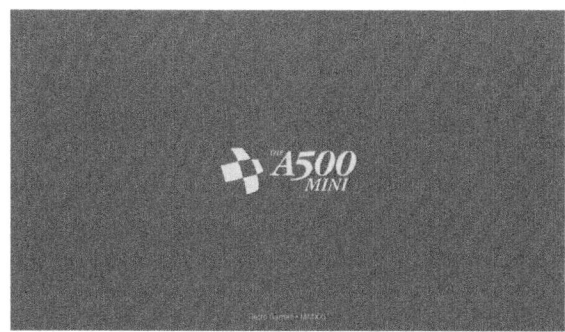

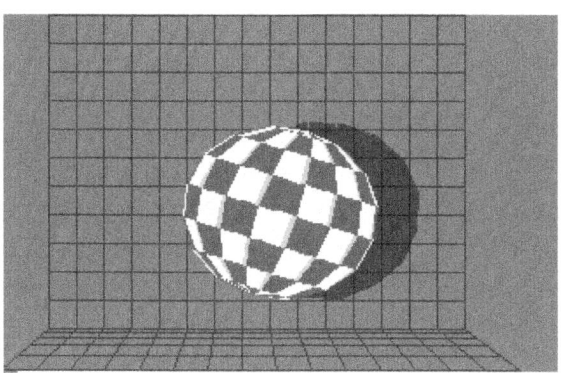

If you like to learn how to operate a real Amiga 500, you should have a look here:

The Complete Amiga 500 User Guide (PDF-Document)

https://ftp.fau.de/aminet/docs/help/A500UserGuide.pdf

4.1: THEHardware

To see the mainboard, you have to unscrew six screws. But only one is visible to the naked eye. Four are under the rubber feet in the corners, and one is under the serial label. You can lift the label with a thin blade without destroying it.

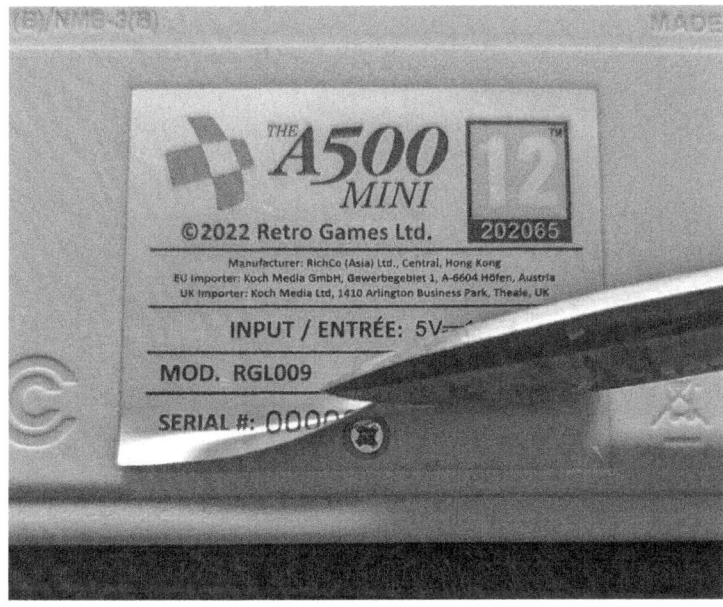

Be careful opening the case, there are two frame clips, one at each side.

The case opens up in two parts. As you can see, there are three weights in the bottom.

The Keyboard is originally black plastic and only painted from above. The Keyboard falls after unscrewing apart in to four seperate parts:

The button from the disk drive has no function. But behind this plate is enough space for a tiny electronic board like an SD-Card adaptor.

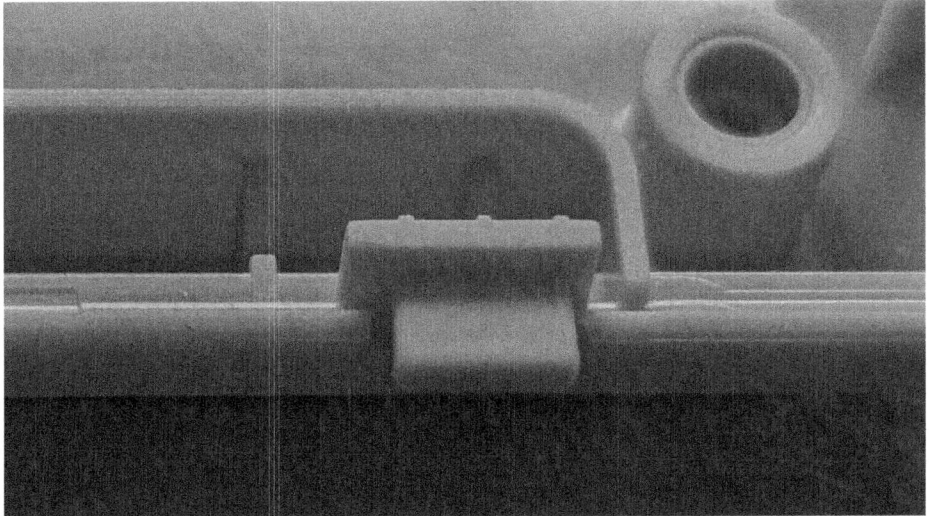

Away from the mainboard is a mini board that holds the power and activity LEDs.

The back of the mainboard has nothing much to see:

But the front is all the more interesting.

A nice litte feature is that RGL gave the mainboard a name like Commodore had with most Amiga boards. "CosmicThing" references a song by the B-52's.

However, the question remains why this title?

Maybe you can find out?

In the coming chapters, all chips are explained.

Question to RGL: There is a push button on the mainboard. What does it do?

Answer RGL: It is sometimes used by the factory for testing.

Q: Why are there two UART/UBOOT connectors on the board? Was there supposed to be a Fan installed? There is a connector name on the board.

A: The initial PCB design was completed before requirements were finalised.

Q: There are some capacitor icons on the board near the USB-Connectors. Why?

A: The PCBs are always over specified and then the component count is reduced to only that needed.

Q: What are GND and ID on the board for?

A: Only for testing purposes.

Q: There are solder points for two LEDs next to the power button. What is that all about?

A: No. These are for diodes, which were not required in the final product.

Q: What represents the Date field? Why is there a line for NAND?

A: Factory tracking and quality assurance.

Q: The main processors clock is 24.000Hertz?

A: No. That's the board clock. The internal clock can go to 1.8GHz

Q: It seems that the power button was soldered by hand?

A: No. Automated soldering (robot) so not the wave soldering that you might expect because of surface mount components on the same side.

4.1.1: THECase & Connectors

4.1.1.1: Power button

Start

To start the Mini, gently press the button once. This triggers a push button in the mainboard, and is held by an arm to the right.

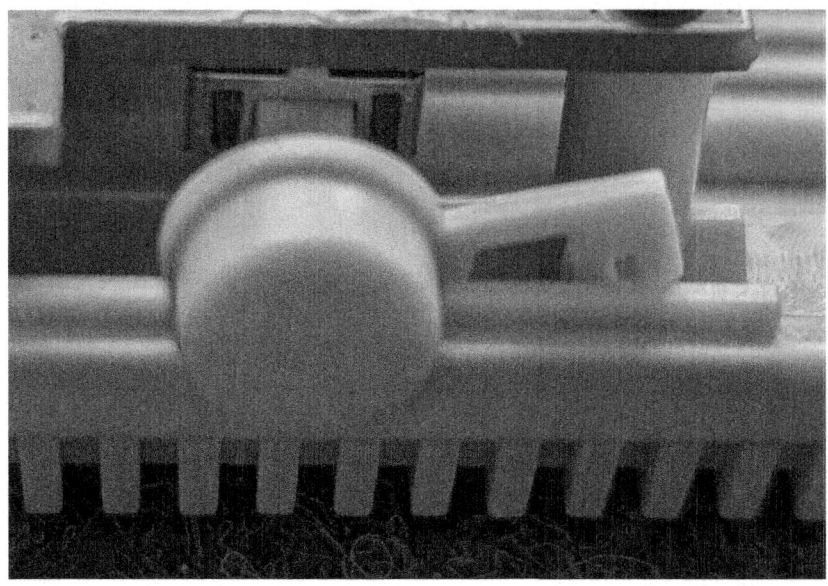

Home

If you press the power button during a game, it acts like the "Home" button, and takes you to the carousel.

Shut down

Hold the button for about 3 seconds or until the red LED turns off.

4.1.1.2: USB-C power connector

Even though a USB-C connector is capable of transferring data, this port is only for power.

You will need a power adpator that delivers at least 1 Ampere.

4.1.1.3: USB

All USB-Ports are type 2.0, and will quickly transport data from any USB-Device into THEA500 Mini.

By now there is no support for other USB-Devices than sticks (thumb drives), hard drives (including SSD), mice and Joysticks/Gamepads (Controller).

Others like a printer or scanner do not work (Firmware 1.0.0).

4.1.1.4: HDMI & Audio

The video output of 720p (1280x720 pixels) was chosen, as FullHD was deemed unnecessary.

No Amiga can produce images larger than 720p. 1080p would need a better GPU, making THEA500 Mini more expensive.

Question to RGL: Why is the audio not separated? There were many questions and suggestions about this regarding the THEC64.

Answer RGL: It adds additional cost, both development and hardware (separate output DAC, amplifiers etc) and we know only a small percentage of users would use this.

Q: I tried connectiong several adaptors to THEA500 via HDMI->DP cable, and HDMI to DP-Adapter to DP input to my Monitor that has no HDMI, but I got no picture

A: The SoC is a true HDMI device, so converting from HDMI to other formats may not work and would depend on the capability of the converter.

HDMI-Audio

Anyone wanting the audio routed to loudspeakers could use a HDMI-Audio Extractor. Different versions are all over the net. This nice, cheap one works absolutely fine.

I had no noticeable delay in the video transfer through the device.

4.1.1.4.1: TV-Out

If you want to connect the Mini to an old TV with a SCART connector, then there are ready-made converters suitable for this.

Unfortunately, I couldn't find one that converts HDMI to the good old FBAS TV-analog signal.

Here is the matching Google search entry: "HDMI+TV+scart+converter"

4.1.1.5: LEDs & Blink codes

See also: "9.10: Guru Meditation" on page 320, "6: THEStart & THEOptions" on page 85

Unlike a real Amiga, THEA500 Mini has no blink codes.

The red and green LEDs display the power and disk drive – e.g. hard drive activities.

In the Options menu in **System options**, you can set the red LED to act like an original Amiga's.

Original Amiga Blink Codes:

- One blink means the Keyboard ROM has a checksum error
- Two blinks means RAM failure
- Three blinks means watchdog timer failure
- There is a connection to the Guru meditation when one occurs.

4.1.2: THECPU (Main Processor)

THEA500 Mini is able to emulate nearly all Processors used by Amiga Computers, ranging from the Motorola 68000 up to the 68030 at 7/14/Max MHz.

But that is not enough. It also emulates the Co-Processors (FPU = Floating Point Unit) 68881 and 68882.

Here are the hard facts:

The Allwinner H6 V200-AI M5121BA 65T2 (Quad Core) CPU is based on an ARM Cortex A53, which is the same chip that powers the Raspberry Pi 3 and Pi Zero 2.

Datasheet

https://linux-sunxi.org/images/5/5c/Allwinner_H6_V200_Datasheet_V1.1.pdf

The CPU Allwinner H6

The Allwinner H6 V200 is a highly cost-efficient quad-core OTT Box processor, which is a part of growing line of home entertainment products that offer high-performance processing with a high degree of functional integration.

The H6 V200 processor has some very exciting features, for example:

- CPU: Quad-core ARM CortexTM-A53 Processor, a power-efficient ARM v8 architecture, it has 64 and 32bit execution states for scalable high performance, which includes a NEON multimedia processing engine.

- Graphics: Mali-T720 Multi-Core, proven Midgard architecture with two shade cores, provides users with superior experience in video playback and mainstream game; OpenGL ES3.1and OpenCL1.2 standards are supported.

- Video Engine: H6 V200 provides multi-format high-definition video encoder/decoder with dedicated hardware, including

H.265 decoder by 4K@60fps, H.264 decoder by 4K@30fps, H.263 decoder by 1080p@60fps, VP9 decoder by 4K@30fps, MPEG1/2/4 decoder by 1080p@60fps, VC1/VP8/AVS/AVS+ jizhun decoder by 1080p@60fps, H.264 encoder by 1080p@60fps.

- Display Subsystem: Supports Allwinner's SmartColor 3.0 for excellent display experience, and three display interfaces including RGB LCD display for LCD, HDMI2.0a output and TVOUT (Controlled by ATE) for TV.

- Audio Subsystem: Supports popular digital audio interfaces such as I2S/PCM, OWA, DMIC and Audio Hub, and supports I2S/PCM for connecting to an external audio codec. To reduce total system cost and enhance high integration, the H6 V200 processor also integrates an audio codec (Controlled by ATE).

- Memory Controller: The processor supports many types of external memory devices, including DDR4/DDR3/DDR3L/LPDDR2/LPDDR3, NAND Flash with full disk encryption, Nor Flash, SD/SDIO/MMC including eMMC up to rev5.1.

- Security System: The processor delivers hardware security features that enable trustzone security system, Digital Rights Management (DRM), information encryption/decryption, secure boot and secure efuse.

- Interfaces: The processor has a broad range of hardware interfaces such as parallel CMOS sensor interface, 10/100/1000Mbps EMAC with EPHY (Controlled by ATE), USB OTG v2.0 operating at high speed(480Mbps) with PHY, USB3.0/2.0 Host with PHY, and a variety of other popular interfaces (SPI,UART,PCIe,One Wire,CIR,TSC,TWI,SCR).

CPU Architecture
- Quad-core ARM CortexTM-A53 Processor
- Power-efficient ARM v8 architecture
- 64 and 32bit execution states for scalable high performance
- Trustzone technology supported
- 3~10x better software encryption performance

- Supports NEON Advanced SIMD(Single Instruction Multiple Data)instruction for acceleration of media and signal processing functions
- Supports Large Physical Address Extensions (LPAE)
- VFPv4 Floating Point Unit
- 32KB L1 Instruction cache and 32KB L1 Data cache per core
- 512KB L2 cache shared

GPU Architecture

- Mali-T720 Multi-Core, proven Midgard architecture with two shade cores
- Supports OpenGL ES 3.1/3.0/2.0/1.1, OpenCL 1.2/1.1, DirectX 11 FL9_3, and Renderscript/Filterscript
- Supports Transaction Elimination, saving external bandwidth and energy
- Supports ASTC, best-in-class compression, reduced size and improved quality
- Supports FAST(4x)FSAA, IO Coherency

More detailed information:

User manual: https://usermanual.wiki/Pdf/AllwinnerH6V200UserManualV11.721716680/help

4.1.3: THERAM (Memory)

If you want to know what the RAM settings are for, then look in the **Game settings**.

This RAM is installed:

NAND RAM: KIOXIA TC58NVG1SSHTA00 21149AE UO1439 (2 Gigabit = 250Megabyte)

Datasheet https://business.kioxia.com/info/docget.jsp?did=14849&prodName=TC58NVG1S3HTA00

DRAM: 2x Nanya Technology NT5CB128M16FP-DI-TR (2 Gigabit DDR3 SDRAM)

Datasheet https://datasheetspdf.com/datasheet/NT5CB128M16FP.html

This emulates up to the following Amiga RAM:

- 8MB Chip
- 1.8MB Slow
- 8MB Fast
- 16MB Fast
- Fast RAM? Chip RAM? Slow Fast RAM?

Memory Map Amiga

The following image shows the three main memory types of the Amiga:

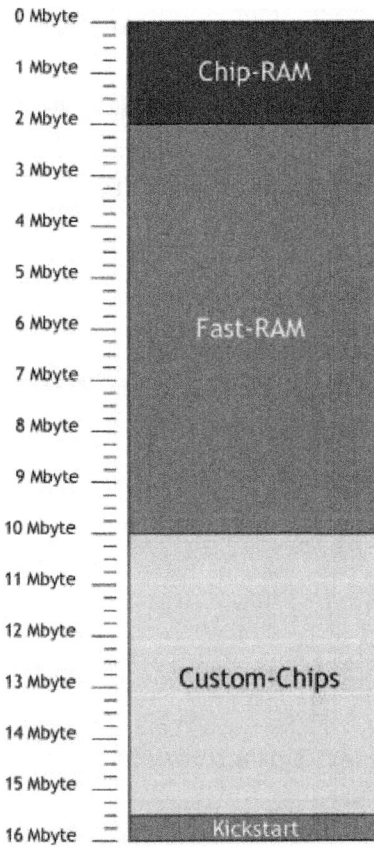

To understand where the differences are you need to know some basics:

The first CPUs used in the Amiga, the 68000s, could address a maximum of 16 MB RAM. All registers of the custom chips as well as the Kickstart ROM have to be placed within these 16 MB to be accessible. However, you have to do without the corresponding amount of RAM. To be prepared for future extensions, the 16 Mbyte address space is divided into several parts.

The first, "lower" part contains the chip RAM, which can contain a maximum of 2 Mbytes. Directly after that comes 8 Mbytes of so-called Fast RAM. This area is also used by the registers of possibly existing Zorro-II add-on cards and is called Zorro-II address space. The rest is occupied by the custom chip registers as well as the kickstart ROM and a few other administrative matters. And now it gets interesting: The lowest part, i.e. the chip RAM can be accessed directly by the processor as well as by the custom chips. The fact that two parties share the access (controlled by Agnus) leads to speed losses in practice, since not everyone can access the memory when they want. In the 8 MB Fast RAM area, only the processor has access, unaffected by the custom chips, and here an advantage of this concept becomes apparent: custom chips (especially the blitter) and processor can work independently of each other in parallel.

Normally, programs and data structures not needed for graphics and sound are stored in Fast RAM and everything the custom chips need ends up in Chip RAM (hence the name). This is not only graphics and sound data, but also things like buffer memory for the floppy drive, which is accessed via the custom chips. This is also the reason why chip RAM is the most valuable memory type on the Amiga. You can have as much Fast-RAM as you want, if you run out of Chip-RAM you still can't open new screens and so on.

The so called Slow-Fast-RAM is a hybrid between both types of memory. Due to technical conditions this memory behaves exactly like the chip RAM, so if a custom chip reads data from the memory, the CPU can't read anything from this memory. The big difference is only that the custom chips can't do anything with the Slow Fast RAM! Therefore, this is probably the worst memory type of all, since it is as slow as chip RAM, but can still only be used by the processor. The original Commodore A501 expansion for the Amiga 500, for example, belongs to this category, but also the various 1.8 MB expansions available from other manufacturers for the 500. At the very end of the address area you find the operating system: 256 or 512 KB ROM, depending on the version.

With the introduction of the 32-bit processors in the Amiga, the maximum amount of memory was raised to about 4 GB. Everything above the 16 MB of the old address space was thus freed for memory expansions and add-on cards using the 32-bit Zorro-III bus. Below that, almost everything remains as before.

4.1.4: THEGraphics

The GPU is the ARM Mali-T720 MP2 which complies with OpenGL ES 3.1, OpenCL 1.1, and is a part of the main processor.

These are the three Amiga graphic modes that are emulated:

OCS

The OCS (abbreviation for Original Chip Set) was the chipset of the early Amiga models. It was used in the Amiga 500, Amiga 1000, Amiga 1500 and Amiga 2000. It consisted of the chips Agnus, Denise and Paula. This division into three chips was due to the limited manufacturing possibilities of the 1980s, in principle the chips are to be understood as a unit.

The OCS has striking similarities in architecture as well as in function division with the core hardware of the Atari 8-bit Computer series, also consisting of three chips, ANTIC, GTIA and POKEY, which was already launched in 1979. Both chipsets were designed by Jay Miner.

ECS

ECS (Enhanced Chip Set) is an improved chipset compared to its predecessor OCS, which was used in the Computers Amiga 500plus, Amiga 600, Amiga 3000 as well as in the CDTV. It is to be seen as a collective term for the interaction of different coprocessors.

The ECS consists of 3 components:
- Big/Fat Agnus,
- Hires Denise and
- Paula

Big Agnus and Hires Denise are further developments of the original Agnus and Denise chips.

AGA

The Advanced Graphics Architecture chipset (AGA) was the last generation of chipsets used in Commodore's Amiga Computer. In Germany, it had to be called AA chipset, since the abbreviation AGA had already been used here for an older PC graphics card (combination of CGA and Hercules graphics).

It was built into the Amiga variants Amiga 1200, Amiga 4000 and Amiga CD^{32} from 1992 on and can display 256 out of about 16.7 million colors (24-bit color depth) indexed in all screen resolutions. In HAM8 mode, an image in all resolutions can contain as many colors at the same time as pixels fit into the chip RAM, minus the first pixel column, i.e. with a maximum chip RAM size of 2 MB, a maximum of 2 million colors. In the highest resolution, however, a maximum of about 830,000 pixels are visible at the same time. These are almost true colors, although this is associated with a not inconsiderable computing effort for optimal display. The chipset enables the display of so-called Productivity Modes, i.e. flicker-free, high-resolution screen modes, without the help of a flicker fixer required for this in the OCS, and has a maximum resolution of 1440 × 576 (hires interlaced, overscan).

Overall, however, the improvements were not sufficient to keep up with the advanced VGA-compatible graphics cards of the time. In particular, a true, unrestricted 24-bit TrueColor mode was sorely missed, and the aforementioned 8-bit HAM mode was not a full replacement. Furthermore, the achievable resolutions and frame rates were no longer competitive. Also, the memory organization via bitplanes at higher color depths was complicated and slow for many applications.

The AGA chipset is also indirectly based on the original Original Chip Set (OCS), but with some changes:

- The Agnus chip of the OCS was replaced here by Alice, it can address up to 2 MB chip RAM.
- The Denise chip was replaced by Lisa, she provides the additional video modes.
- The Paula chip was used unchanged.

The successor chipset Advanced Amiga Architecture (AAA) for AGA was already developed, but never came to market due to Commodore's bankruptcy.

Big/Fat Agnus

The name Agnus is derived from the word "Address Generator Unit". The chip works as a chip-RAM Controller and generates the necessary addressing for the DMA channels. It also contains the two coprocessors Blitter and Copper and generates the various video synchronization signals.

Compared to the OCS, these Agnus versions could address more chip RAM, 1 and 2 MB respectively.

Hires Denise

The name is derived from the English words "High Resolution Display enCoder/Programmer". The chip controls the graphics output.

Compared to the OCS, this Denise version could display some higher resolutions (Productivity Mode), but at the expense of the number of colors that could be displayed simultaneously.

Paula

The name Paula is derived from the English words peripheral and audio. The chip controls the following tasks in the Amiga:

- Input and output control for floppy drives
- Audio output
- Polling of the analog inputs

4.1.5: LAG & Latency

To let you know why lag and latency are often mentioned, here is the explanation:

Lag is a synonym of latency.

As nouns the difference between latency and lag is that latency is the state of being latent while lag is (countable) a gap, a delay; an interval created by something not keeping up; a latency.

In a few tests, it was found that THEA500 Mini has a latency of just under 44ms (milliseconds), which is really very little and should not be noticeable when playing. While I was playing, I didn't notice any noticeable lag.

There are two possible latencies/delays we're having with THEA500 Mini.

On one hand the input delay like through a Keyboard and a Joystick or Mouse, and on the other hand the output like the HDMI signal going to a Monitor or TV.

My tests with a regular Monitor (no special gaming Monitor) and my regular several years old 1080p TV, showed no delay measurable. All games and actions felt like they are instantaneous.

However, maybe someone else will experience a delay, and here I explain what this is about.

This delay is the time it takes for a keystroke or Joystick action through the processing of the emulator, the game, and finally to the display. For an excellent gaming experience, a display with high input delay must be avoided, as the gameplay feels sluggish and insensitive.

Problems can occur because:

Most TV today are still 1080p and the mini output is 720p, so the TV have to upscale the picture which may result in a lag.

Another possibility to solve this is to disable all HDMI-Features in your TV. Every feature like motion smoothing or noise reduction cost some processing time which will increase the delay a bit.

One other thing to try would be to change the HDMI port as on some TVs one port is specially for or just runs a little better for gaming.

Secondly the screen mode you choose changes the delay a bit. THEStart & THEOptions.

4.1.5.1: Display-Lag Database

The input delay database helps to avoid delay indications, as it is the world's largest database for it. We therefore recommend the devices marked Excellent or Great, as they offer the least input delay in Game mode. The displays of the same model series have an almost identical input delay across all size ranges. Most displays can be ordered via a direct link to Amazon. Share it with your friends! Thank you.

Go to: https://displaylag.com/display-database/

UART Interface Root access

As with the THEC64, on THEA500 mainboard is an UART interface.

The clever and experienced JJ0 already had found out some very interesting things about the access to the system via the UART interface. Similar to what was done with the THEC64.

If you are also interested in it, take a look here:

Hacker's Guide to UART Root Shells
https://www.youtube.com/watch?v=01mw0oTHwxg

THEA500 Mini hacking development
https://thec64community.online/thread/1220/thea500-mini-hacking-development

What is UART?

A universal asynchronous receiver-transmitter (UART /ˈjuːɑːrt/) is a computer hardware device for asynchronous serial communication in which the data format and transmission speeds are configurable. It sends data bits one by one, from the least significant to the most significant, framed by start and stop bits so that precise timing is handled by the communication channel. The electric signalling levels are handled by a driver circuit external to the UART. Two common signal levels are RS-232, a 12-volt system, and RS-485, a 5-volt system. Early teletypewriters used current loops.

It was one of the earliest computer communication devices, used to attach teletypewriters for an operator console. It was also an early hardware system for the Internet.

A UART is usually an individual (or part of an) integrated circuit (IC) used for serial communications over a computer or peripheral device serial port. One or more UART peripherals are commonly integrated in microcontroller chips. Specialised UARTs are used for automobiles, smart cards and SIMs.

A related device, the universal synchronous and asynchronous receiver-transmitter (USART) also supports synchronous operation.

Question to RGL: Why are there two UART/UBOOT connectors on the board?

Was there supposed to be a Fan installed? There is a connector name on the board.

Answer RGL: The initial PCB design was completed before requirements were finalised.

Q: There is a push button on the mainboard. What is it good for?

A: It is sometimes used by the factory for testing.

4.2: THEEmulator

See also: "2.4: Dimitris Panokostas (THEDeveloper of AmiBerry)" on page 17

Amiberry is an optimized Amiga emulator designed for ARM-based SoCs (such as the Raspberry Pi, Odroid XU4, ASUS Tinkerboard, etc.), that brings you the highest performance Amiga emulation. Be it a classic A500, A1200, CD32 or up to a high-end model equipped with a 68040 and a graphics card, we've got you covered. The code is based on WinUAE for the core emulation, but with some parts stripped down and optimized specifically for lower-powered boards. Additionally, there are several features that were developed specifically for Amiberry, such as WHDLoad support, custom events, support for RetroArch mapping, etc.

It's an open-source project (under GPLv3) that started back in 2016, build with the efforts of several people and based on previous work of others. You are welcome to join the project and help make Amiberry the best Amiga emulator for ARM devices! Visit the project page on GitHub for more.

Nowadays, Amiberry is already included in several popular distros (like RetroPie, DietPi, Amibian, The RetroArena, Batocera, Pimiga and others) and in many cases it can be installed or upgraded from within their ecosystems. Additionally, you can of course install it on a standard Linux distro (e.g. Raspbian, Ubuntu, Arch, Manjaro), or even on macOS (both on x86 and Apple Silicon). It supports both 32-bit and 64-bit platforms, and although it was originally intended for ARM devices only, there are now some x86 targets available also.

Question to RGL: What are the restrictions and changes to the emulator compared to the software version?

Answer RGL: Mainly that it's hidden behind our UI, so the emulator options are not directly accessible. Most of the work to the emulator was to port it to our hardware, integrate with our frontend and maximise performance.

Q: What has led to the decision for the Amiberry. Where other emulators in questions before?

A: This was a decision made by Chris Smith as being the most suitable for the needs of the project.

Q: Is there an original Diskdrive sound emulation? WinUAE has this feature. If not, maybe in an update?

A: No. Only WHDLoad is currently supported, so no emulated floppy disk access and no floppy disk sound.

AmiBerry main page: https://blitterstudio.com/amiberry/

At **THEInterviews** you find Dimitris Panopkostas who is the main developer of AmiBerry.

4.3: THEPeripherals

As usual Retro Games Limited provided us not just with the fantastic THEA500 Mini, but with excellent peripherals as well.

Trackball

Question to RGL: What is about the support of a Trackball? Some very good and fun Amiga games are only really good playable with a trackball.

Answer RGL: USB trackballs might work; we have not tested this since there is no game in the mini that needed one.

The author: I have tested my external Keyboard with an integrated trackball which worked fabulously. So you look forward into adding a modern USB-Trackball.

4.3.1: THEGamepad

See also: "6.4: Help for a game" on page 116, "7.1: Built-In" on page 123, "6.1: Starting a carousel game" on page 92

Quote from Chris Smith: The CD32 pad was not well received at the time for a variety of functional and ergonomic reasons.

Hint! You can use two or more Gamepads at the same time for playing a game – for example, Kick Off 2!

Here are some facts about the Gamepad:

Comes with a 1.8m USB cable

Connects by a standard USB-A plug

The precision DPad has a short, responsive travel for quick action gaming

Four main action buttons and two function buttons

Has two short-travel click switch shoulder buttons

Compatible with THEC64, THEC64 Mini, THEA500 Mini, PC, Mac & Linux.

You can configure the Gamepad in the **Game settings** choosing **Map Gamepad.**

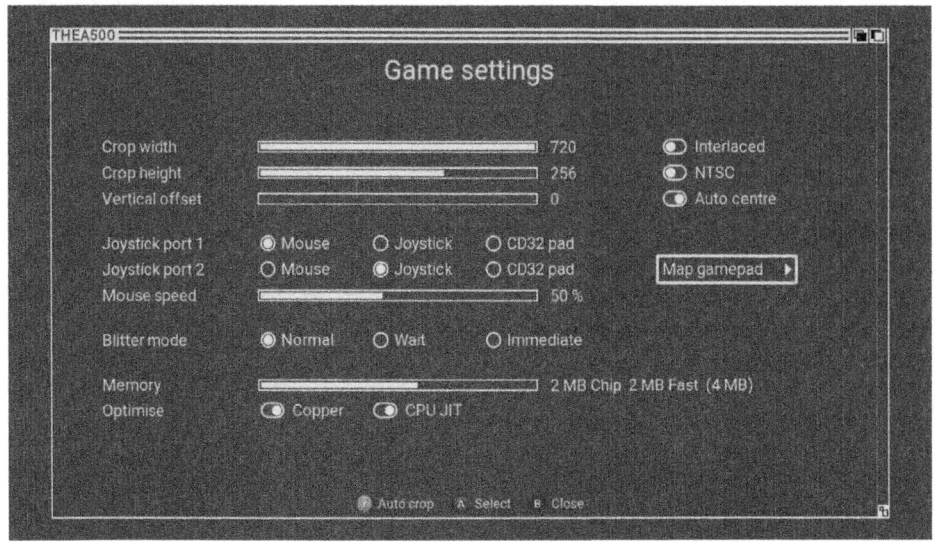

Question to RGL: How and why came up the idea to engineer your own Gamepad?

RGL: We wanted THEA500 to be as authentic as possible. The Amiga did not have an official Joystick, so it was difficult to choose the "correct" style of Joystick to use. However, when the CD32 arrived it came with a Controller (so really it is the only "official" Amiga Controller) and lots of games are compatible with that. Unfortunately, the CD32 Controller was not very good for many reasons, so we took its styling and created THEGamepad which is what the CD32 pad could have been like if it had been done properly. We chose the colours to match THEA500 and THEMouse, and maintained the button colours from the CD32 Controller to keep compatibility with games that use on-screen button colour prompts such as "Press RED".

Q: Why not using an existing one?

A: It wouldn't have been in keeping with the authenticity of THEA500 and we couldn't control the supply and quality if we used a third-party product.

4: THEA500

https://retrogames.biz/products/theGamepad/

Hint! The colored buttons are acting like the function keys F1 to F4.

Red (A) = F1

Blue (B) = F2

Yellow (Y) = F3

Green (X) = F4

All buttons are fully customizable in the **Game Settings** menu at Map Gamepad!

Hint! The buttons A/B/X/Y are represented by the corresponding keys on an external Keyboard!

Here are some pictures that shows how THEGamepad looks from the inside.

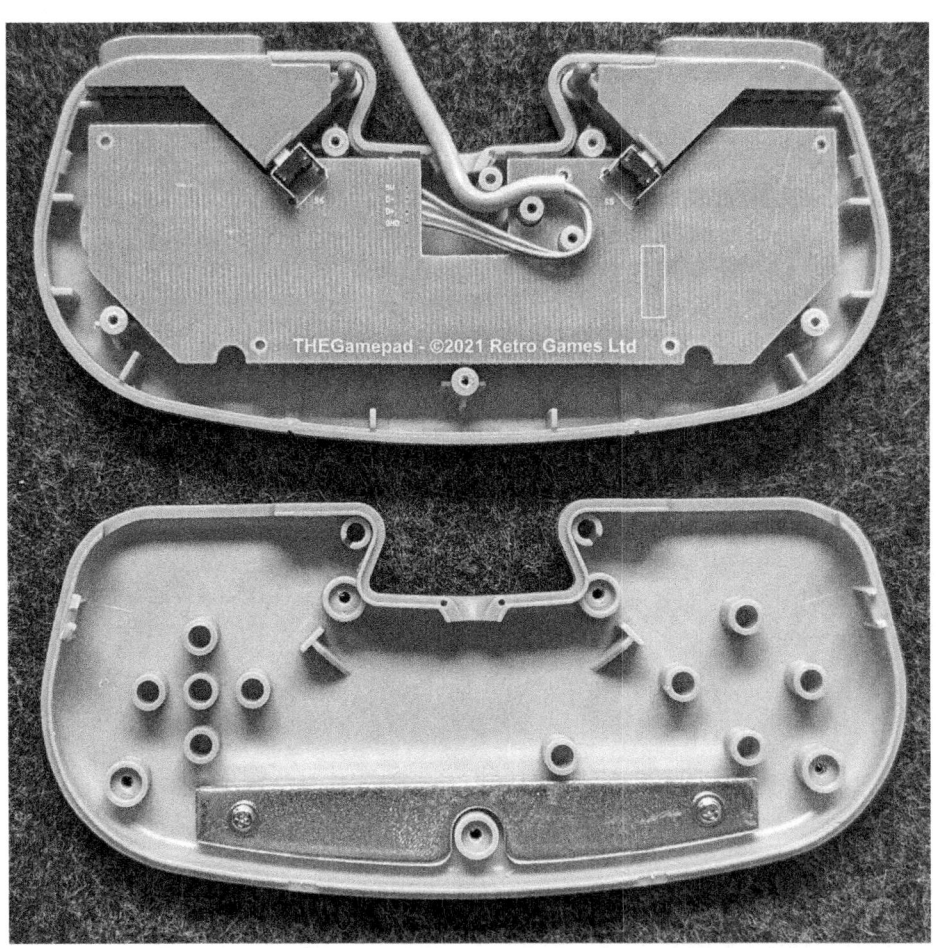

4: THEA500

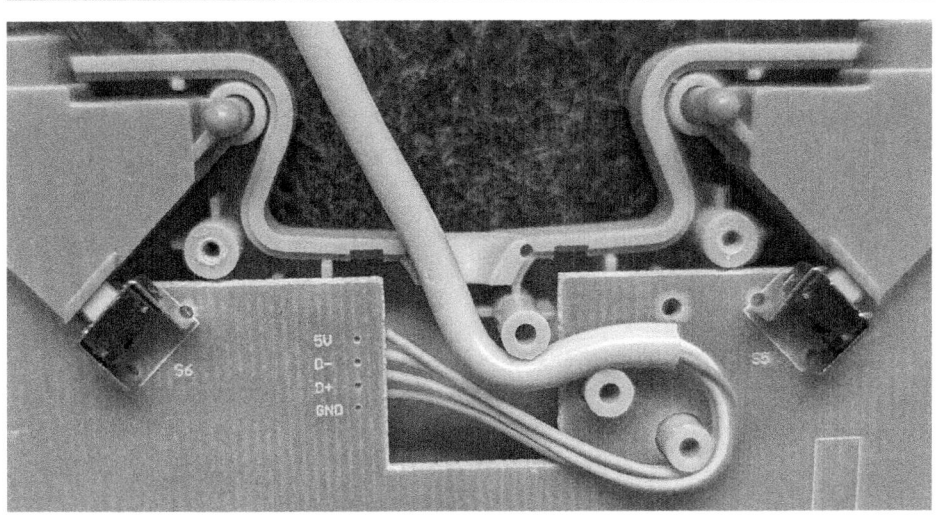

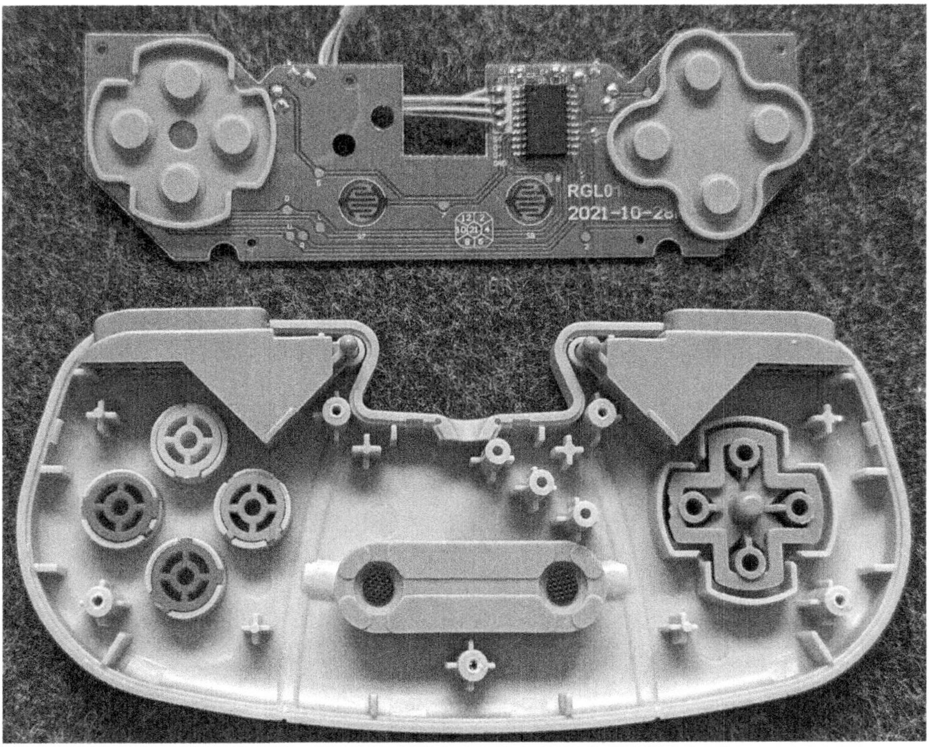

The Gamepad is also available as standalone in black:

4.3.2: THEMouse

See also: "7.1: Built-In" on page 123

The Mouse of THEA500 is needed for a few of the built-in games and you will certainly want to use it for other games as well.

Note that you can get more information about the key assignment and control of the Mouse in the carousel via the Gamepad with the menu button.

In this book, all functions are illustrated for the respective game.

Hint! You can use two or more mice at the same time for playing a game – for example, Worms!

Compatibility

Yes, it is fully compatible with both THEC64 and the THEVic20, and is working on any Computer via USB.

Question to RGL: How and why came up the idea to engineer your own Mouse?

Answer RGL: The original Amiga came with a Mouse – therefore it was necessary to supply THEA500 Mini with a Mouse. The original Mouse is no longer manufactured, and needed to be USB, so we had to create our own.

Q: In Facebook you're writing "original style 2-button Mouse". You constructed the Mouse new or is it based on original data?

A: We reproduced the shape of the original Mouse to create a new USB Mouse that is optical and not roller-ball based. We deliberately chose to use an infrared LED so the Mouse does not produce any light because the original Mouse did not produce any light!

Q: What are the specs for the Mouse like datarate, Hz., and so on.

A: The Mouse is a standard IR optical Mouse. These values are reported when THEMouse is plugged into a standard Linux desktop that uses the default 125Hz sample rate:

T: Bus=01 Lev=02 Prnt=03 Port=01 Cnt=01 Dev#= 13 Spd=1.5 MxCh= 0

D: Ver= 1.10 Cls=00(>ifc) Sub=00 Prot=00 MxPS= 8 #Cfgs= 1

P: Vendor=1c59 ProdID=0027 Rev= 0.21

S: Manufacturer=Retro Games LTD

S: Product=THEMouse

C:* #Ifs= 1 Cfg#= 1 Atr=a0 MxPwr=100mA

I:* If#= 0 Alt= 0 #EPs= 1 Cls=03(HID) Sub=01 Prot=02 Driver=usbhid

E: Ad=81(I) Atr=03(Int.) MxPS= 4 Ivl=10ms

Here are some pictures that shows the size difference and how THEGamepad looks from the inside.

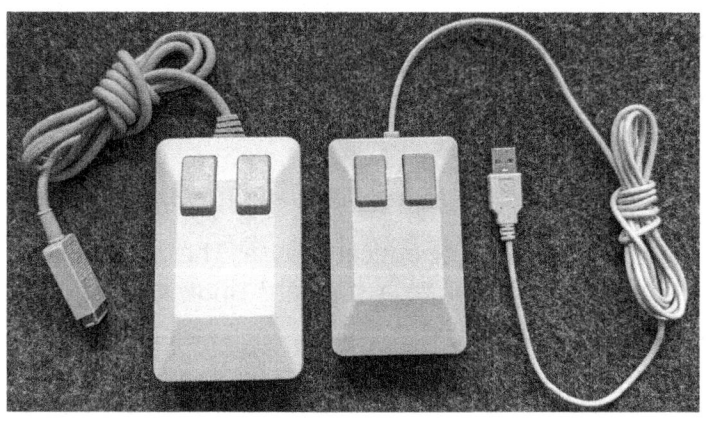

Commodore
327124-05 03/92
057845 MADE IN MALAYSIA

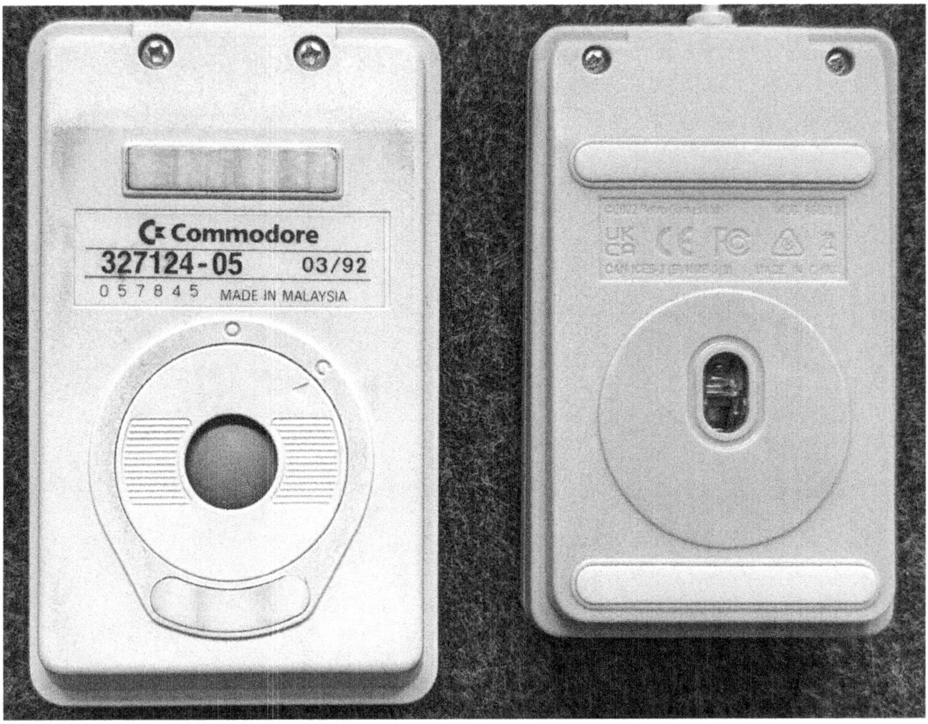

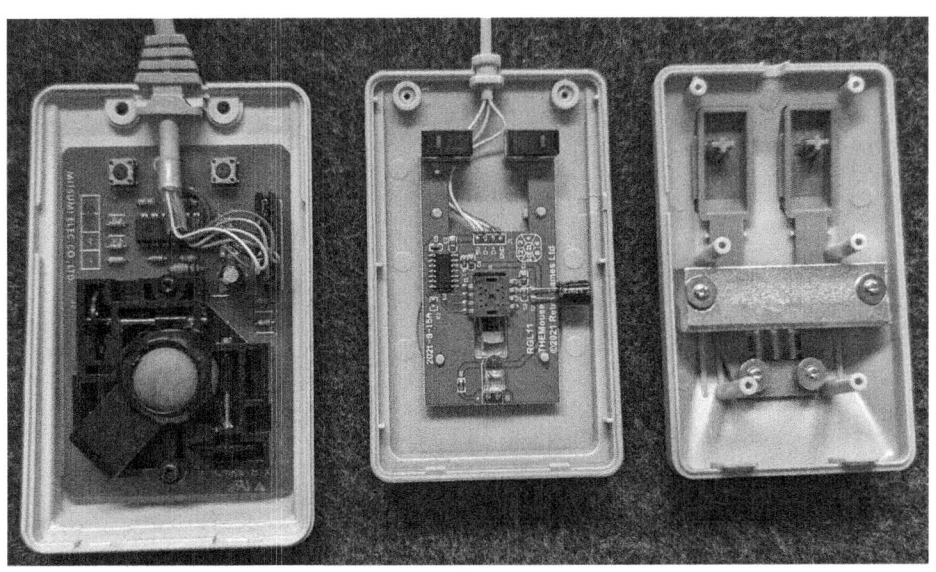

Unlike an original Amiga Mouse which uses a ball, 3 rollers and two small light barriers to electronically convert the position data into digital data, the Mouse of THEA500 has only two diodes.

And here is an original Amiga Mouse.

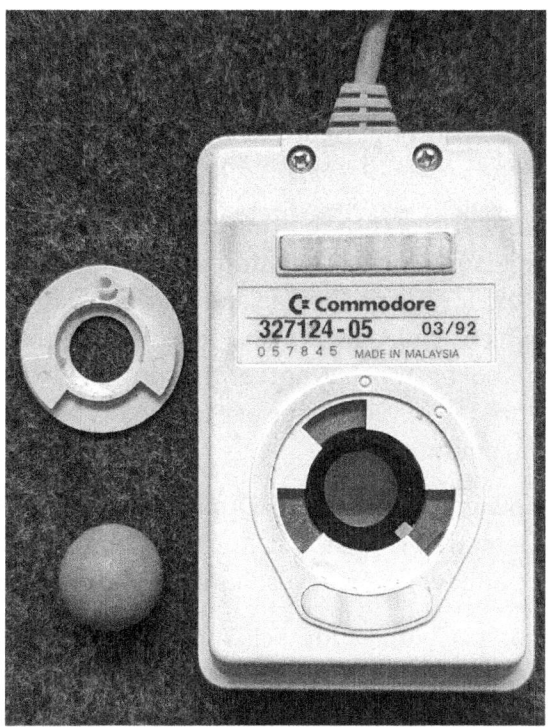

4.3.3: THEJoysticks (THEC64 joystick) fire buttons

The default mapping of the fire buttons for THEJoystick have been swapped, so button A is left fire, button B is right fire, button X is left triangle, button Y is right triangle.

Fire button is on the right

Question to RGL: On the Competition Pro Joystick (USB) in the first Firmware 1.0.0, the fire button is on the right. On the C64 mini it was left. How can one change that?

Answer RGL: The Joystick fire button choice is complicated because THEJoystick is impersonating a 12 button Controller, so some games will only have one button for fire on the pad and thus one button on the Joystick (unlike THEC64 which could have many Joystick buttons simultaneously mapped to fire for most games). Whether that button is the left or right fire button is a matter of taste. We appreciate that users have preferences and we are considering options.

Q: There are no plans to make an THEAmiga Joystick? I believe it would be a seller. Am Gamepad is nice, but not the same feeling as a Joystick. THEJoystick is nice and works well, yes, but it is not an Amiga Joystick.

A: There was no "official" Amiga Joystick. Amiga owners used whatever was their preference. The nearest to an "official" Controller was the CD32 Pad, which is why we created THEGamepad.

Joystick and a Gamepad together – BE AWARE!

This concerns only games for 2 players and more with Firmware 1.0.0!

If the Mini is already started and the Joystick is plugged in first and then the Gamepad, the Joystick is player 1 and if it has additional buttons like the Competition Pro, also the control unit for "Home" and "Menu". The Gamepad is automatically Player 2 and the "Home" and "Menu" buttons no longer work .

If you leave the game with "Home" and then start it again with the Gamepad which has its functions in the carousel again, the roles of Gamepad and Joystick are reversed in the game!

Additional buttons

While some Joysticks may have more than 2 fire buttons, the additional buttons mostly perform the same functions as the Gamepad.

E.g. the Competition Pro USB.

On a Competition Pro with triangle buttons, the left one acts like "Home" and the right one like "Menu." The left fire button acts like fire and the right like the A or Start button. In a game, the right fire key calls the virtual Keyboard.

Since the update to 1.1.1 the buttons have swapped to its normal functions.

4.3.4: THEKeyboards

Physical controller swap (since Firmware 1.1.1)

This feature aims to allow users to play games with a two or four button joystick such as a USB Competition Pro, which cannot launch games from Media select because it does not have the required buttons. With this feature, you launch the game with THEGAMEPAD as usual, and then switch to the button-limited joystick by pressing and holding HOME and then press button X.

This will swap the controller in hand (THEGAMEPAD used to launch the game) with the next controller THEA500 Mini has detected. Invoking the controller swap function a second time will swap the joystick back.

Keyboard control (since Firmware 1.1.1)

THEA500 Mini now allows the user interface to be controlled using the keyboard. The cursor keys act as the DPAD, keys A, B, X, Y, R and L act as the buttons of the same name on THEGAMEPAD with H and M acting as HOME and MENU.

Question to RGL: Have you ever considered making an external Keyboard with Amiga keys? If not, why not?

Answer RGL: If significant numbers of customers want one, we could consider it.

Hint! I suggest you connect a real Keyboard. It will make typing in names much easier, and you can use cheat codes more simple.

I have connected various USB Keyboards to the A500 Mini and had no problems at all. Quite the opposite, in fact, because a Keyboard with a built-in trackball worked quite wonderfully as a mouse replacement.

Cherry Ultraslim Trackball Keyboard G48-4400

If you use a Windows Keyboard, the Windows keys to the left and right of the Space and Alt keys work like the matching Amiga keys on an original Keyboard.

If you plug any standard USB keyboard into one of THEA500 Mini's USB ports, that keyboard will function much like an original Amiga keyboard.

QWERTY, QWERTS, AZERTY...

If you use a keyboard with a US QWERTY layout, most of the keys will function as you would expect. For other layouts, press the key in the same physical position as the key you wish to press on a standard US QWERTY layout. For example, if you have a French AZERTY layout keyboard, pressing "A" will act as if you had pressed "Q" on the Amiga keyboard.

Some Amiga keyboard keys do not exist on a modern USB keyboard, so are mapped to the following **Keys**:

Amiga key	USB keyboard key(s)
𝐴 Left solid Amiga 'A'	⊞ Left Windows logo / Left Meta / Insert
𝔸 Right hollow Amiga 'A'	⊞ Right Windows logo / Right Meta / Home
Help	Page Down

On the Amiga keyboard there are also the "(" and ")" keys on the numeric keypad. These cannot be pressed using a USB keyboard, but can be pressed using the virtual keyboard

Hint! A Keyboard can be plugged in any time. Even if you only realise while playing a game that you need to type or press keys, just plug a Keyboard in. This also works if you have to unplug another peripheral first.

AmigaOne Keyboard

The AmigaOne Keyboard USB (German key layout) in black, with silver AmigaOne logo and with the Amiga keys as boingballs. A "Help" key for Amiga applications, as on previous Amiga Keyboards, is also present. The Keyboard is designed to match the new Amiga Boingball Mouse.

The AmigaOne Keyboard can be used with any Amiga with USB interface.

https://www.amiga-shop.net/Amiga-Hardware/Amiga-Eingabegeraete/AmigaOne-Tastatur-Deutsch::458.html

Fun fact! Perifractic has already announced in a video about the THEA500 Mini that they are already building a real keyboard for the Mini :)

If you want to find out what the status of the thing is, check his YouTube page:

https://www.youtube.com/channel/UC6gARF3ICgaLfs3o2znuqXA

or search YouTube for: Retro Recipes

4.3.5: Virtual Keyboard

You can start the virtual Keyboard pressing "Menu" on the Gamepad.

The virtual keyboard can be accessed without having first to map its activation function to a Gamepad button. To activate the Virtual keyboard you can press hold HOME and then press MENU. To close the virtual keyboard, press MENU on its own.

A	B	C	D
E	F	G	H
I	J	K	L
M	N	O	P
Q	R	S	T
U	V	W	X
Y	Z	1	2
3	4	5	6
7	8	9	0
␣	↑	↵	⌫
←	↓	→	Del
!	"	£	$
%	^	&	*
-	_	=	+
(	)	\	¦
[	]	#	@
{	}	;	:
<	>	,	.
/	?	`	~
⇧	Ctrl	Alt	⇧
CL	A	A	⇥
F1	F2	F3	F4
F5	F6	F7	F8
F9	F10	Esc	Help

To navigate over the Keyboard, use the D-Pad on the left side on the Gamepad.

While playing a game, the virtual Keyboard will appear on the right-hand side of the screen. This allows you to virtually press any of the standard Amiga Keyboard keys.

Move the selector to key you wish to virtually press and press A.

Hint! While the virtual Keyboard is in operation the game will not respond to THEGAMEPAD. This is most useful for typing, for example entering your name for a high score table.

There are also some special shortcut functions you can quickly access using THEGAMEPAD:

THEGAMEPAD button Virtual Keyboard key

B = Return

X = Backspace

Y = Space

To close the virtual Keyboard and resume gameplay with THEGAMEPAD, press M.

4.3.6: Using third party devices

While THEA500 Mini has been designed to work best with the included peripherals, THEGAMEPAD and THEMOUSE, it is also compatible with Retro Games' THEJOYSTICK, as well as some third-party controllers and joysticks.

The button designations of most USB controllers follow one of the three conventions established by Microsoft (Xbox), Sony (PlayStation) and Nintendo. The following table shows how the buttons of these, and THEJOYSTICK, correspond to those of THEGAMEPAD.

4: THEA500

Xbox	Playstation	Nintendo	THEJOYSTICK	THEGAMEPAD
A	✕	B	Right fire	Ⓐ
B	○	A	Left fire	Ⓑ
X	□	Y	▽ ◣	Ⓧ
Y	△	X	◤ ◢	Ⓨ
LB	L1	L	○●○○	(L)
RB	R1	R	●○○○	(R)
Back	Select	Select	○○●○	(Menu)
Start	Start	Start	○○○●	(Home)

4.4: THEMaking of THEA500 Mini

4.4.1: Introduction

The very first release Video: THEA500 Mini (English)

https://www.youtube.com/watch?v=yKUgEOpr4Qs

The first Ad was the "THEA500 Mini Ad (UK, Ireland & Benelux)":

https://www.youtube.com/watch?v=cMIcOgQIMCA

Behind the scenes

THEA500 Mini – Behind the Scenes – January 2022

https://www.youtube.com/watch?v=AdTOt3DV9Z4

Question to RGL: Tell me about the hassle with getting enough chips for THEA500 Mini.

Answer RGL: As we booked well in advance our manufacturing partners had no more issues than any other company. We work with large professional companies, and build to scale, as opposed to small companies making say 1000-2000 units of a small niche project, so because we ordered and planned well in advance we did not encounter huge issues other than constantly increasing prices for electronic components and global shipping costs, as everyone has the same issue right now.

Q: Was the decision to make THEA500 unrelated to the global chip problem?

A: This was on our road map from a very early stage and once THEC64 was in production stages we moved the development from that to THEA500.

Q: What have you learned fromTHEC64/VIC20 projects (mini/maxi) that flow into THEA500? Please be detailed.

A: Almost every lesson and experience we learnt about manufacturing, designing, planning, licensing of THEC64 range was carried over to THEA500, and of course as the team and our partners became more experienced in this particular market that has been useful. It should be remembered that Daren for example has been in the games industry since his late teens for some of the biggest game companies in the world, Paul has been releasing media products into retail and digitally for over 22 years and was working within global blue chip companies since leaving school prior to that, Chris has worked at many tech companies and until working full time for Retro games was the 'Chief Software Architect' for Companies House in the UK, plus our partners Koch are a global publisher distributors and manufacturers. So while we are all learning new things every day, and we all adapt to a constantly changing world the team is very experienced in many disciplines.

Q: Did you ever received a letter or mail regarding the THEC64/VIC20 or since the announcement of the A500 by a celebrity? Or something that was really remarkable?

A: A UK MP often posts online how much he loves his THEVIC20, and some TV personalities like Dara Ó Briain' (https://en.wikipedia.org/wiki/Dara_%C3%93_Briain) actually had a THEC64 in the background on one of his shelves when he live hosted the BAFTA game awards in the UK.

4.4.3: Production Update

Here you will find a video that shows how the Mini is built.

THEA500 – Production update – November 2021 https://www.youtube.com/watch?v=BRqFCGPCOOI

4.4.4: Prototypes

There are not many pictures from the original THEA500 Mini prototypes available.

But here is one of the first produced ones:

The well-known Perifractic shows on his YouTube Channel "Retro Recipes" the very first prototype with serial No. 1!

4: THEA500

THEA500 Mini® Prototype Serial #01

Most of the differences indicate that this is not a 3D printed model, but only an unpainted production model.

The colour of the case is still rather grey, and not Commodore beige.

In contrast to the light rubber feet on the retail version, they are black on the prototype.

The power button is white and not beige.

The Keyboard does not have its own colours yet and is not labelled.

The label is a bit different.

4: THEA500

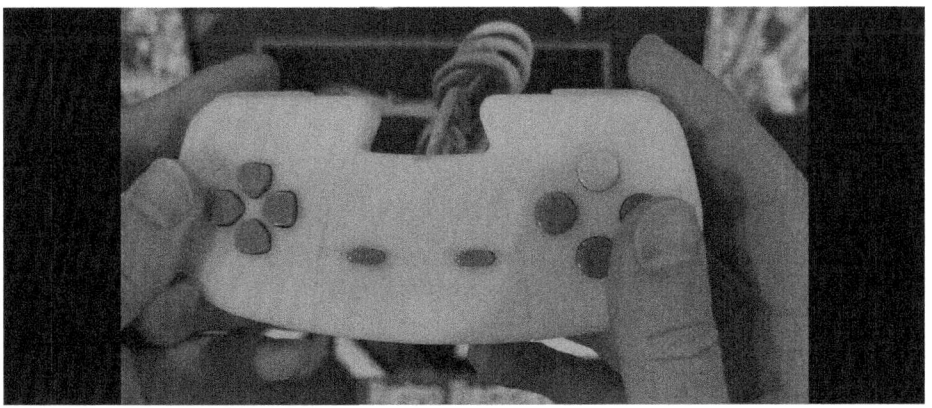

THE prototype Mouse

THE prototype Gamepad

4.5: Troubleshooting

Power indicator does not light up

To turn on THEA500 Mini, press the power button once. If after a few seconds the power LED does not light up and you see nothing on the TV, check that you are using a suitable 5V/1A (5W) USB power adapter, and that the power adapter is working. Unplug any controllers or USB sticks that you have attached to THEA500 Mini. Also check the power cable and test by exchanging it for a cable you know works.

Blank screen seen on the TV

If THEA500 Mini power indicator is lit but the TV shows no picture, check the HDMI cable is correctly connected at both ends, and if necessary try a different cable that is known to be working. Also it may be that THEA500 Mini is using a video output mode that your TV does not support. See "I have chosen a video output mode that is not supported by my TV".

No sound heard from my DVI Monitor

THEA500 Mini is not designed to be used with a DVI monitor nor is it supported when done so. THEA500 Mini may appear to be compatible with DVI monitors through an HDMI-to-DVI converter, but the DVI standard does not support audio, so even if you see a picture you will hear no sound. It may be possible to use a converter that is capable of feeding audio separately, but this is done at the user's own risk.

THEGAMEPAD or THEMOUSE is not responding

Do not unplug or plug in a THEGAMEPAD or THEMOUSE while a game is running as they may stop responding. If this happens, give the power button a short single press. This will suspend the current game and return you to the game carousel. After a few seconds THEGAMEPAD or THEMOUSE should be detected, but if not, unplug the input device and then plug back in after 5 seconds.

I have chosen a video output mode that is not supported by my TV

If you have accidentally chosen an output mode in Television settings that your TV cannot display, or are now using a TV that doesn't support that mode, there are two options. Either:

- Plug THEA500 Mini into a TV that does support the current output mode and then change the mode in Options → Advanced settings → Television settings (See "Television settings" on page 4). Or,

- Force a factory reset. If turned on, turn THEA500 Mini off by pressing and holding the power button for approximately two seconds (until the power indicator goes out). Wait 10 seconds. Perform the factory reset by pressing and holding the power button until the welcome logo appears.

You will then be guided through the initial setup sequence which includes choosing an output mode supported by the TV.

Note: Forcing a factory reset will delete your saved games and settings.

The edges of the TV picture are being chopped off

It is likely that your TV cannot display a full 720p picture or that you have some picture scaling options turned on in your TV settings.

Make sure to disable any scaling options in your TV settings so it is able to display a full unmodified 720p picture. If your TV cannot display a full 720p picture, turn off THEA500 Mini's setting Use screen edges in **Options → Advanced settings → Television settings**. This will usually help reduce or even eliminate the issue with the TV.

The TV picture appears to lag behind the game action

HD TVs often employ digital processing of the incoming TV picture. Aware of how this affects video games, they usually provide a setting to enable "gaming mode" (or a similarly named feature). Ensure that you enable this setting for the video input channel you are using for THEA500 Mini.

USB stick is not recognised

THEA500 Mini will only recognise USB sticks that are formatted with the FAT32 filesystem with a Master Boot Record (MBR). This is a standard format that can be created with all operating systems.

THEA500 Mini gets warm

This is normal. THEA500 Mini contains a powerful processor that works very hard to recreate the authentic gaming experience of the original Amiga, and in doing so it generates a little heat. THEA500 Mini contains lots of vents on the upper and lower surfaces of the case for this reason, and it is important not to block or impede this ventilation (see "Ventilation" on page ii).

THEA500 Mini should be moved away from other sources of heat and it should be ensured that there is plenty of airflow around the case.

Stuck in a game

If you play a game and don't have the Gamepad assigned to anything thus rendering the menu button useless, you may think you're stuck. Hoever, press the power button shortly not longer than one second and it will take you back to the menu automatically.

No virtual keyboard:

If you can't reveal the virtual keyboard with the menu button, you have to open up the mapping in the option menu then exit back out. The virtual keyboard will then work when you press the menu button.

Slowing down a carousel game:

If a game seems to be too fast, you have to edit the settings file it creates for it. In the .uae file (generated when you go into Game Settings for the game), add 'cpu_speed=real'. This should do the trick.

USB Save States missing:

When you save a game to the USB saves and they disappeared once you quit the game, you have to log into the game again, then go back to the USB menu the saved states. Your saved progress will then be visible again.

5: THEUpdates & Firmware

See also: "7.3.1: Install and Update WHDLoad" on page 256

Your very first step should be to upgrade the Firmware of your Mini. This will make everything much easier for you!

Attention! You cannot install a firmware that is older than the build version currently installed!

E.g. you can't install V1.0.0 when V1.0.2 is installed. You can only install more recent versions.

Why can't the firmware be downgraded? Will this be possible in the future?

Retro Games: Being able to downgrade firmware would make the upgrade user interface much more complicated. For users to be confident in what they are doing, Retro Games made the procedure and user interface as simple as possible. As such, the Mini detects the most recent upgrade on the USB-Drive and tries to install that.

The official link: https://thec64.com/upgrade/

Question to Retro Games Ltd (RGL): Are there plans for updates that doesn't make it in the first release and why?

Answer from RGL: We're very pleased with the firmware, but yes, it's likely to have then to add further file compatibility.

Always and constantly look for updates!

On one hand because of getting rid of bugs, get some new features like support for more filetypes, and of course for more official games in the carousel.

The best way is to watch and subscribe the Retro Games Ltd. YouTube and Facebook pages:

Facebook: https://www.facebook.com/THEC64andMoreByRetroGamesLtd

YouTube: https://www.youtube.com/c/THEC64/

If a new firmware or WHDLoad-version is launched, there you will find the announcement.

How to update WHDLoad, is shown in this chapter.

The newest files together with a change history, will be available on the official support pages:

Firmware THEA500 Mini https://retrogames.biz/support/thea500-mini/upgrade/

WHDLoad for THEA500 Mini: https://retrogames.biz/support/thea500-mini/whdload/

USB-Drive

Upgrading the firmware requires an USB-Drive, formatted using FAT32 with MBR (Master Boot Record).

With most formatting utilities, MBR isn't explicitly stated as an option so it isn't immediately obvious if your USB-Drive has it or not.

How to update

The update process is very easy. All you need is the firmware file, and a USB-Drive.

1. Download the newest file thea500-x_x_x.bin
2. Insert a FAT32 formatted USB-Drive
3. Copy the file to the root of the USB-Drive. Don't place the file inside a folder on the stick or rename the file. If you do, the firmware upgrade will not be recognised.
4. Plug the USB-Drive into THEA500 Mini
5. Start THEA500 Mini if he isn't already started :)
6. Choose the menu "system information"

5: THE UPDATES & FIRMWARE

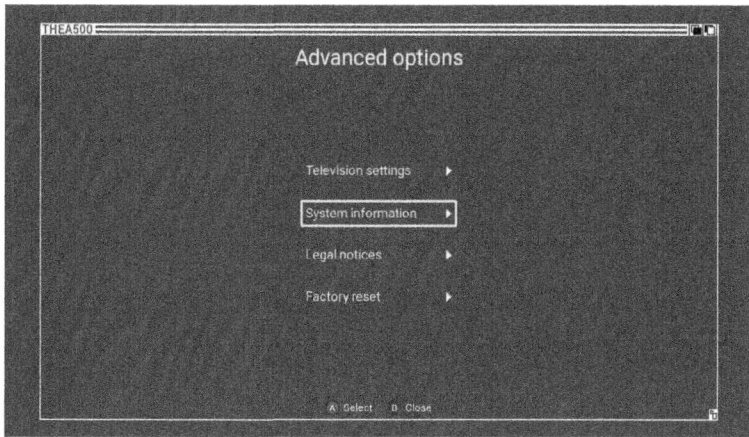

7. The upgrade file will be detected and you will be given the choice to "Apply the upgrade" or "Cancel" the screen. If you do not wish to upgrade at this time, select Cancel. If you Apply the upgrade, the following screen will appear showing the upgrade process:

!!!! Do not interrupt the upgrade or turn THEA500 Mini off while the upgrade is in progress. After a successful upgrade the console will restart automatically.

Note that you cannot install a firmware earlier than the build version currently installed.

81

5.1: Formatting a USB-Drive

THE USB FORMATTING PROCESS

You must format your USB-Drive on a suitable Computer before connecting it to THEA500. Most Computer operating systems (typically Windows, Linux or macOS) have an in-built tool for formatting a USB-Drive to the required standard.

Firstly, choose a USB-Drive that you are happy to wipe clean of all files and folders.

Connect your chosen USB-Drive to the Computer intended for formatting the stick. What you do next depends on which operating system is running on the Computer.

WINDOWS 10/8/7 (USB-Drive CAPACITY UP TO 32 GB)

If a window doesn't automatically display the content of the USB-Drive after connection, press + E to open File Explorer.

1. In File Explorer, right-click over the drive icon for the USB-Drive you want to use. Please ensure that you have selected the correct device before you proceed any further!
2. Select Format In the 'File System' category, and then select FAT32 (Default). Note that Windows will not offer to format a USB-Drive using FAT32 if the capacity (size) of the partition is greater than 32 GB.
3. We recommend that you don't tick the 'Quick Format' option. As a result, the format will take longer, but it checks for errors on the stick as part of the formatting process. Also, not using 'Quick format' ensures that MBR will apply
4. Select 'Start' to begin. In Windows 10, you can check for MBR after formatting is complete.
5. Right-click over the USB-Drive in Windows Explorer
6. Select 'Properties' from the bottom of the menu
7. Select the 'Hardware' tab
8. Select your USB device from the list

9. Select the 'Properties' button
10. Select 'Volumes' tab
11. Select 'Populate'
12. Select 'Volumes' tab (again)
13. Select 'Populate' (again)

For earlier versions of Windows (e.g. Windows XP/2000/NT4), you will need to source a separate utility that can format FAT32 with MBR. Use your preferred search engine to find one online.

USB-Stick correct formatted

It seems that simply formatting a USB-Drive with FAT32 is not enough. The Mini also expects an MBR (Master Boot Record) within the first 512 bytes of the stick.

The easiest way is to use a third-party formatting tool that works with USB-Drives and/or SD cards. Here is a search via Google (Format USB FAT32 with "MBR").

If you are curious and want to understand the details: Google Search for: What is an MBR?

MACOS

The following instructions apply to high Sierra (10.13.6), but we cannot guarantee that they apply to all releases of macOS.

1. After connecting the USB-Drive, a USB icon appears on the desktop. Now run Finder.
2. Select Applications > Utilities > Disk Utility, then select your USB-Drive. Please ensure that you have selected the correct device before you proceed!
3. Select the 'Erase' option. You can 'Name' the USB-Drive if you like
4. Select 'FAT32' or 'FAT' from the Format menu. If FAT32 is grayed out, select FAT instead. As far as this process is concerned, they achieve the same result

5. Finally, select the 'Erase' button to begin the formatting process. Note that unlike Windows, macOS will format a 64 GB USB-Drive using FAT32.

LINUX

You need to know the root password for your Linux Computer before you can format your USB-Drive using the guidance below.

1. The quickest and simplest method for Linux users to format a USB-Drive is to open a new terminal session and enter the df command
2. All available storage devices are now listed, but the only one that is of interest to you is the USB-Drive
3. Determine which item in the list is your USB-Drive. Please ensure that you have identified the correct device before you proceed!
4. We are using the example of /dev/sdb1 in the remaining instructions. Just substitute this with your own if it is different
5. Type umount /dev/sdb1 and press Return. This unmounts the USB-Drive, ready for formatting by the next command
6. Now type sudo mkfs.fat –F32 –v –I –n THEC64 /dev/sdb1 and press Return. Note that the name of the stick ("THEC64") is just an example. Use another name, or just omit the '–n THEC64' to not name the USB-Drive
7. Supply your root password and then the formatting will begin.

6: THEStart & THEOptions

See also: "4.1.1.5: LEDs & Blink codes" on page 36, "9.4: Disk Images & File Formats" on page 306

Before you start gaming and after you have chosen the language and the video output for 50 or 60Hz, I suggest you go through some more options first.

Mainly the **Display options** for the right video emulation you prefer like using the CRT filter, and **Game settings** for choosing what kind of input devices you prefer like either a Joystick and a Mouse, or a Gamepad.

Press **Menu** on the Gamepad to enter the option.

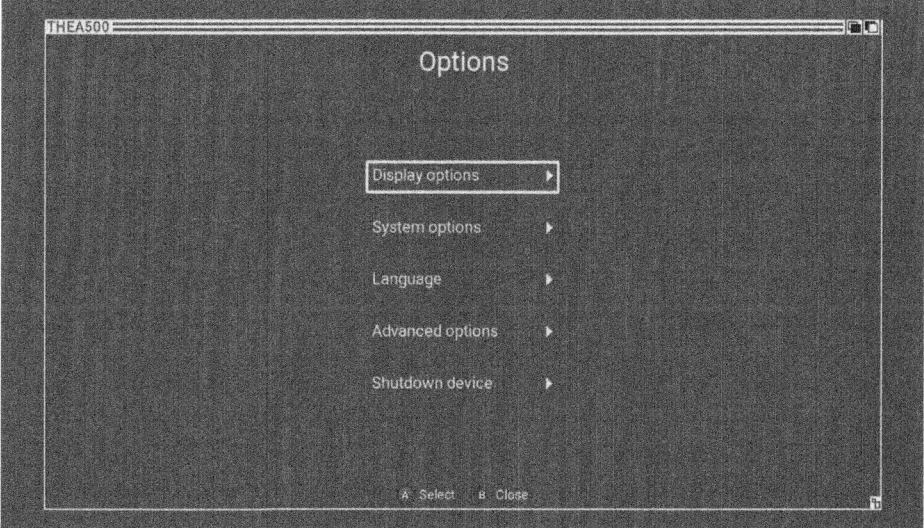

Language

This menu allows you to change the language THEA500 Mini uses to display the game descriptions and menus. The choices are English, Deutsch, Français, Italiano, Español and Polski. It does not affect the 25 included games, which are in English.

Tip: Most of the built-in games were developed in Europe where 50 Hz was common, so it is best to choose the 50 Hz output, if your TV supports it. Otherwise 60 Hz output will work just fine, as THEA500 Mini employs some clever techniques to manage the output difference. If you are not sure if your TV supports 50 Hz, THEA500 Mini will test this before continuing.

Television settings

Before you can proceed, you must test and confirm that your TV will work with the chosen video output mode by pressing X. THEA500 Mini will perform the test by switching to the chosen video output mode for 20 seconds. When the test starts you may see your TV screen go blank for a few seconds.

If your TV successfully resumes displaying the Television settings menu with the new mode selected, press Y to accept the mode. If the video test is not successful, identified by whether or not you can clearly see the Television settings menu during the test, wait until the test completes and THEA500 Mini will revert to the previous output mode.

Modern TVs and Monitor are together with THEA500 Mini, fully compatible and fast enough that you should see no difference if you choose 50 or 60hz. But there are still some devices that causes some troubles. You will soon find out, and just have to adjust this settings.

Use screen edges

Enable this option if your television can display a full 720p image without cropping. Disable this option if you find the edges of the image are being clipped off. This is enabled by default.

Starting the Option menu

The get to the Options menu, just press **Menu** on the Gamepad.

Display options

Fixed size

This does not scale the game image, and it will be surrounded by a black border.

Moderate zoom

This will attempt to scale the game image by a whole number of pixels, but only when it will still fit on the TV screen without being cut off at the top or bottom. Therefore some game images will appear the same size as with Fixed size scaling, and others will be larger. The amount of black border around the image will vary with the scaling applied.

Screen fit

This will adaptively scale the game image so that it will fill the TV screen from top to bottom, maximising the size of the image. The scaling may not be a whole number of pixels, which can occasionally produce very slight scaling artefacts.

Enabling Image smoothing or CRT effect will remove these. With this scaling mode, only minimal black borders are seen to the left and right of the game image.

If you are playing a game and wish to zoom the image, you can press and hold HOME and then press button Y. This will perform a crop and zoom of the image without you needing to exit back to the Game settings screen to change the crop setting there. However, when you do a hot-crop, the resulting image size is not stored, so if you want it to persist you need to configure it in the Game Settings screen.

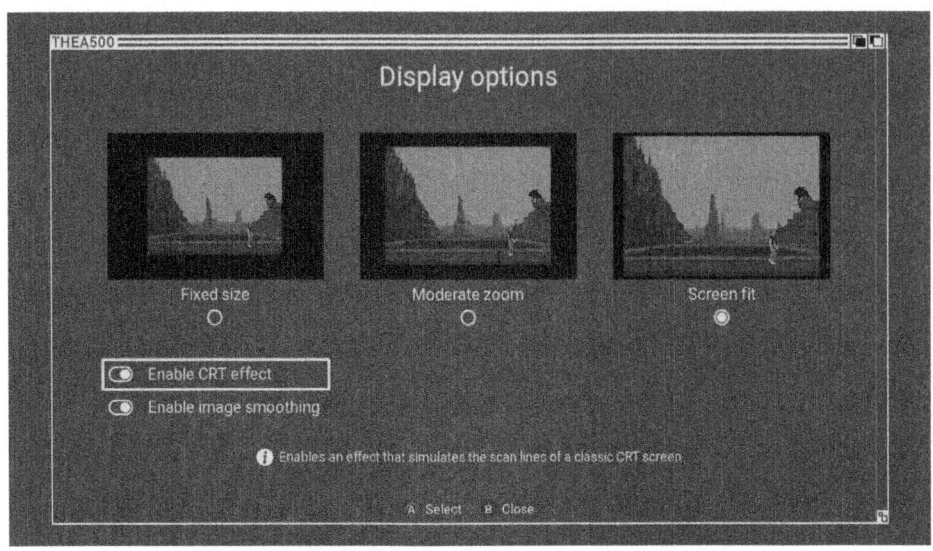

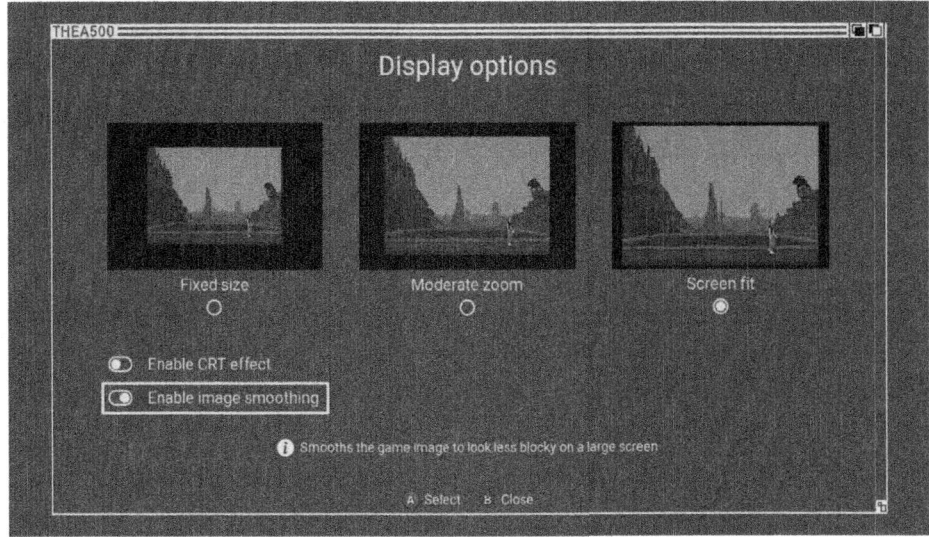

The CRT Effect puts some very thin lines in the video output, so that you have a feeling like looking on a tube Monitor.

The image smoothing smooths the pixels. There is now preview of this effect. You have to start a game, change the effect and find out what you like more.

System options

These settings are very subjective. You have to try out some settings till they fit what you prefer.

Mouse sensitivity

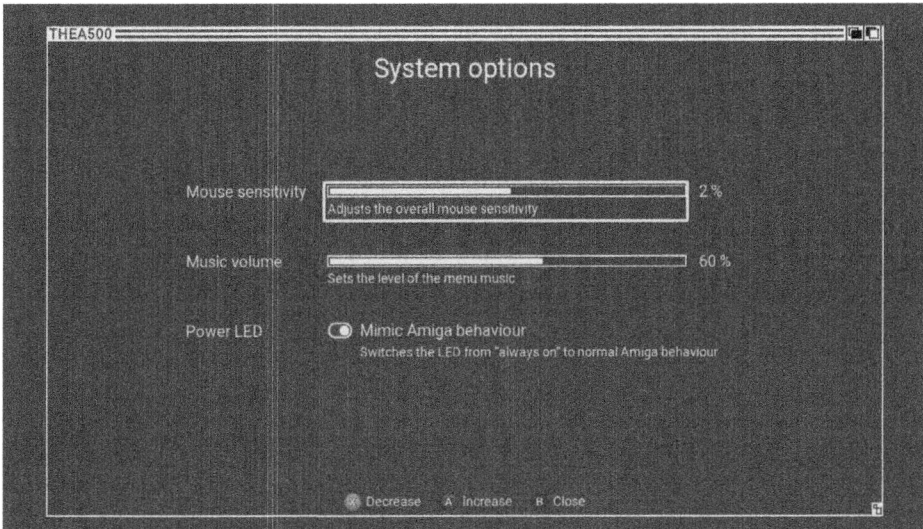

Music Volume

This setting is only for the Carousel background music:

If you want to mute the music, set the setting to 0.

Question to RGL: Chris made the Intro sound for THEA500. Was this his idea?

Answer RGL: Yes. Chris was unhappy with the available choices for music and wanted something that would set a certain mood, so he composed and recorded the piece himself.

Q: What is the background of Chris and music?

A: Primarily a guitarist and bass player. As a hobby he composes and records original pieces, produces and engineers songs for others and arranges songs for choir.

Q: Is this a special composition or part of a bigger soundtrack?

A: It's a special composition and arrangement for THEA500.

Power LED

When the option to Mimic Amiga behaviour is turned on, THEA500 Mini's power LED will mimic the behaviour of the original Amiga's power LED: that of being controlled by the running game. When this option is turned off, the power LED will remain lit while THEA500 Mini is turned on (this is the default behaviour).

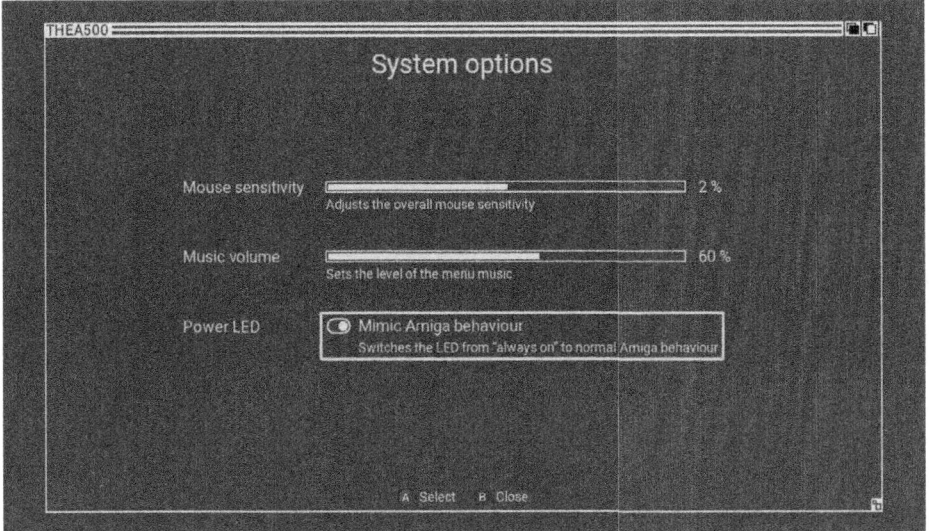

Shutdown device

This option safely shuts down THEA500 Mini. This will discard any suspended game and power off the device. Alternatively, you can shut down the device by pressing and holding the power button for two seconds.

Advanced options

This menu contains options for more advanced users and rarely used functions.

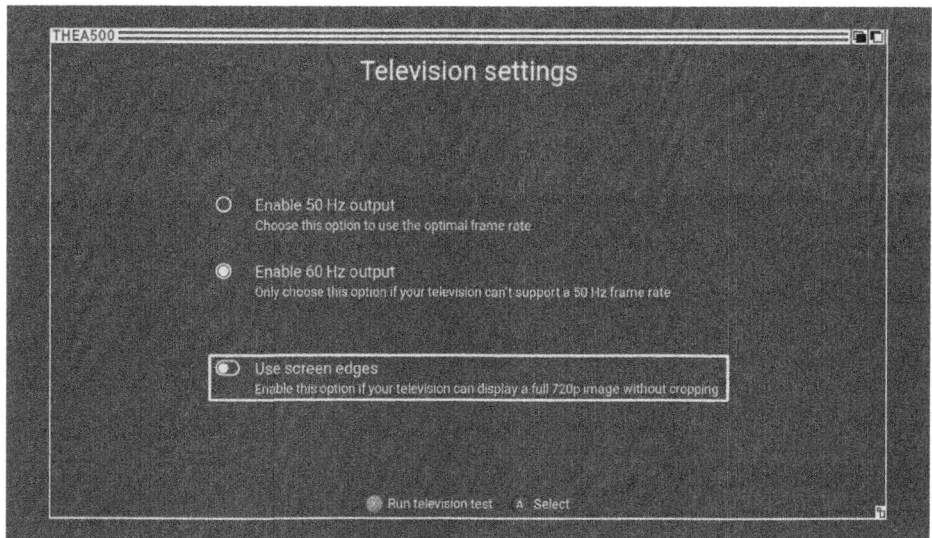

Read more about this options at "**Starting you own games.**"

System information

This shows THEA500 Mini's current firmware build, and will also allow you to upgrade to a newer firmware build if one is present on an inserted USB stick THEUpdates & Firmware.

Legal notices

This option displays legal notices relevant to THEA500 Mini. The text may be scrolled up and down using the up and down arrows on the D-Pad.

Factory reset

This will reset all settings to their default values and erase all saved games for the 25 installed games. This function can also be initiated by holding the power button down while THEA500 Mini powers on.

A factory reset will not revert any firmware upgrades, nor will this erase the Saved game slots and settings for user supplied programs held on USB stick.

6.1: Starting a carousel game

See also: "7.1: Built-In" on page 123, "4.3.1: THEGamepad" on page 51

Start InBuild Games in the Carousel

1. Current game title
2. Current game description
3. Current game information icons
A. Control type icons

These indicate what types of control are needed for the game.

All built in games show indicating they can be played with THEGAMEPAD, and some also show indicating they can additionally be controlled using THEMOUSE, depending on preference.

B. Number of players icon

This shows for single player games, for two player games, and for games that can have more than two players. Such multiplayer games may be simultaneous or round robin style play.

C. Favourite stars

This shows the number of favourite stars you have given this game.

D. Saved games indicator

This shows whether any saved games have been stored for this game.

The number of filled circles shows how many saved game slots are occupied.

4. Carousel of games

This carousel shows the box covers of the games included in THEA500 Mini, with the current game highlighted.

5. Suspended game

While a game is suspended, a miniaturised view of the suspended game is shown floating at the top-right of the screen. This suspended game may be resumed, or saved into one of four saved game slots per game.

Selecting a game

Use – to scroll through the carousel of games and select the game you want. As each game is selected, the game title, description and information icons displayed at the top-left of the screen will update accordingly.

Giving a game a favourite rating

Press X to add a favourite star to the current game. If the game already has four favourite stars, this will reset its number of favourite stars to zero.

Sorting the games

Press Y to sort the carousel of games by different criteria. These are Title (the default), Author, Genre, Year of release, Publisher, and number of Favourite stars.

Playing a game

Select the game you wish to play from the carousel of games using – and press A to start it from the beginning.

If a game is started before a suspended game is saved, the suspended game will be discarded.

All of the included games can be played with the THEGAMEPAD, though some may also be played using THEMOUSE, as indicated by the control type icons.

Some games have more controls than there are buttons on THEGAMEPAD.

Where this is the case, those that are needed less frequently are assigned to a secondary group of controls activated by pressing and holding R.

This causes the other Gamepad buttons to switch to their secondary control assignments.

6.2: ADF File support

As you may already know THEA500 Mini allows you to load your own programs from a USB drive. For this THEA500 Mini uses a program format called WHDLoad which was developed for the Amiga to allow floppy disk-based programs to be quickly loaded from a hard disk without the user needing to swap floppy disks.

There are four requirements that must be met for THEA500 Mini to recognise and load a WHDLoad program:

- the USB stick is formatted with a FAT32 MBR filesystem
- the USB stick has THEA500 WHDLoad Package installed on it
- the WHDLoad program is an LHA file
- the WHDLoad program is a complete archive of the program and not the program's WHDLoad installer.

THEA500 WHDLoad contains information on thousands of WHDLoad programs. Insert a USB drive, an additional item will appear on the game carousel titled USB Media Access.

If not you see this picture:

In the chapters **THEUpdates & Firmware** & **Formatting a USB-Drive** you can read how to get the WHDLoad package and get it on a USB drive.

Browsing programs on the USB stick

Select the USB Icon in the carousel and press A to browse and run the programs.

Only directories and files with an .lha file extension will be shown (at least with Firmware 1.0.0. In later updates other file formats will be visible too, like .adf.

Use the Gamepads D-Pad to navigate through the contents of the USB stick.

To select a program or directory, press A. To step back press Y.

Hint! You must always select a game with A before you can start it. Otherwise it can happen that you are on a game and press **Home** to start, but the last played game is still under **Current Media** and then this is started again.

Once you have selected a program, its filename will be displayed in the Current media section at the bottom of the screen. To start the selected program press **Home**, and to adjust its settings press **Menu**.

To return to the game carousel press B.

Start Games with WHDLoad

Before you start a game, it's best to set the right Joystick, Gamepad and Mouse combination. You probably already know this for your favourite games.

Hint! It is important to make the settings before starting a game, because every change requires a restart of the game. This can't be avoided with a save state!

It will happen that a screen like this shows up:

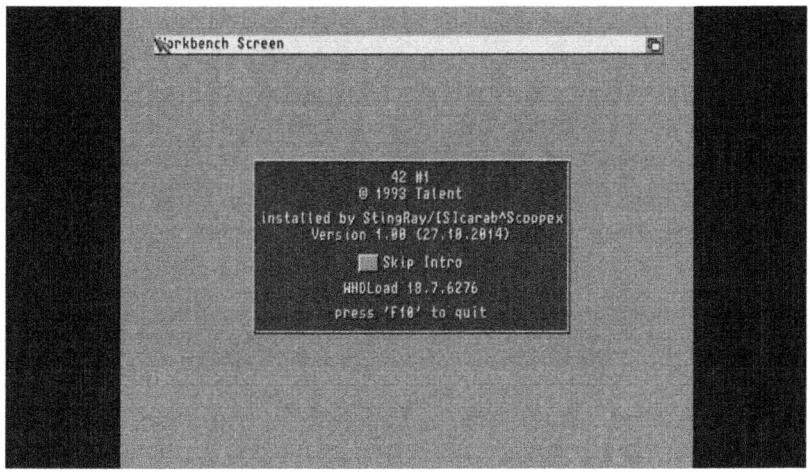

You can't use a Joystick or Gamepad to move the Mouse cursor, you have to take a Mouse or Trackball. Even if one is plugged in, you must first make sure that it is selected as the input device and on the correct port. Because unfortunately every program always wants the other port than the one you just preset. Murphy sends his regards :)

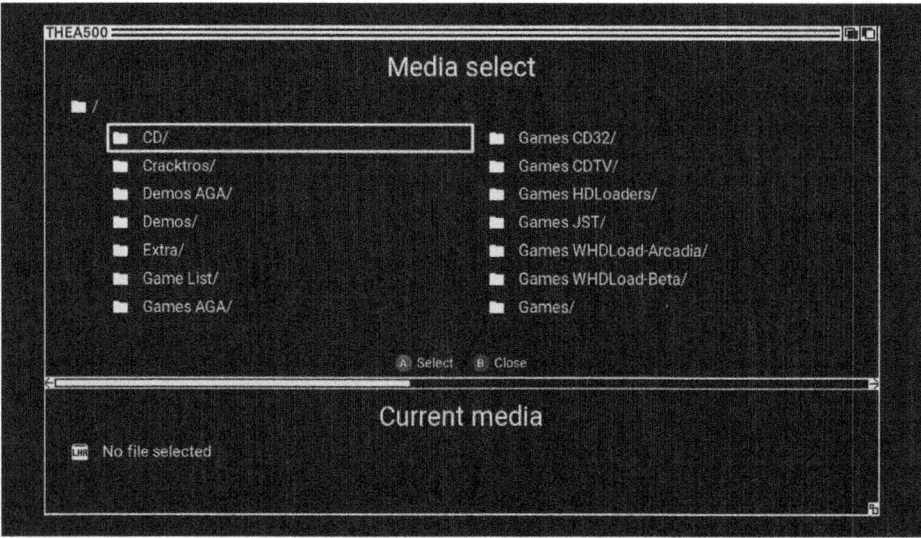

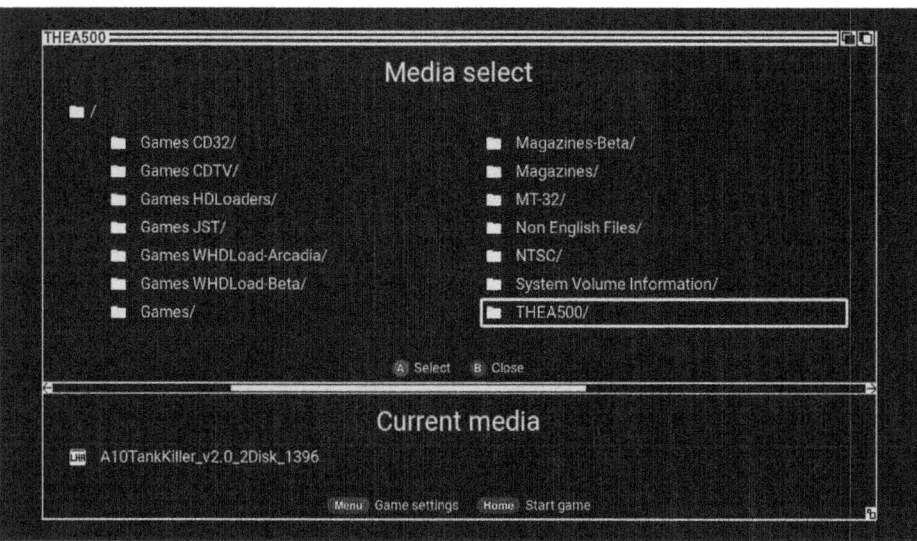

I connected a USB hard disk and provided it with several directories in which I stored Amiga games and demos. So I could easily try out which ones worked.

For example, I quickly found out that games for the Amiga CD32, the Amiga CDTV and also games in JST archives are playable.

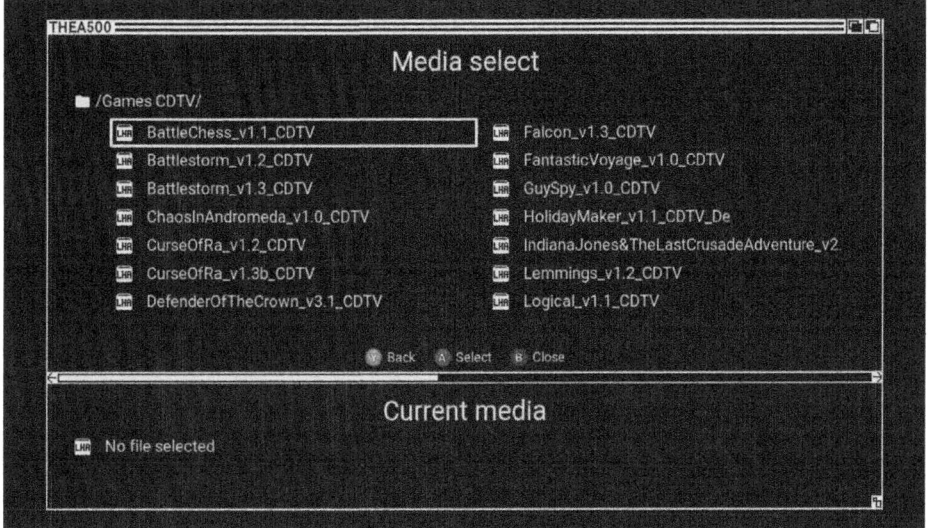

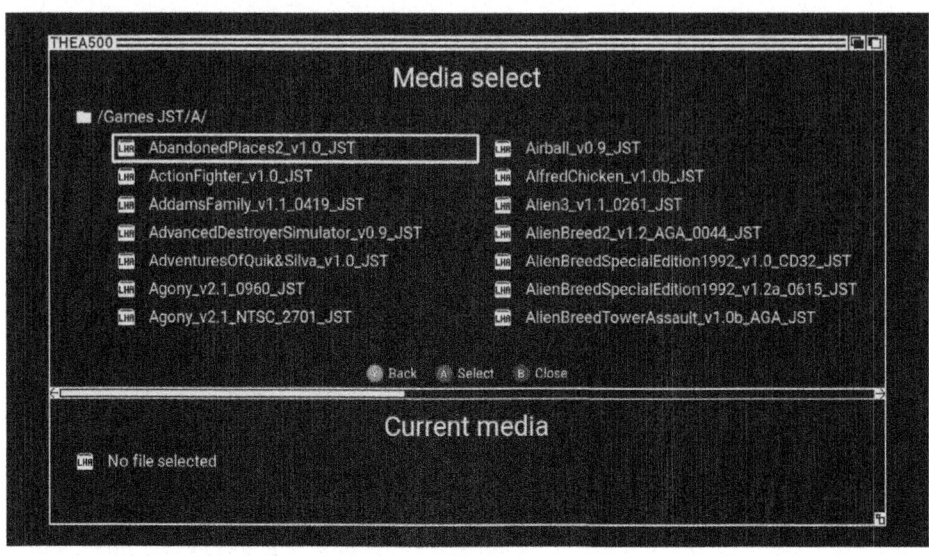

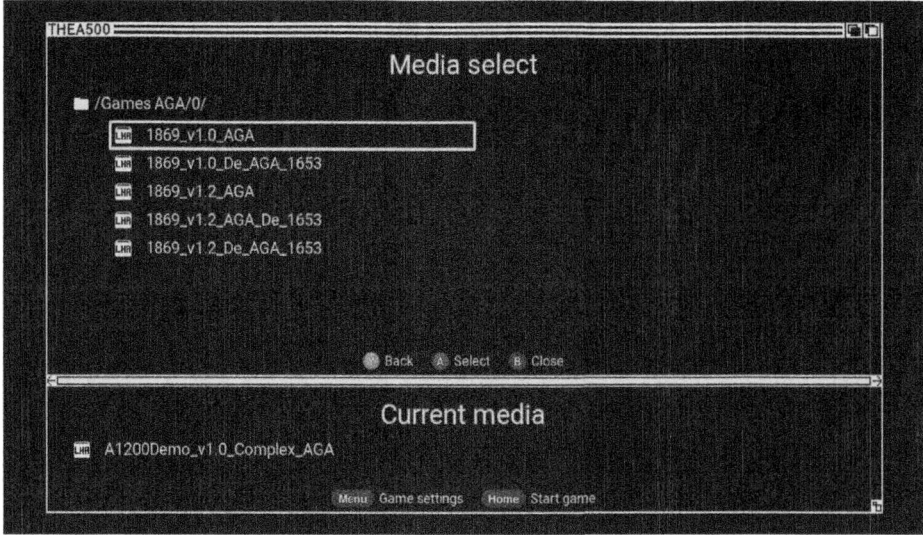

If there are several slaves to choose from, they are displayed one below the other and can be selected with the arrow keys (Up) & (Down) or via the button "A" on the Gamepad and confirmed with the button "B".

6.3: Game Settings

Game Settings

If you have started a game and you don't like the resolution (i.e. the image is too small overall or too large or compressed), you can change this in two ways and adjust it per game.

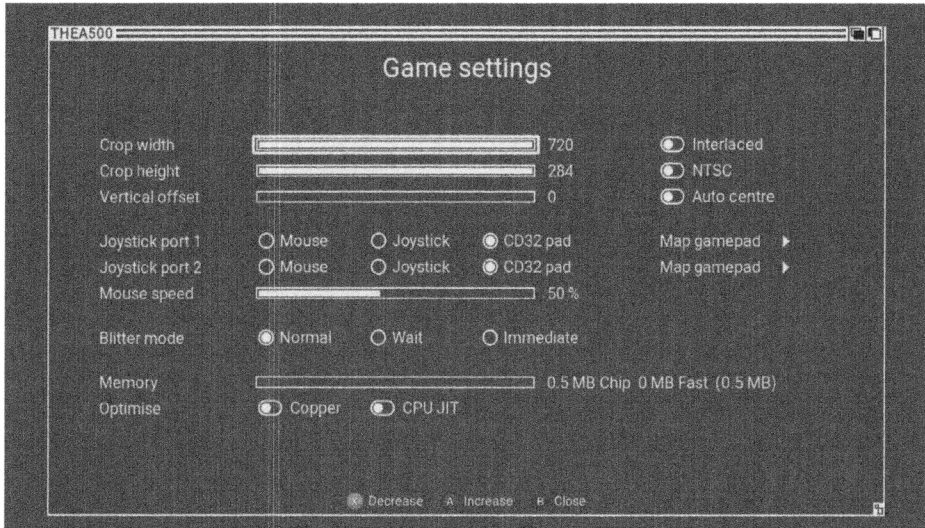

Crop width, heights and Vertical Offset

The first two settings allow you to change/crop the height and width of the game. Specially in very old games this is useful to map the video to a nicely fit the screen resolution.

The same applies to **Interlaced** and **NTSC**. Both switches make for a more pleasing video output depending on the game you start.

With Vertical Offset, you can change the graphic center of the game and move it in height.

Auto centre fits the screen usually in the right place for you. I suggest you always try this first.

Auto crop

This function attempts to automatically set the size of the image to minimise the black borders shown at the top and bottom of the screen (particularly when using the Screen fit display mode).

The Auto crop function is only available for a game that is currently suspended. In this case an additional button Y for Auto crop will be shown at the bottom of the Game settings menu.

When activated, the Auto crop function will analyse the image at the point it was suspended and automatically calculate the Crop rectangle and position.

This is nearly always successful and only occasionally requires a slight tweak to the settings afterwards.

1. Select the program to launch from USB drive
2. Enter **Game settings**
3. Enable **Auto centre**
4. Configure the mouse and joystick ports
5. Launch the program and proceed to the main game play screen
6. Suspend the program by pressing **Home**
7. Enter **USB Media Access** → **Game settings**
8. Activate Auto crop by pressing Y
9. Press B twice to return to the game carousel
10. Resume the program by pressing **Home**

If you find that the image moves around too often with Auto centre enabled, repeat the procedure but instead disable Auto centre at step 3.

Your changes will be saved in the settings of the game on the USB drive.

6: THESTART & THEOPTIONS

Joystick, Mouse, Gamepad and Keyboard settings

Here you can choose which device should be available in which Amiga port. The original Amiga had two joystick ports to which a mouse and/or joysticks could be connected.

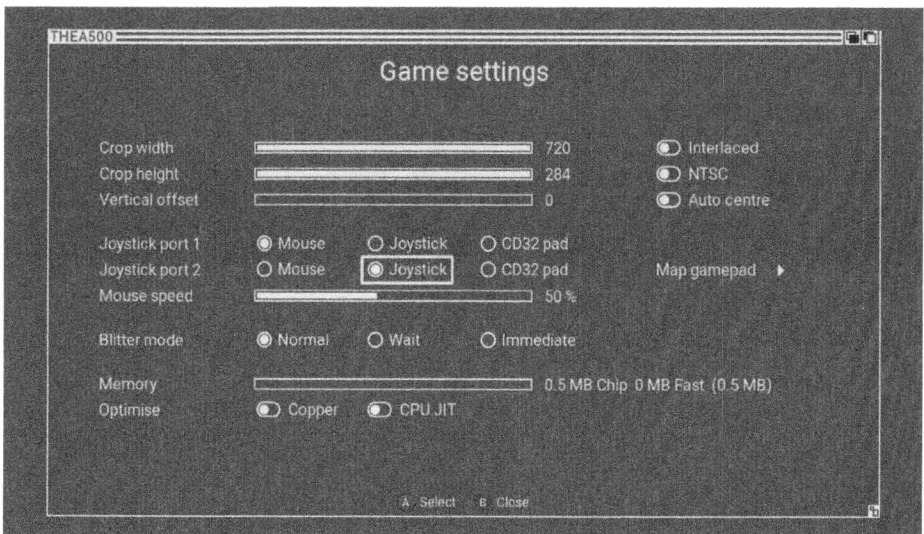

103

Hot-Crop

If you wish to zoom the image while playing, press and hold Home and then Y. This will crop and zoom the image directly. This is not stored! If you want it to persist, you need to configure it in the Game Settings screen.

Via "Map Gamepad" you can configure each device separately and change the key functions. The name is a bit confusing because you can also configure a Joystick, Mouse and a Keyboard here.

This settings are set for all additional devices you add. This way two Joysticks have the same configuration.

If there are multiple THEGAMEPADs connected to the USB ports of THEA500 Mini, THEGAMEPAD that launches the program is the one that will be designated as connected to the first Amiga port which is not configured for a mouse.

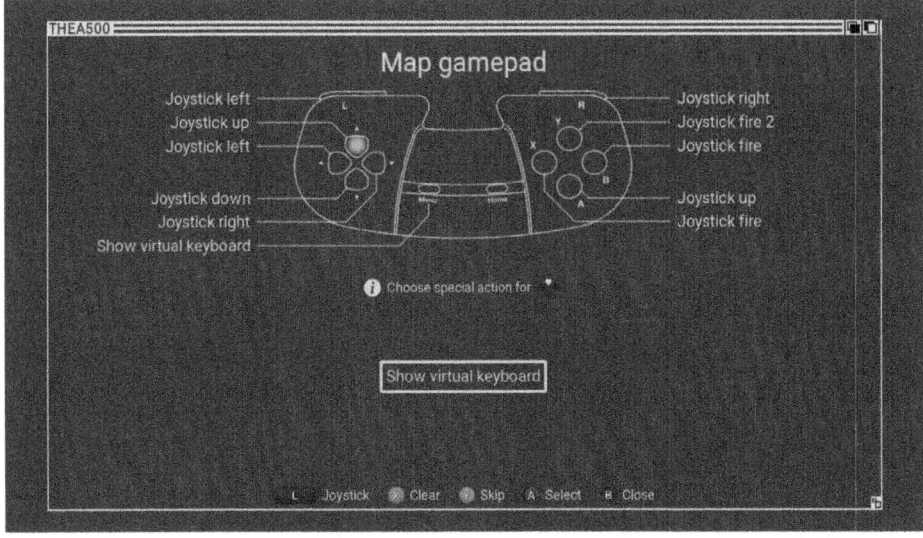

6: THESTART & THEOPTIONS

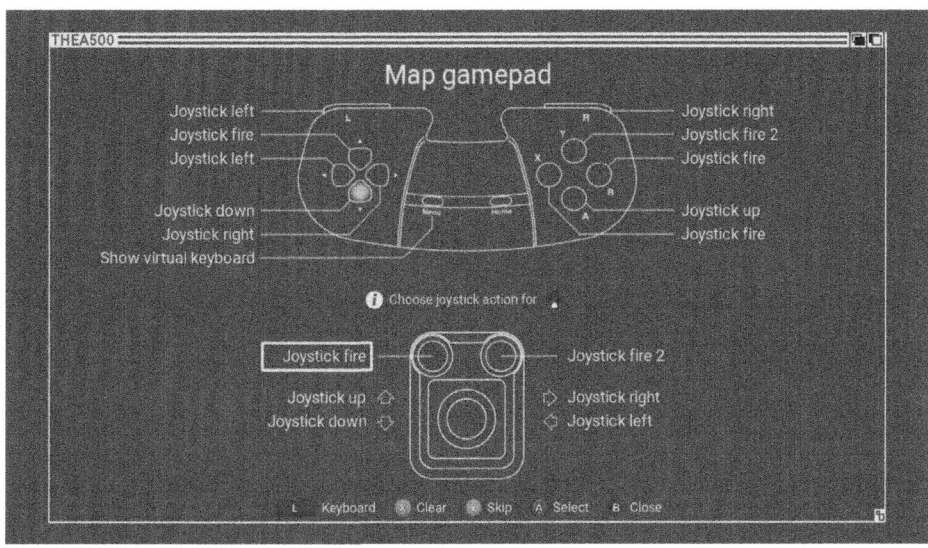

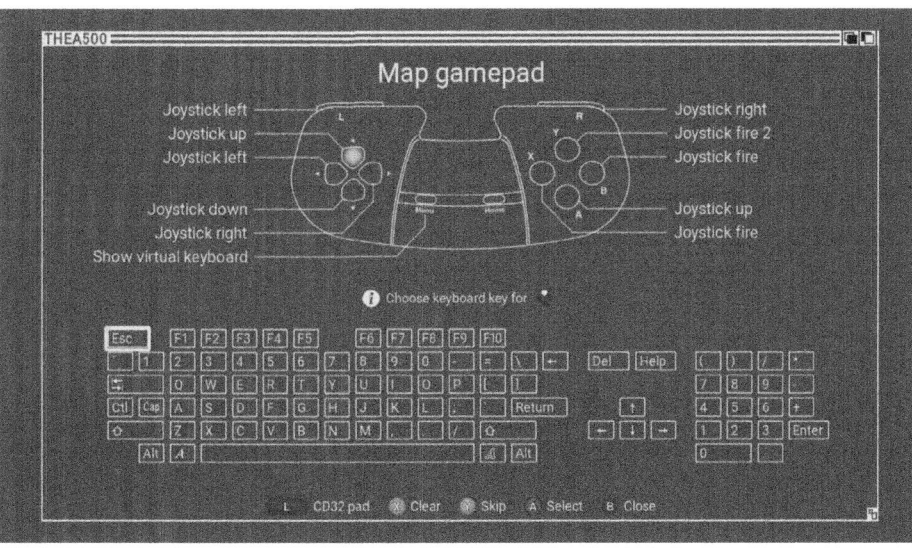

A HOBBYIST'S GUIDE TO THEA500 MINI

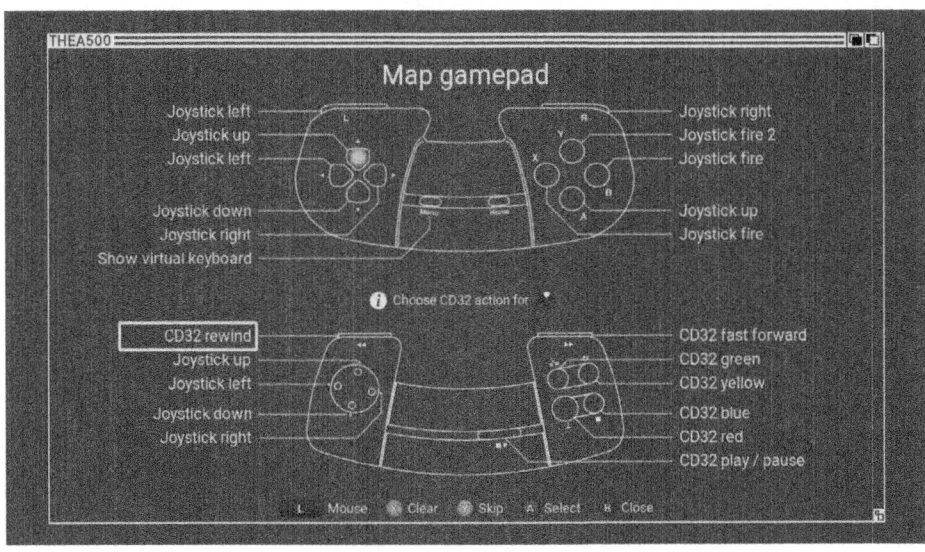

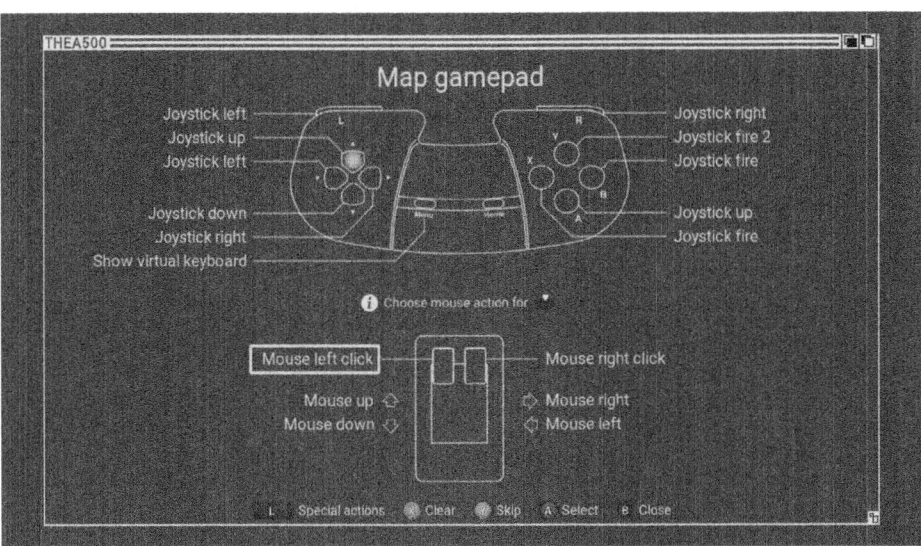

Mapping the Gamepad

When a port is configured as a Joystick or CD32 pad the connected THEGAMEPAD can be reconfigured to assign any control or action to any button, choosing from a combination of Joystick actions, CD32 pad actions, Keyboard actions, Mouse actions and Special actions such as opening the virtual keyboard.

The current action maps of a port can be viewed and edited by selecting its Map Gamepad option. This will show a diagram of THEGAMEPAD with a label on each button showing the current assigned action.

By pressing and holding R, the diagram labels will switch to show any secondary actions that have been assigned (the secondary action map).

To edit the primary action map, press A. To edit the secondary action map, press R+A.

Note: When the secondary action map is edited, any action on the R button on the primary action map will be overwritten with the Secondary controls action. If this is subsequently edited to become any other action, the secondary controls will not be accessible during game play.

When you start editing the map you are first shown the group of Joystick actions to choose from, represented as a labelled diagram of a joystick. This diagram will change as you cycle through the other action groups of Joystick, Keyboard, CD32 pad, Mouse and Special by pressing L.

Assigning joystick actions

While editing, THEA500 Mini positions a light blue indicator over THEGAMEPAD button currently being assigned. For this button:

- To change the assigned action, use 5 to select the joystick action you want to assign and press A
- To keep the assigned action, press Y
- To clear the assigned action (leaving that button unassigned), press X
- To make a selection from a different action group, press L

Once an assignment is made, cleared, or skipped, THEA500 Mini will move the blue indicator to the next button, where you repeat the process until all buttons have been assigned, cleared, or skipped.

When assigning Joystick actions, pressing L will switch to the group of Keyboard actions.

Assigning keyboard actions

THEA500 Mini will display a representation of an Amiga keyboard and allow keys to be assigned to THEGAMEPAD buttons.

Note: You can only assign a single keypress to a THEGAMEPAD button.

Assigning CD32 pad actions

Assigning CD32 pad actions to THEGAMEPAD follows the same process as assigning Joystick actions. THEA500 Mini will display a representation of a

Assigning special actions

This follows the same process as assigning Joystick actions. Typically this would be assigned to **Menu**.

Press L to switch to the group of Joystick actions.

Secondary controls

The Gamepad has a second pack of buttons which you can configure with pressing the right shoulder button R = **Secondary controls**.

6: THESTART & THEOPTIONS

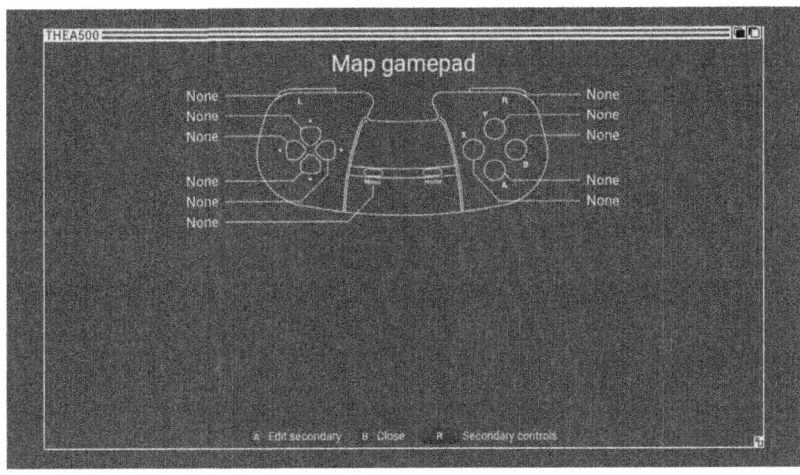

Gamepad keys on Keyboard

When you have a Keyboard attached, you can choose the games by these keys:

A	F9
B	F10
Menu	F11

Numpad	
Up	6 + 7
Down	4 + 3
Left	8 + 1
Right	9 + 2
/	Y
.	A
*	X

Since the Firmware 1.1.1:

109

Cursor Left/Right	Left/Right
Cursor Up/Down	Up/Down
A/B/X/Y	A/B/X/Y
M	MENU
H	HOME

Mouse speed

Programs that use the mouse will typically vary in sensitivity to its movement.

The Mouse speed setting allows you to adjust this for individual programs, perhaps to achieve a consistent response across all programs, or just to make some easier to control.

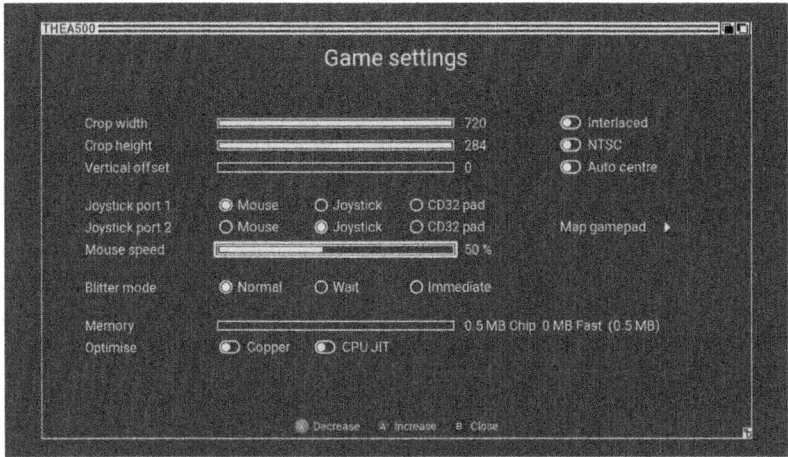

This is different from changing the sensitivity of the mouse itself, which will affect every game equally. To do this, go to Options → **System settings** and adjust **Mouse sensitivity**.

Expert Mode

To activate some additional settings which are very useful for your own games, you first have to enable this mode. Open the **Advanced options** and choose **Expert mode** and enable.

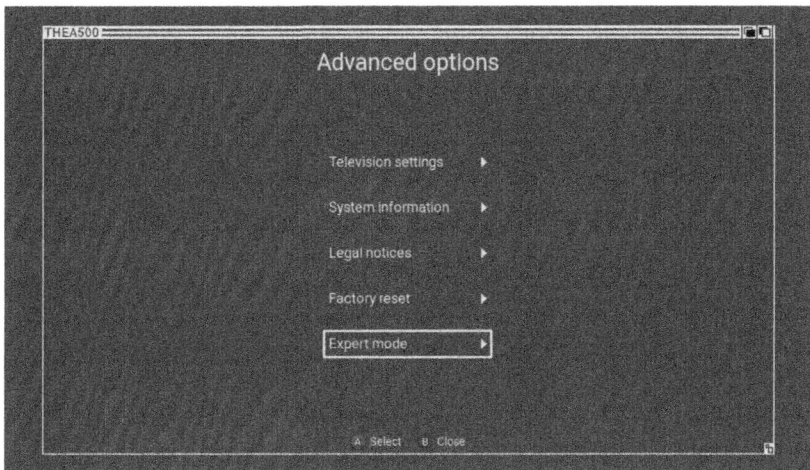

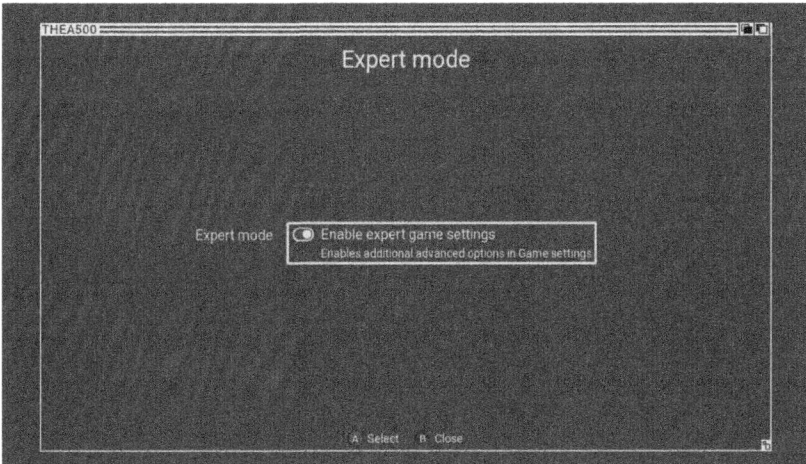

Then you will see this:

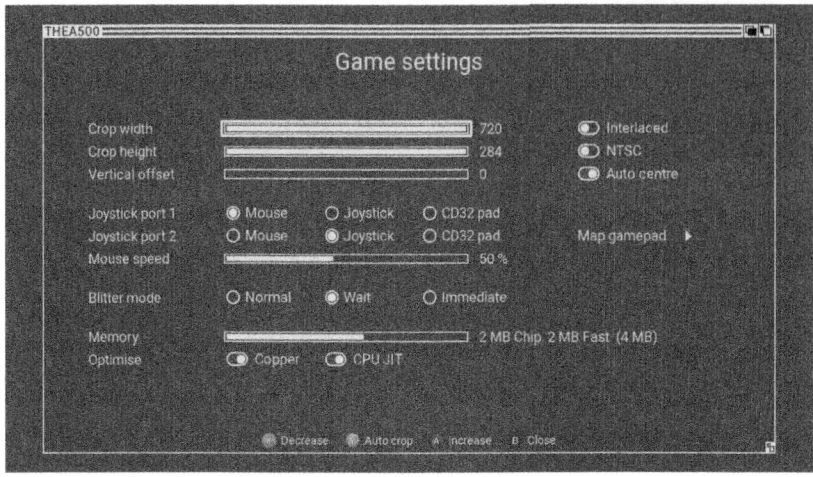

Blitter mode

An important setting can be the correct Blitter mode. Unfortunately, you only find this out when you play the game.

Since the processor of the THEA500 is very fast, it can lead to timer problems, especially with games of an older generation which were programmed for the Amiga 500.

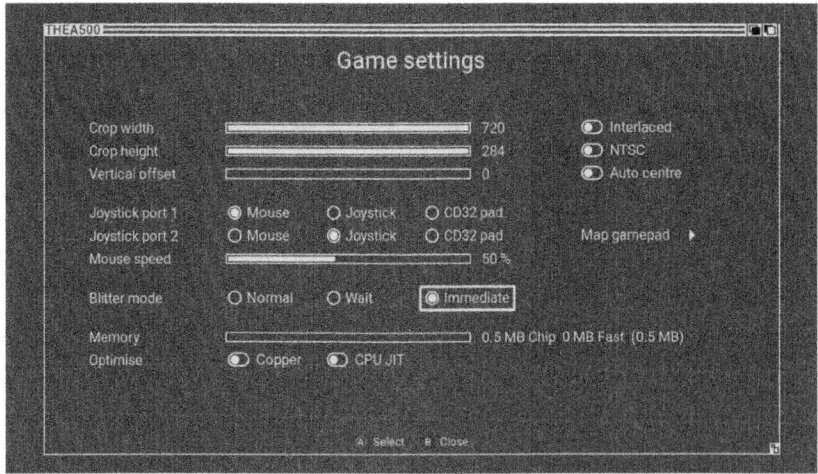

The modes can be described like this:

Normal – For games that already run on all Amigas without problems.

Wait – This mode helps most with old programs to adapt the speed of the blitter to them.

Immediate – Turbo mode for programs of the newest generation.

Memory

THEA500 gives every program the possibility to access up to 2MB Chip RAM and 8MB Fast RAM. Since there are programs that don't run with too little of one or the other RAM, but also some that don't like too much RAM, there is the possibility to choose from a standard Amiga 500 with 512Kilobyte up to a well-equipped Amiga 1200.

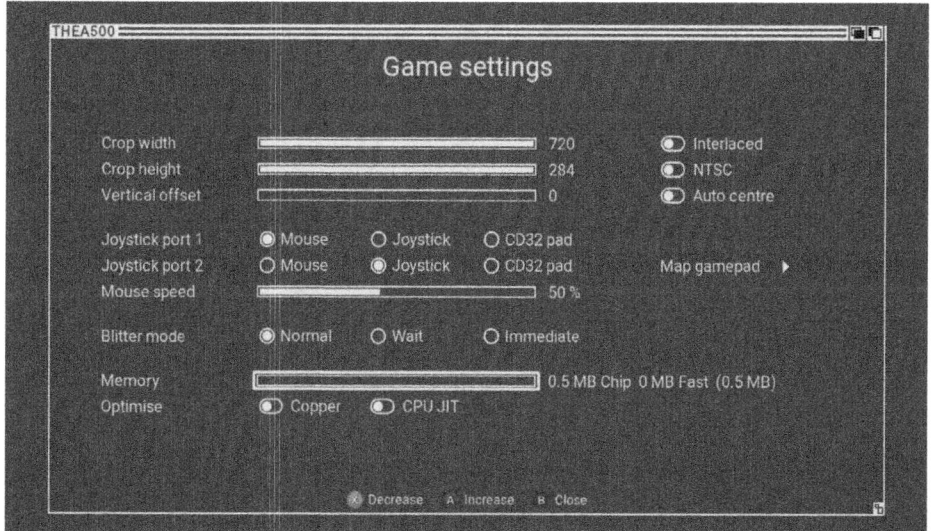

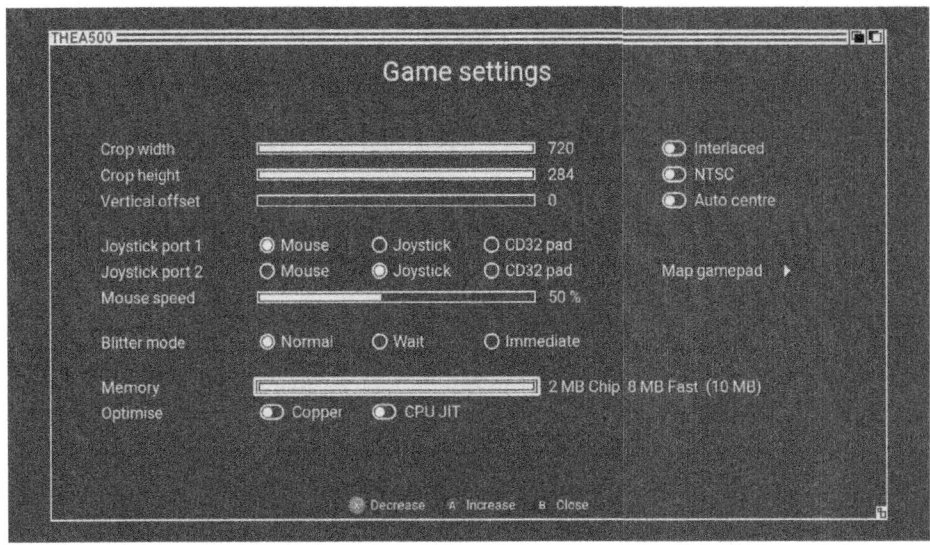

Optimise

If you see unusual artifacts and streaks in places where there shouldn't be any in the game, switch the Copper mode to Optimise.

The Copper (co-processor) mode provides even more performance.

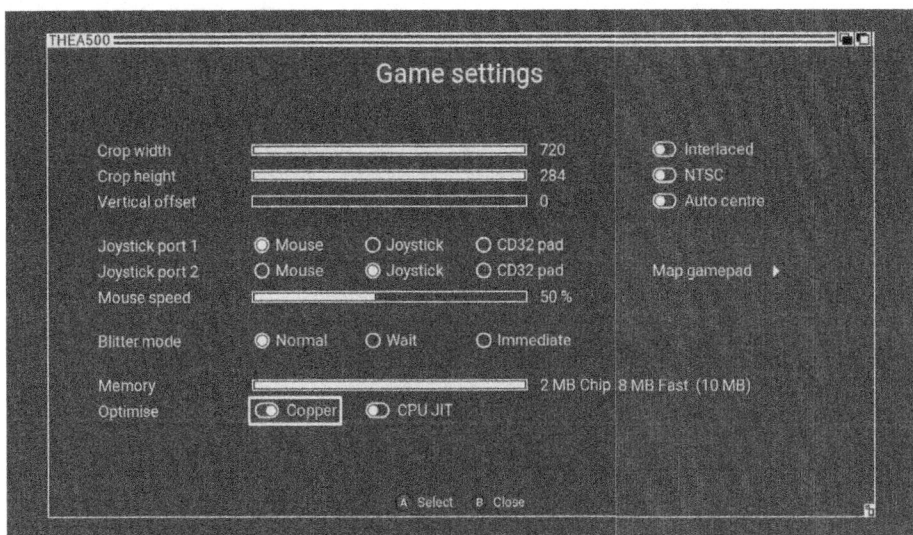

CPU JIT

CPU Just In Time – is mainly needed for games and demos that are complex and generate a lot of CPU load.

It prioritise the CPU's efficiency over compatibility. Because compatibility is reduced, this should be used with care.

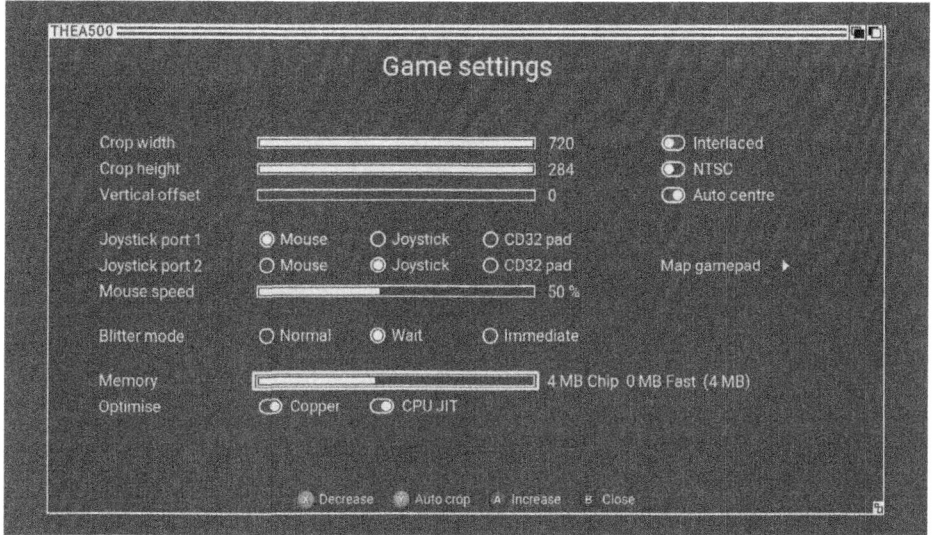

6.4: Help for a game

See also: "4.3.1: THEGamepad" on page 51

In the carousel you always get useful help when pressing the Menu-Button. An extra menu appears, showing the button layout of the Gamepad as they are mapped during the game.

For example Alien Breed and Worms:

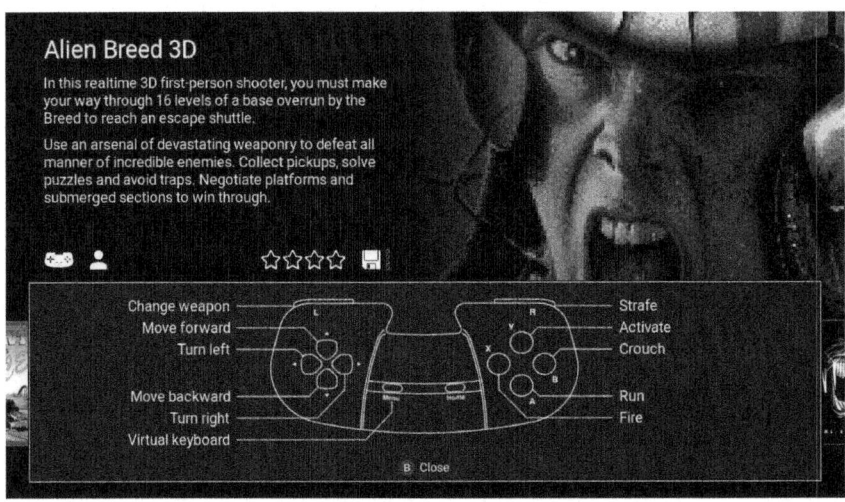

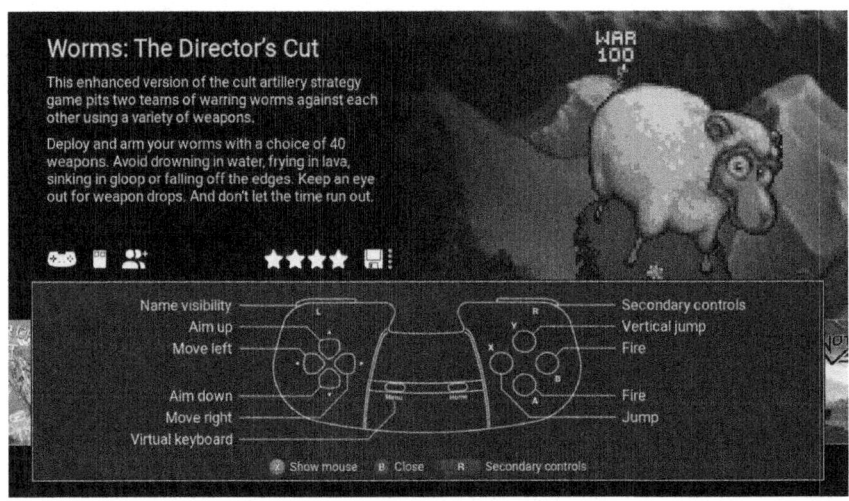

Press on the D-Pad Arrow up to view the help for the current game. This will show a diagram of the Gamepad with each button labelled with its function within the game.

Some games have a set of secondary controls. For these games press and hold R to show the secondary control functions of the Gamepad buttons.

For games that have support for mouse control, press X to toggle between diagrams of the Gamepad and the mouse to view the help for each.

Tip: The included games that use a mouse will have the mouse controls duplicated by THEGAMEPAD. This allows the game to be played with THEGAMEPAD alone if necessary. Such mouse controls are usually assigned to the secondary controls of THEGAMEPAD.

For full instructions on how to play each of the 25 included games, visit retrogames.biz/thea500/games

6.5: Exiting, resuming and suspending a game

Question to RGL: Are the original functions for save states and high scores still available?

Answer RGL: The user should use THEA500 Mini save states. The save/load provided by the game might work, or maybe it will not work at all. We can't make any guarantees for third party programs.

Hint! A high score or game progress can only be saved when you are in the carousel and if the USB-Drive is still plugged in. If the drive is disconnected before saving, the save state display disappears and only the carousel is visible again.

Suspend a carousel game

To suspend a game and return to the game carousel, press H, or the power button once. A miniaturised view of the suspended game will appear floating in the top right corner of the screen.

Tip: Try not to suspend a game while in the middle of an intense action phase, as this can result in a game that is difficult to play when resumed.

Saving or loading a suspended USB program

Select the USB Media Access, press down on the D-Pad to show the Saved game slots for the program currently selected.

To load or save a suspended program, you first need to make sure it is the one currently selected on the USB drive.

Resuming a suspended game

Press Home on the Gamepad to resume a currently suspended game.

6.6: Save & load suspended games

Pressing the down arrow on the D-Pad will show the Saved game slots for the current game, where you can save a currently suspended game, or resume a previously saved game.

Each game has four slots for saved games, represented by four floppy disks.

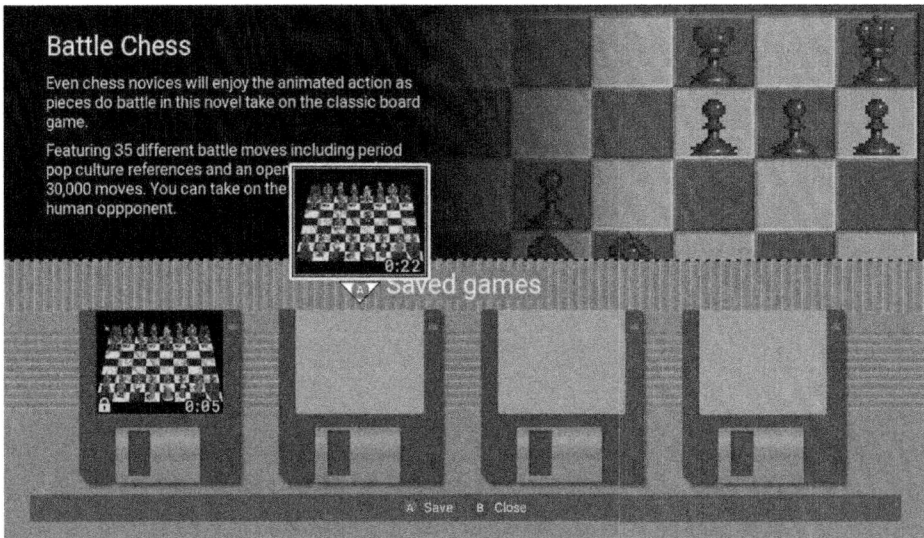

1. Filled saved game slot
2. Empty saved game slot
3. Elapsed game time
4. Locked game slot indicator
5. Suspended game

Saving a game

If there is a currently suspended game, the miniaturised suspended game will move down and hover above the first available Saved game slot (either the first blank slot, or otherwise the first unlocked slot). Pressing – will move the hovering suspended game to another slot.

Press A to save the game in the chosen slot. This will overwrite any game already in that slot. If a slot has been locked you will not be able to save a game into that slot until you unlock it.

Loading a game

If there is a currently suspended game, the miniaturised suspended game will move down and hover above the first available Saved game slot. If this is the case and you want to discard it and load a previously saved game, press 2 to move the selector down to one of the occupied game slots.

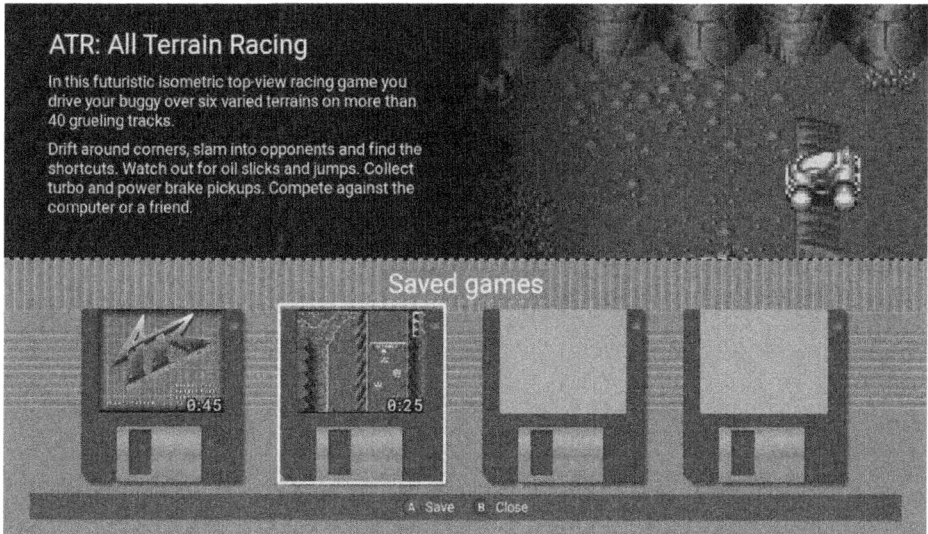

If there isn't a currently suspended game, the selector will automatically move to the first occupied game slot.

Press A to select the saved game you wish to resume, and press A to load it.

Note: Loading a previously saved game will discard any suspended game.

Locking/unlocking a saved game slot

Move the selector to one of the occupied saved game slots and press X to lock that slot. This will prevent any game from being saved into that slot.

Press X on an already locked slot to unlock it.

7: THEGames

Here you will find the compete overview of all games that are available in THEA500 Mini:

https://retrogames.biz/games/thea500-mini/

For each game there are a manual, screenshots, Gamepad layout and more.

And much more like hints, cheats and developer names, you will find in this book :)

Hint! High scores will NOT be saved automatically! And High scores can't be saved via the save function of any game. You NEED to make a save state to save your High scores and other settings!

CD32/CDTV Compatibility

Question to RGL: Is an update to the CD32 and CDTV or a compatibility planned? or can this already be used now?

Answer RGL: WHDLoad CD32 titles are supported. Native support for CD32 is being investigated.

Q: Can one run programs that influence a game? like a grabber or cheat? if not why not?

A: Not currently – you can only boot a single game/program/ for simplicity, as it is what most users want to do.

Q: Will there be more games?

A: Not at present, maybe in the future depending on storage capacity.

Q: Will it be possible to use the Keyboard to navigate the carousel and open the menu while in a Game?

A: This is already in test and will be part of a future firmware upgrade.

Q: Will it be possible to add your own games to the carousel?

A: No, first because all the internal storage is used, second because the firmware would require a lot of additional functionality to support this and the user would require multi-platform tools to package the game and assets into the correct format. Though we might look at options around this in the future.

7.1: Built-In

See also: "4.3.2: THEMouse" on page 57, "4.3.1: THEGamepad" on page 51

7.1.1: Alien Breed 3D

Released: 1995

Other Platforms: Amiga CD32 1995

Developed by: Team17 Software Limited

Published by: Team17 Software Limited

Distributed by: Ocean Software

Design: Andrew Clitheroe, Michael Green, Ben Chanter, Jackie Lang, Kai Barrett, Charles Blessing

Manager: Martin O'Donnell

Coder/Programmer: Andrew Clitheroe

Graphics: Andrew Clitheroe, Michael Green, Charles Blessing

Musician/Composer/Sound Effects: Bjørn Lynne

Original Game Soundtrack (13 Tracks): https://www.discogs.com/release/4840368-Bjorn-Lynne-Alien-Breed-3D-Original-Game-Soundtrack

Introduction

A 3D-Action first-person shooter, the fourth game in Team17's Alien Breed franchise, a series of science fiction-themed shooters.

Team17 made the source code for Alien Breed 3D freely available in March 1997. They released the source code to the sequel, Alien Breed 3D II: The Killing Grounds, on the cover CD of Amiga Format magazine and although not mentioned in the accompanying magazine, the source code to Alien Breed 3D was also included on the CD.

Gameplay

It is a first-person shooter. The game has maps of varying depths with platforms and floors above others.

Game modes: You can play in three modes: Easy, Normal & Hard.

Number of Levels: 16

Reception

The game was ranked the 12th best game of all time by Amiga Power.

Predecessor/Successor

- 1991: Alien Breed
- 1992: Alien Breed: Special Edition 92
- 1993: Alien Breed 2
- 1994: Alien Breed: Tower Assault
- 1995: Alien Breed 3D
- 1996: Alien Breed 3D II: The Killing Grounds

Hardware Requirements

Minimum CPU Class Required: Amiga 1200

Minimum OS Class Required: Kickstart 3.0

Minimum RAM Required: Attribute Image 2 MB

Media Type: 3.5" Floppy Disk

Video Modes Supported: AGA

Input Devices Supported: Keyboard, Mouse

Controller Types Supported: Digital Joystick, Joypad

Multiplayer Options: Null-modem cable

Number of Players Supported: 1-2 Players

Save Game Methods: Password

Miscellaneous Attributes: Hard Drive Installable, Amiga CD32

Number of Players Supported: 1-2 Players

Save Game Methods: Password

Miscellaneous: Audio CD Tracks

Joystick/Mouse/Gamepad:

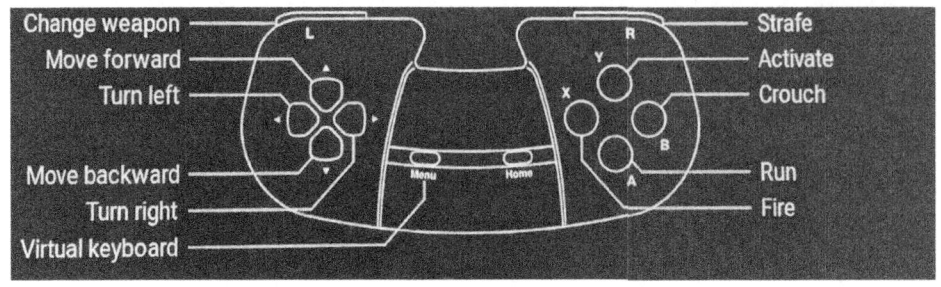

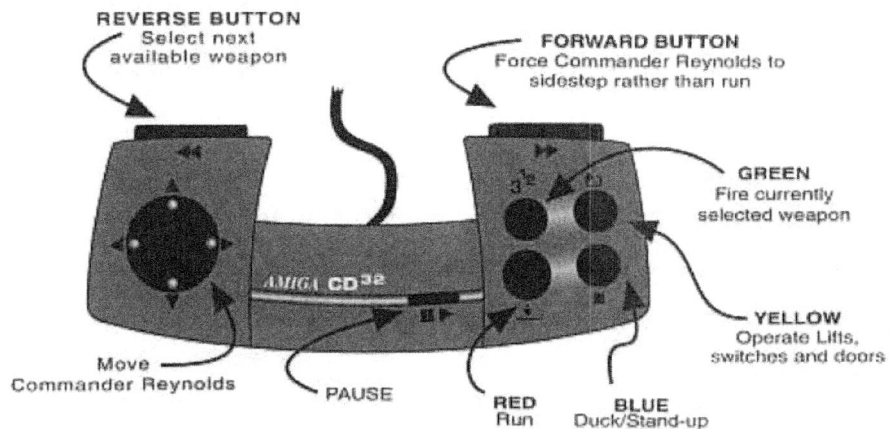

Keys

The "ENTER" key can be used to switch to the full screen.

Cursor up: Move forward

Cursor down: Move back

Cursor left/right: Turn Left/Right

. = Sidestep Left

/ = Sidestep Right

Alt Right = Fire

Shift Right = Run

D = Duck

L = Look Behind

Amiga = Force Sidestep

P = Pause

Esc = Quit

1 = Pulse Rifle

2 = Shotgun

3 = Plasma Gun

4 = Grenade Launcher

5 = Rocket Launcher

J = Joystick

K = Keyboard

M = Mouse

Space = Operate Door/Switch

Walkthrough

Video: https://www.youtube.com/watch?v=-CwgXt75csU

Walkthrough: https://youtu.be/y7k4o_VgbK4

Cheats, Hints, Tips & Tricks

1. Note the number of the level you are stuck on, quit the game and load your workbench. Here you rename your level file, for example "Level_1"; "Level_2"; and so on. Now the order of the levels is messed up, but you start the harder level first with lots of power and ammo!
2. If you would like to have full ammo for all weapons, then replace the last 8 digits of the level code with "J"
3. **Upgraded weapons:** Replace the last eight letters of any level code with "IIIIIII"

4. **Extra items:** Replace the last eight letters of any level code with "MMMMMMMM"
5. **Infinite ammo:** Replace the last eight letters of any level code with "EEEDCGN"
6. **More firepower:** Replace the last four letters of any level code with "AIHP"
7. **Increased health level:** Replace the last two letters of any level code with "00"

Levelskip

Level	CodeInfo
01 The Gate	
02 KOLKFNFFNFFNFFFF	Storage Bay
03 OKLKFHFFNFFNFFFF	Sewer Network
04 KPLKFPFFNFFNFFFF	The Courtyard
05 PLOPNFFFNFFNFFFF	System Purge
06 POOPNNFFNFFNFFFF	The Mines
07 KKLKNHFFNFFNFFFF	The Furnace
08 PPOPNFFFNFFNFFFF	Test Arena Gamma
09 LLLKHFFFNFFNFFFF	Surface Zone
10 LOLKHNFFNFFNFFFF	Training Area
11 PKLKHHFFNFFNFFFF	Admin Block
12 LPLKHPFFNFFNFFFF	The Pit
13 OLLKPFFFNFFNFFFF	Strata
14 OLLKPNFFNFFNFFFF	Reactor Core
15 LKLKPHFFNFFNFFFF	Cooling Tower
16 OPLKPPFFNFFNFFFF	Command Center

Skip to Level With Extra Items

These codes will allow you to skip to the level shown, but with extra items too:

Effect	Password
Go to level 02	CMOFFJENMMMMMMMM
Go to level 03	MIOOEDEOMMMMMMMM
Go to level 04	KPKOFOPOMMMMMMMM
Go to level 05	NLIAMBOOMMMMMMMM
Go to level 06	FOIINMPOMMMMMMMM
Go to level 07	CCCGIDOPMMMMMMMM
Go to level 08	PPKKIKKPMMMMMMMM
Go to level 09	LLKOHBLPMMMMMMMM
Go to level 10	BMAGHMLPMMMMMMMM
Go to level 11	HCIGGHLPMMMMMMMM
Go to level 12	LNIECOLPMMMMMMMM
Go to level 13	OLKOPFKPMMMMMMMM
Go to level 14	EOIGLMKPMMMMMMMM
Go to level 15	LKKOPPKPMMMMMMMM
Go to level 16	GNAEPPKPMMMMMMMM

Skip to level with upgraded weapons

These passwords will skip you to the level shown, and you will have upgraded weapons.

Effect	Password
Go to level 02	CMOFFJENIIIIIIII
Go to level 03	MIOOEDEOIIIIIIII
Go to level 04	KPKOFOPOIIIIIIII

Effect	Password
Go to level 05	NLIAMBOOIIIIIIII
Go to level 06	FOIINMPOIIIIIIII
Go to level 07	CCCGIDOPIIIIIIII
Go to level 08	PPKKIKKPIIIIIIII
Go to level 09	LLKOHBLPIIIIIIII
Go to level 10	BMAGHMLPIIIIIIII
Go to level 11	HCIGGHLPIIIIIIII
Go to level 12	LNIECOLPIIIIIIII
Go to level 13	OLKOPFKPIIIIIIII
Go to level 14	EOIGLMKPIIIIIIII
Go to level 15	LKKOPPKPIIIIIIII
Go to level 16	GNAEPPKPIIIIIIII

Contributed By: TheProdigy.

Glitches: Extra Gear

To start with extra items, skip the first 8 letters of any password, then replace the next 8 letters with 'M'.

Example: Level 6 password

(POKKNMPLGNNLPOF)

becomes

POKKNMPLMMMMMMMM

7.1.2: Alien Breed: Special Edition '92

Released: 1992

Other Platforms: MS-DOS 1992, BlackBerry 2013

Developed by: Team17 Software Limited

Published by: Team17 Software Limited

Coder/Programmer: Andreas Tadic, Peter Tuleby, Stefan Boberg

Graphics: Rico Holmes

Musician/Composer/Sound Effects: Allister Brimble, Christopher Brimble, Lynette Reade, Martyn Brown (Spadge)

Introduction

An interlude between Alien Breed and its sequel. The gameplay is the same as in the predecessor – each level is a maze through which you have to move while fighting hordes of aliens. Special Edition 92 includes 12 new levels and a number of new features: A "dark mission" where only the blue glowing eyes of the aliens can be seen, a level without aliens but with the destruction sequence already initiated, the possibility to access the levels by means of a code (you don't need to cheat to start the game where you failed).

Gameplay

The game is a top-down linear shooter, inspired mechanically in some places by Gauntlet, that has taken a lot of influence from Alien movies, especially the return of Aliens. The game can be played as a single or doubles game, with the aim of advancing the mazey fields of an abandoned space station while surviving intrusive attacks by aliens with limited ammunition, with the main goal of triggering a self-destruct mechanism from each floor, then advancing to the elevator to reach the next level. The game focuses a lot on finding keys to open various lock doors and upgrading weapons to be the most destructive for alien mass vases. Ammunition and equipment can be purchased at the terminals in the game with credits found in the fields. There are a total of six fields in the game (Special Edition includes 12 fields).

Reception

CU Amiga magazine rated the game 90% in its review.

Predecessor/Successor

- 1991: Alien Breed
- 1992: Alien Breed: Special Edition 92
- 1993: Alien Breed 2
- 1994: Alien Breed: Tower Assault
- 1995: Alien Breed 3D
- 1996: Alien Breed 3D II: The Killing Grounds

- 2009: Alien Breed Evolution for Xbox 360
- 2010: Alien Breed 2: Assault for Steam
- 2010: Alien Breed 3: Descent for Steam

Hardware Requirements

Minimum CPU Class Required: Amiga 500

Minimum OS Class Required: Kickstart 1.3

Minimum RAM Required: 2 MB

Media Type: 3.5" Floppy Disk

Video Modes Supported: OCS/ECS/AGA

Input Devices Supported: Keyboard, Mouse

Controller Types Supported: Digital Joystick, Joypad

Multiplayer Options: Null-modem cable

Number of Players Supported: 1-2 Players, Simultaneous

Save Game Methods: Password

Miscellaneous Attributes: Hard Drive Installable

Controls/Joystick/Mouse/Gamepad

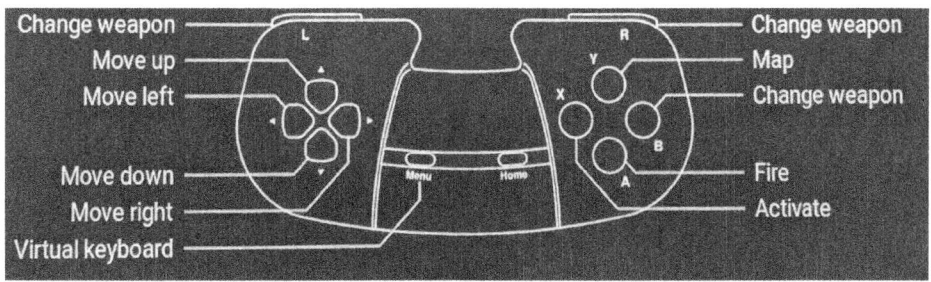

The game supports one player using the Keyboard. A Joystick is requires for more than one player, and both players can use a Joystick if desired.

Up: ↑

Down: ↓

Left: ←

Right: →

Fire 1: Right Shift

Fire 2: /

Keys

Pause = P

Escape = Esc

Exit to Dos = F1

Cheats, Hints, Tips & Tricks

5 million credits: Select two-player mode and enable the "Share Credits" option. Begin game play and type PPPEAB when logging on to the Intex Computer on level 1. The game will resume on level 10. Locate the Computer a few screens above the starting location on this level and log on to collect 5 million credits.

Select the two-player mode and switch the share credits option on. Then start the game. on the first level, go to the Computer and log on. Instead of typing {PPEAB} which would advance you to level 10, type "PPPEAB" (note 3 P's) when you now log off, you'll go straight to level 10. If you go straight to the Computer (a few screens above where you start) and log on, you'll find that you have a staggering five million credits, which really helps!

Make your way to the third level without spending any money. Now log on to the first Intex Computer you find. You should have about 6000 credits. Buy nothing, then log off. It is important that no fire doors have been closed. Now do a complete circuit of the level. If you log back onto the same Intex Computer, you will find you have loads of money.

A hint that might work on Level two: https://youtu.be/285JB0h0QxY?t=801

Levelcodes

2: XXDFA 3: RTHAA 4: LAEEA 5: UYTTA 10: PPEAB	
Level 2	AAJIGDDC
Level 3	GGHDGGDG
Level 4	HDICICCII
Level 5	IDHEHDGCC
Level 6	IJIIDIHEC
Level 7	CFDFEFEFJ
Level 8	JIIJIIIIC
Level 9	AAAABAAAA
Level 10	CCGDGBBBB
Level 11	HHIAAJJIG
Level 12	GGDDJJHFD
Level 13	JIECBFGFF
Level 14	HGGEDDCCB
Level 15	HHHGFGDCC
Level 16	IHDCHGHFF

Jump to the next level (Contributed by B.L. Stryker)

Type "tuleby" (surname of the game programmer) in game and you will jump to the next level

By entering the following words, into the Intex Computer, you get these extras:

Log into one of the Computers during the game and enter any of the codes listed below for different effects:

- AHH BUT WILL SHE SWALLOW IT: Infinite energy player two
- ALIENS ARE BENDERS: Infinite Energy

- ALIENS LIKE MICHAEL BOLTON: Make aliens weak
- BANK RAID: Infinite money player two
- ELVIS MODE: King-Sight
- FUCK OFF: Computer Reset
- HARD BARSTEDS: Invincibility
- HARD BASTARDS: Aliens faster
- I JUST LOVE TEAM17 SOFTWARE: Score + 100.000
- JANUARY SALE NOW ON: Speeds up aliens
- JESUS THIS JIM BEAMS IS GOOD STUFF: Infinite energy player one
- JUST CALL ME MOGGY: 9 lives player one
- KATRINA HAS FARTED AND ITS A BEAUTY: Aliens disappear
- KEY TO THE CITY: Infinite keys player one
- KNACKERED JOYSTICK/MOUSE/GAMEPAD: Joystick reversed
- MR YALE OR WHAT: Infinite keys player two
- PC EMULATOR: No Intex-Computer
- PPEAB: Level 10
- SALMAN RUSHDIE PLAYS ALIEN BREED: Player invisible
- ST EMULATOR: Bad graphics
- STEVIE WONDER: Pink Screen
- THE IRAQIS MADE THE WEAPONS: Weak Weapons
- WHY NOT CALL ME MOGGY AS WELL: 9 lives player two
- WON THE POOLS: Infinite money player one
- I WANT FISH: Following keys are active:
    - [F1] – Quits the game for player 1.
    - [F2] – Quits the game for player 2.
    - [F3] – Extra keys.

- [F4] – Kills player 1.
- [F5] – Kills player 2.
- [F6] – Blow up deck.
- [F7] – Skips the current level.
- [F9] – Allows you to walk through walls and gives you all weapons.

Press 'QAZWSXEDCRFVTGBYHNUJMIKOL' repeatedly and at some point you will skip the current level.

Play to level 3 and turn right from the lift. Don't close any fire doors and head for the Intex console. You should have about 60,000 credits, so buy what you need and go around the map (which is square). Return to the Intex console and you will have 3,500,000 credits.

7.1.3: Another World

Released: 1991 under the name "Out of this World"

Other Platforms: 3DO, Apple IIgs, Atari ST, DOS, Genesis, Jaguar, Macintosh, SNES, Symbian, Windows, Windows 3.x, Zodiac

Developed by: Éric Chahi

Published by: Interplay Productions, Inc. (US)/Delphine Software International (France)/US Gold (Rest of World)/ERBE (Spain)

Design: Eric Chahi

Coder/Programmer: Eric Chahi

Graphics: Eric Chahi

Musician/Composer/Sound Effects: Jean-François Freitas

Official Game Soundtrack: https://blackscreenrecords.com/products/jean-francois-freitas-another-world-official-soundtrack?variant=12439536173104

Introduction

A cinematic platformer action-adventure game designed by Éric Chahi and published by Delphine Software. The game tells a story of Lester, a young scientist who, as a result of an experiment gone wrong, finds himself on a dangerous alien world where he is forced to fight for his survival.

Another World was innovative in its use of cinematic effects in both real-time and cutscenes, which earned the game praise among critics and commercial success. It also influenced a number of other video games and designers, inspiring such titles as Ico, Metal Gear Solid, Silent Hill, and Delphine's later Flashback.

Gameplay

Another World is a platform game, featuring a control scheme where the player uses either the Keyboard, Joystick or Gamepad to make the protagonist run, jump, attack and perform other, situation-specific actions, such as rocking a cage back and forth. In the initial part of the game, the player's character Lester is unarmed. He is able to kick at small creatures, but is otherwise defenseless.

Later in the game, the player acquires a laser pistol from a fallen foe. The pistol has three capabilities: a standard fire mode, the ability to create force fields to block enemy fire, and a powerful charged shot that can break through force fields and some walls.[5] Enemies also have the same capabilities, requiring the player to take advantage of the three gun modes and the environment to overcome them.

Reception

Was named as number one top new Amiga game of 1992 by Amiga World. FLUX Issue #4 – #73 in the "Top 100 Video Games of All-Time" list.

Successor

Heart of the Alien (1994)

Official Webpage:

http://www.anotherworld.fr/anotherworld_uk

Specials

A short film "Project 23" https://vimeo.com/96120254

Hardware Requirements

Minimum CPU Class Required: Amiga 500

Minimum OS Class Required: Attribute Image Kickstart 1.2

Minimum RAM Required: 512KB

Media Type: 3.5" Floppy Disk

Video Modes Supported: OCS/ECS

Input Devices Supported: Keyboard, Mouse

Controller Types Supported: Digital Joystick

Multiplayer Options: No

Number of Players Supported: 1

Miscellaneous Attributes: Hard Drive Installable

Controls/Joystick/Mouse/Gamepad

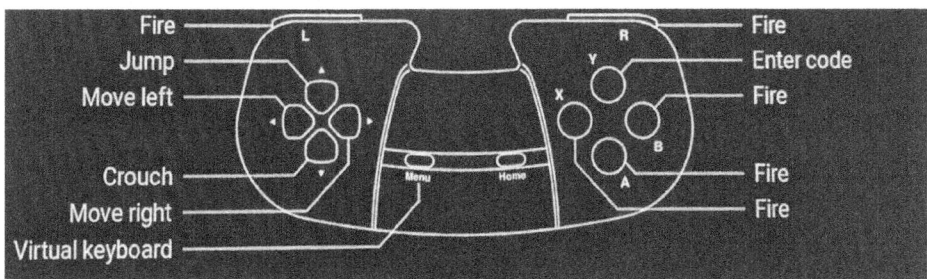

← Move left

→ Move right

↑ Jump forward / Move up

↓ Duck / Move down

Enter/Space: Kick/Fire weapon. Hold down while moving to run.

When you press the fire button, he deals a kick or uses the weapon he is holding.

Joystick Up – Your character jumps.

Joystick Down – Your character ducks. When you press the fire button, he deals a kick or uses the weapon he is holding.

Joystick to the right or left Pressed – Your character walks in the selected direction. When you hold the button, he runs.

Keys

C = Enter level code

S = Toggle sound

P = Pause

F1 = Switch back to normal screen

F2 = Switch to wide screen

F3 = Switch to vertical screen mode

F4 = Switch to small screen (high resolution)

Cheats, Hints, Tips & Tricks

It is worth remembering after the blast run in the arena. The directions for pressing the correct buttons are:

Fire, down, fire, left 2, down, fire, up 3, and fire. You will now be launched into the female sanctum.

Press "C" during play and enter one of the following passwords:

Code	Info
HICI	In prison/Im Gefängnis
CLLD	In the ventilation shaft/Im Belüftungsschacht
LIBC	In the charging station/In der Aufladestation
CCAL	In the caves/In den Höhlen (1)
FADK	In the caves/In den Höhlen (2)
KCIJ	Fortress/Festung
EDIL	At the empty waterhole/Am leeren Wasserloch
LDCI	At the full waterhole/Am vollen Wasserloch (1)
ICAH	At the full waterhole/Am vollen Wasserloch (2)
LAEA	At the full waterhole/Am vollen Wasserloch (3)
FIEI	At the full waterhole/Am vollen Wasserloch (4)
FLAK	At the full waterhole/Am vollen Wasserloch (5)
LDIJ	At the full waterhole/Am vollen Wasserloch (6)
KCGB	At the full waterhole/Am vollen Wasserloch (7)
GABK	At the full waterhole/Am vollen Wasserloch (8)
LALD	At the hole/Am Loch
KJIA	At the arena/An der Arena
LFEK	At the swimming pool/Im Schwimmbad

7: THE GAMES

SectionCodes	
01	In the lake EDJI
02	In the prison HICI
03	In the sewer FLLD
04	First recharger LIBC
05	In the cave CCAL
06	End of caves EDIL
07	T-shaped rock FADK
08	Temple entrance KCIJ
09	Blast run LALD
10	Tower bath LFEK
11	By the pool ICAH
12	Powerline FIEI

LevelCodes	
Level	Code
1	HTDC
2	CLLD
3	FXLC
4	KRFK
5	XDDJ
6	LBKG
7	KLFB
8	TTCT
9	DDRX
10	TBHK

LevelCodes	
Level	Code
11	BRTD
12	CKJL
13	LFCK
14	BFLX
15	XJRT
16	HRTB
17	HBHK
18	JCGB
19	HHFL
20	TFBB
21	TXHF
22	JHJL

7.1.4: Arcade Pool

Released: 1994

Other Platforms: Amiga CD32, Blackberry, DOS

Developed by: Team17 Software Limited

Published by: Team17 Software Limited

Manager: Martyn James Brown

Design: Mario Savoia

Coder/Programmer: Mario Savoia

Graphics: Mario Savoia

Musician/Composer/Sound Effects: Allister Brimble

Introduction

It is a pool simulation game developed and published in 1994 by Team17, initially for the Amiga. The game was later ported to MS-DOS. An CD32 release soon followed.

The game is a top-down pool simulator. Although simple, the physics are surprisingly accurate. The game featured many British and American variations of pool as well as two variations of ball set (standard UK red and yellow, and standard US circles and stripes).

Gameplay

Arcade Pool has been in development for well over two years and that's an incredibly long time for a budget game. The time was obviously spent on making sure the game was a realistic as possible and to achieve this the graphics had to be as close to the real thing as possible.

Reception

Amiga Format (May, 1994) 94/100: This game is incredibly addictive. It's not realistic as Archer Maclean's Pool but hey, it's an arcade game so monkeys to it. I defy anyone to play one game and walk away from the machine. Go out and get a copy.

Successor

Arcade Pool 2 (II) 1999 by Hasbro Interactive

Hardware Requirements

Minimum CPU Class Required: Amiga 1000

Minimum OS Class Required: Kickstart 1.3

Minimum RAM Required: 1 MB

Media Type: 3.5" Floppy Disk

Video Modes Supported: OCS/ECS, AGA

Input Devices Supported: Keyboard, Mouse

Controller Types Supported: None

Multiplayer Options: In sequence

Number of Players Supported: 1-8 Players

Save Game Methods: Password

Miscellaneous Attributes: Hard Drive Installable

Controls/Joystick/Mouse/Gamepad

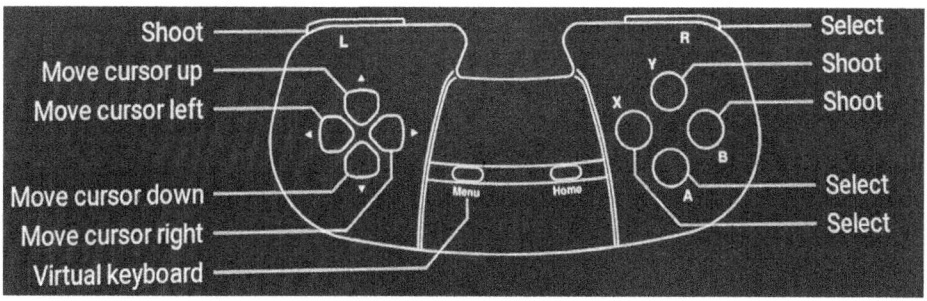

Use the Mouse

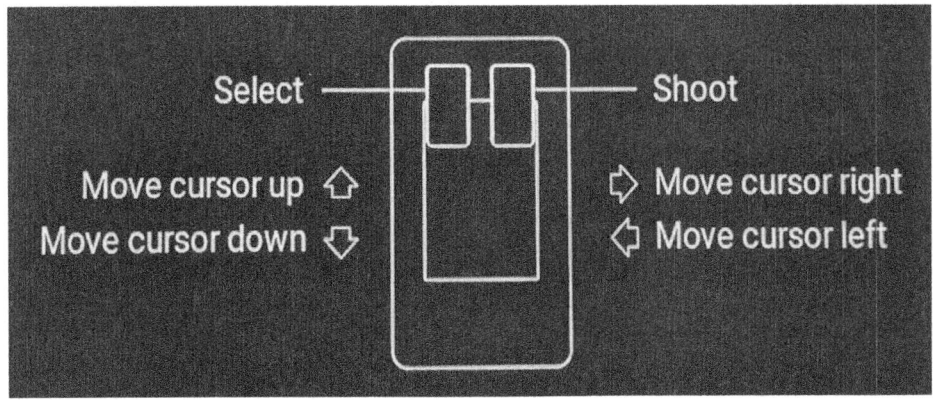

Gameplay

Video https://www.youtube.com/watch?v=8vABB7rVTmI

Cheats, Hints, Tips & Tricks

I've got rather a naughty little tip for Arcade Pool in two-player mode.

After your opponent fouls in US pool, grab the cue ball and before you take your shot, push it in between the two other balls that are close together on the table so that the cue ball touches both of them. This nudges the balls a bit and if they are in the right place you could set yourself up a treat, or ruin your mate's plans. The Computer players don't mind but your mate will.

Another cheat for Arcade Pool. It works on any of the play modes but it's only really useful on Speed Pool. To get as low a time as you like, pot all of the balls apart from one, then line the last one up on the pocket. Select save, then New to start with one ball left on 0 minutes and 00 seconds.

7.1.5: ATR: All Terrain Racing

Released: 1995, also for Amiga CD32

Other Platforms: BlackBerry 2013

Developed by: Team17 Software Limited

Published by: Team17 Software Limited

Distributed by: Mirage Software

Design: Daniel J. Burke

Manager: Martyn James Brown

Coder/Programmer: Jamie Woodhouse

Graphics: Daniel J. Burke

Musician/Composer/Sound Effects: Allister Brimble

Gameplay

Like many Amiga racers from the era, ATR was a top-down racer. This just meant that the camera would be looking down onto the track. Handling was based on drifting around corners and slamming into opponents.

Reception

Amiga Dream 17 (Apr 1995) 90%

Hardware Requirements

Minimum CPU Class Required: Amiga 500

Minimum OS Class Required: Kickstart 1.3

Minimum RAM Required: 1 MB

Media Type: 3.5" Floppy Disk

Video Modes Supported: OCS/ECS/AGA

Input Devices Supported: Keyboard

Controller Types Supported: Digital Joystick

Multiplayer Options: Same/Split-Screen

Number of Players Supported: 1-2 Players

Miscellaneous Attributes: Hard Drive Installable

Controls/Joystick/Mouse/Gamepad

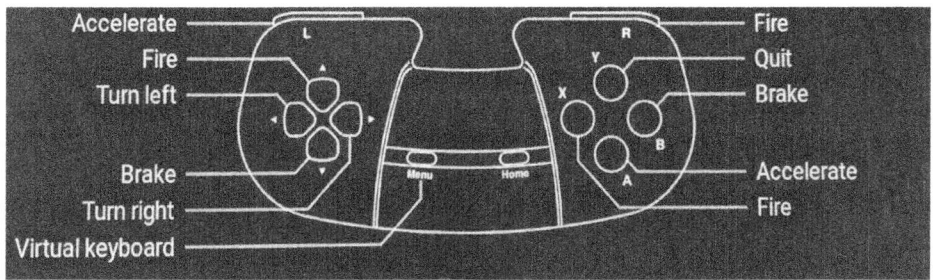

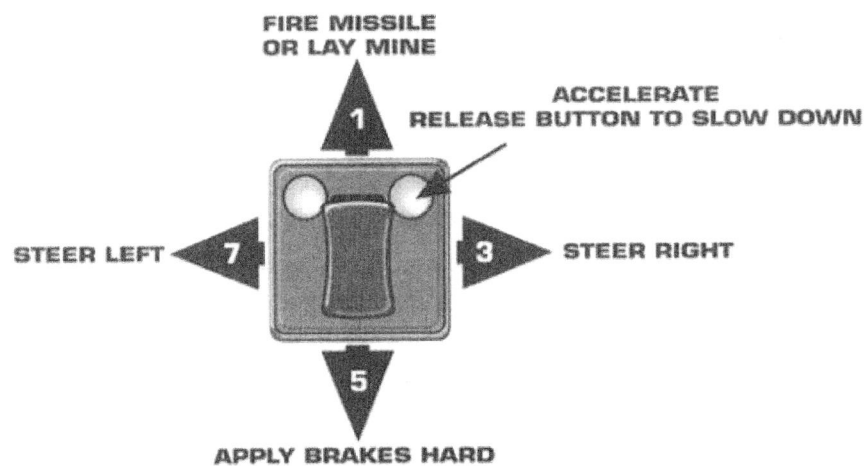

Keys

P = Pause

Esc = Exit Game

Gameplay/Walkthrough

A Playguide and Review: https://www.youtube.com/watch?v=jacwhE3P9Vo

Cheats, Hints, Tips & Tricks

On the starting grid, do not accelerate before the green light, otherwise You are penalised and held back slightly.

Do not try and accelerate around corners; take Your foot off the gas going into tight bends and accelerate out.

Do not spend vital seconds chasing after a pick-up – concentrate on the race.

In two player games, it's important to keep ahead. Save Your missiles for when you need to get in front.

Use Your money wisely and power-up Your car sensibly.

In order to play the later tracks in two-player mode you first have to reach them in single-player game. Then lose a race and enter your name as "ATR". Now go back to a two-player battle and you can select any of the hidden tracks.

Select battle mode and choose Forest World. Select track two and race in a formula car. Intentionally allow player one win all the races. Select battle mode after returning to the title screen. Space World will now be selectable.

7.1.6: Battle Chess

Released: 1988, Amiga CD32 and CDTV

Other Platforms: 3DO, Acorn Archimedes, Apple II/IIGS, Apple IIGS, Apple Macintosh (Classic), Atari ST/E, Commodore C64/128, Fujitsu FM Towns/FM Towns Marty, NEC PC-98, Nintendo NES (Famicom)/Sharp Twin Famicom, PC (DOS), PC (Windows), Sharp X68000, Tandy PC/IBM PCjr

Developed by: Electronic Arts

Published by: Interplay Productions, Inc.

Distributed by: Mediagenic

Manager: Brian Fargo

Coder/Programmer: Michael Quarles. Jay Patel, Troy Worrell

Graphics: Todd J. Camasta, Bruce Schlickbernd

Musician/Composer/Sound Effects/Sound Effects: Kurt Heiden

Introduction

Battle Chess is a Computer game version of chess in which the chess pieces come to life and battle one another when capturing. The game itself was inspired by the 3D chess sequences from Star Wars Episode IV: A New Hope and Futureworld.

Gameplay

The battles cannot be influenced by the players, unlike in the previously released Archon, which was only loosely based on chess. The "winner" is always the striking piece.

Reception

90% Amiga User International (Dec, 1988) Ken St. Andre reviewed the game for Computer Gaming World, and stated that "Quibbles aside, every chess player will want a copy of this program, and every Amiga owner owes it to him/herself to see Battlechess in action. highly recommended."

Successor

Battle Chess II: Chinese Chess 1991, Battle Chess 4000 1992

Hardware Requirements

Minimum CPU Class Required: Amiga 500

Minimum OS Class Required: Kickstart 1.2

Minimum RAM Required: 512KB

Media Type: 3.5" Floppy Disk

Video Modes Supported: AGA

Input Devices Supported: Mouse

Controller Types Supported: Digital Joystick

Multiplayer Options: Null-modem cable

Number of Players Supported: 1-2 Players

Save Game Methods: Password

Miscellaneous Attributes: Hard Drive Installable

Controls/Joystick/Mouse/Gamepad

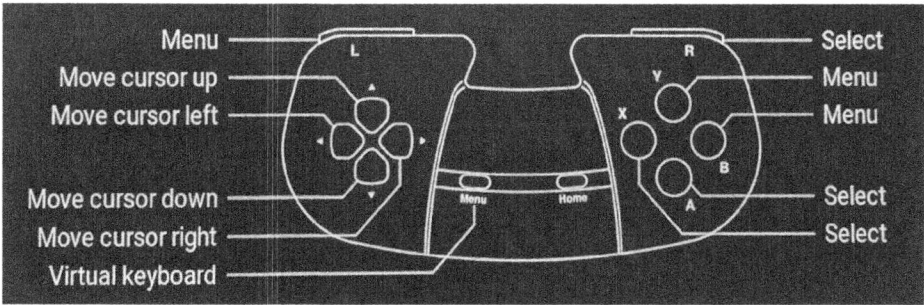

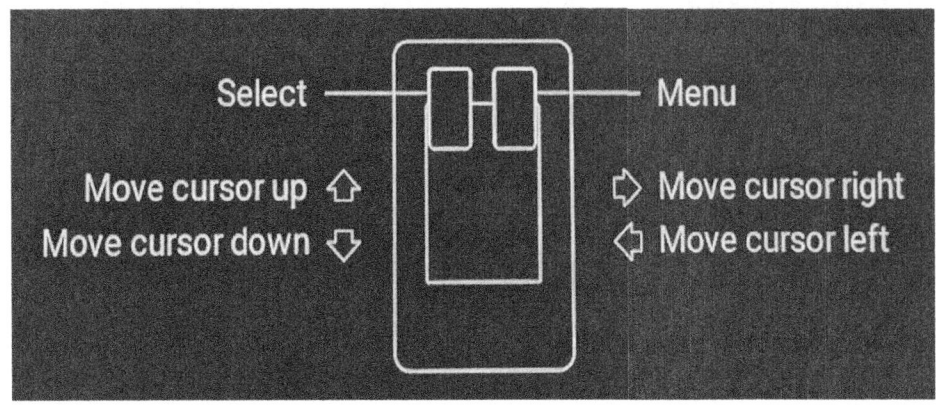

To move one of your chess pieces, first move the Mouse pointer to the square the piece stands on, and then click. Moving the pointer around, you will note that legal move squares for that particular piece will be highlighted as you move the pointer over them. Select the desired legal destination square by clicking on it with the left Mouse button. The piece will then walk over to the new position.

Keys

If you don't want to use the menus with the Mouse, certain shortcut keys are available in combination with the "open Amiga" key. They are as follows:

AMIGA+F = Force Move

AMIGA+M = Suggest Move

AMIGA+T = Take Back

AMIGA+S = Toggle Sound on/off

AMIGA+R = Replay

Walkthrough

Longplay: https://www.youtube.com/watch?v=MMjSweUlXAU

7.1.7: Cadaver

Released: 1990

Other Platforms: Atari ST, PC, Archimedes

Developed by: Bitmap Brothers

Published by: Image Works/Renegade

Design: Mike Montgomery, Steve Kelly, Eric Matthews, Phil Wilcock

Manager: Graeme Boxall

Coder/Programmer: Mike Montgomery, Sean Griffiths

Graphics: Daniel Malone, Robin Chapman

Musician/Composer/Sound Effects: Richard Joseph

Introduction

The game consists of five levels representing different floors of Castle Wulf. Entering the castle via the sewers, Karadoc works his way up from the dungeons, through guard chambers, royal hall, the king's private chambers and finally the battlements with Dianos's sanctum.

Gameplay

The game is played using a Joystick, with which you can control the movement of Karadoc in 8 directions. The directions are not as one would expect in a game from today – instead, they are rotated. If you push the Joystick up, Karadoc will run "north", which is right-up on the screen. If you want Karadoc to move up on the screen (which is "north-west" in the game), you need to push the Joystick left-up. The fire button of the Joystick is used to jump.

Reception

Golden Chalice 1990 Adventure Game of the Year, Generation 4 1990 Best Foreign Adventure

Successor

Cadaver – The Payoff 1991

Hardware Requirements

Minimum CPU Class Required: Amiga 500

Minimum OS Class Required: Kickstart 1.3

Minimum RAM Required: 2 MB

Media Type: 3.5" Floppy Disk

Video Modes Supported: ECS/OCS

Input Devices Supported: Keyboard, Mouse

Controller Types Supported: Digital Joystick

Gamepads Supported: Joypad

Multiplayer Options: No

Number of Players Supported: 1 Player

Save Game Methods: Password

Miscellaneous Attributes: Hard Drive Installable

Controls/Joystick/Mouse/Gamepad

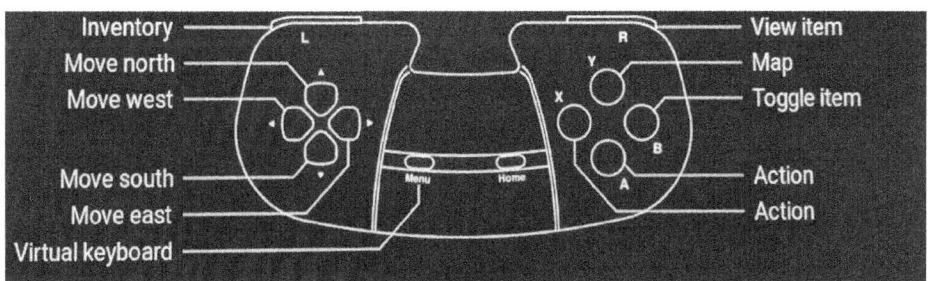

North: Cycle through items in rucksack/Scroll map up

South: Cycle through items in rucksack/scroll map down

East: Cycle through icons/Scroll map right

West: Cycle through icons/Scroll map left

Fire: Jump/Use weapon/Throw objects

Keys

RETURN: Displays the whole rucksack. When pressed a second time, it returns you to the small rucksack display.

SPACE BAR: Displays a single item from the rucksack. When pressed a second time it returns you to the main game.

UP/DOWN CURSOR KEYS: Zoom In/Out of the map

CLR/HOME: Centre the map display (ST)

DEL: Centre the map display (AMIGA)

S: Save the game position (only available if you have enough money)

L: Load a saved game position

H: Toggles a held object on and off

P: Toggles Pause/UnPause

C: Clear all game messages from screen

F1: Map

F2: Toggles between using fire or ENTER to access icons

F3: Toggles between icon displayed as soon as you make contact with object, or after first pressing the fire button.

F4: Toggles between moving in 8 directions or moving in 4 directions

0-9: Numeric Save/Load a game after the appropriate key has been pressed.

Walkthrough

Longplay: https://www.youtube.com/watch?v=nAWjNRXn6_E

Cheats, Hints, Tips & Tricks

To get the second key, go to the guards on level four. Ignore the levers until you have the guard key from the north passage, the candle and the shuriken (in the pillow). Open the wall above the bed to get the second key.

7.1.8: California Games

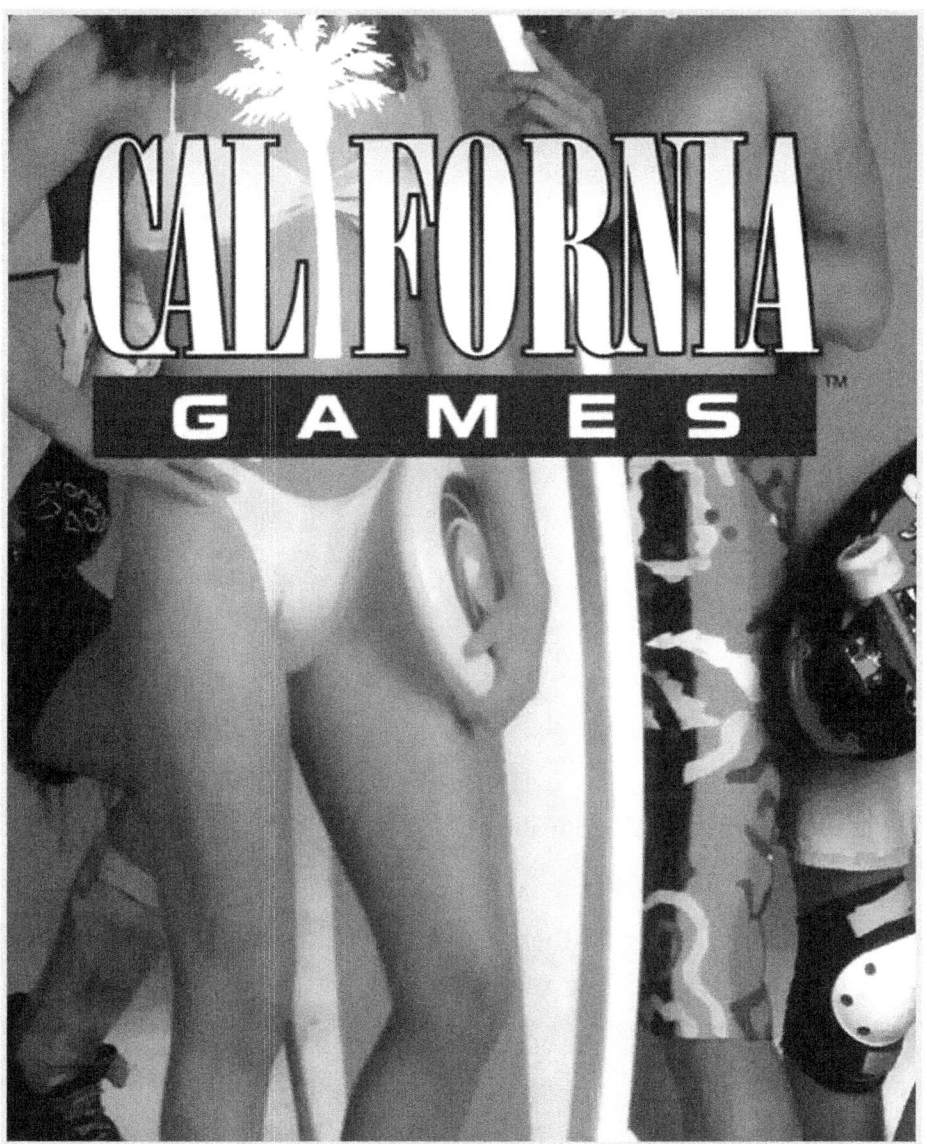

Released: 1987

Other Platforms: Apple II, Commodore 64, Amstrad CPC, Apple IIGS, Atari 400/800/1200XL/2600/7800, Atari Lynx, Atari ST, Mobile (J2ME), MS-DOS, MSX 1/2, NES, Sega Genesis/Master System, Tandy PC, Sinclair ZX Spectrum, WII, IBM PCjr

Developed by: Epyx, Westwood Associates

Published by: Epyx, U.S. Gold

Design: Chuck Sommerville, Ken Nicholson, Kevin Norman, Kevin Furry, Jon Leupp

Graphics: Jenny Martin, Susan Greene, Sheryl Knowles, Paul Vernon

Musician/Composer/Sound Effects: Chris Grigg, Karl Lehenbauer, David Hayes, Steve Hales, Chris Ebert, Gil Freeman, David Wise (NES)

Gameplay

The events available vary slightly depending on the platform, but include all of the following:

- Half-pipe
- Roller skating
- Surfing (Starring Rippin' Rick)
- BMX
- Footbag
- Flying disc

Reception

73% The Games Machine (UK) (Apr, 1989). California Games was a commercial blockbuster. With more than 300,000 copies sold in the first nine months, it was the most-successful Epyx game, outselling each of the four previous and two subsequent titles in the company's "Games" series.

Successor

California Games 2 (II) 1992

Hardware Requirements

Minimum CPU Class Required: Amiga 500

Minimum OS Class Required: Kickstart 1.2; Not fully Kickstart 1.1 compatible (graphics artifacts may occur).

Minimum RAM Required: 512KB

Media Type: 3.5" Floppy Disk

Video Modes Supported: OCS/ECS

Input Devices Supported: Keyboard, Mouse

Controller Types Supported: Digital Joystick

Multiplayer Options: Null-modem cable

Number of Players Supported: 1-8 Players

Save Game Methods: Password

Miscellaneous Attributes: Not Hard Drive Installable

Controls/Joystick/Mouse/Gamepad

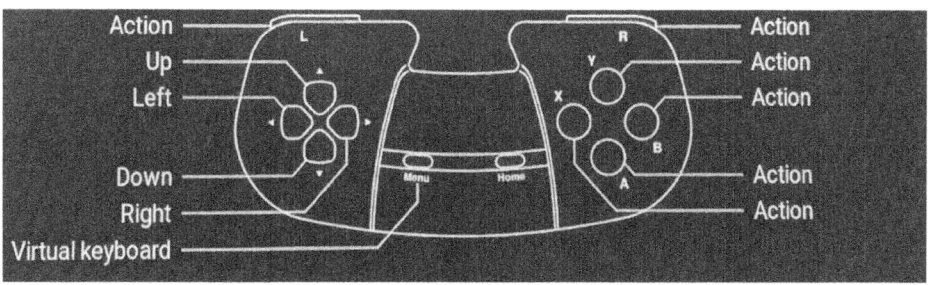

Walkthrough

Playguide: https://www.youtube.com/watch?v=KYrSL3WQJf8

Cheats, Hints, Tips & Tricks

Easter Eggs:

While skateboarding, the H of Hollywood falls during rare upcoming earthquakes.

At Footbag you can meet a seagull.

In surfing, sometimes a laughing shark, dolphin or seagull appears.

In Frisbee, if you have a few misses and wait too long, your partner will be abducted by aliens.

7.1.9: The Chaos Engine

Released: 1993 by the name "Soldiers of Fortune"

Other Platforms: Acorn Archimedes, Amiga CD32, Atari ST/E, Blackberry, DOS, Nintendo SNES (Super Famicom), PC (DOS), Sega Mega Drive/Genesis, Mobile (J2ME), Linux, Macintosh, Windows

Developed by: The Bitmap Brothers

Published by: Renegade Software

Design: Simon Knight, Eric Matthews

Manager: Graeme Boxall

Coder/Programmer: Steve Cargill, Mike Montgomery

Graphics: Dan Malone

Musician/Composer/Sound Effects: Richard Joseph, Farook Joi, Haroon Joi

Introduction

Chaos Engine (Soldiers of Fortune in the US) is a run-and-gun overhead shooter. Sixteen levels (in four groups of four) await the players in the game. The basic gameplay is similar to Gauntlet, but in an open-air setting, with bridges across rivers and other features in the maps. The visuals are in the ‚metallic and blue' style Bitmap Brothers appeared to favor.

There are six characters available in the game, each with different strengths and weaknesses, and different starting prices. In two-player mode each player chooses a character and plays co-operatively, but in

Gameplay

The setting is a steampunk Victorian era England. A time traveller on a reconnaissance mission from the distant future became stranded in the England of the late 1800s, and his technology came into the hands of the Royal Society, led by Baron Fortesque (based upon Charles Babbage), a grand inventor. Fortesque then retro engineered many of the futuristic contraptions, creating an entirely different, alternate timeline.

Reception

Amiga Down Under 3 (Jul – Aug 1993) 9.5/10 – Electronic Gaming Monthly gave the Super NES version a 6.8 out of 10, summarizing it as "A decent overhead shooting game in the spirit of Technoclash and Gauntlet." They gave the Genesis version a 6.4. GamePro remarked of the Genesis version that "Overhead-view gunfighting has never played better", citing the heavy challenge, solid controls, and use of teamwork. They criticized the sprites as overly small, but also noted that the sharp artwork ensures that it is still easy to make out what is happening on screen.

Hardware Requirements

Minimum CPU Class Required: Amiga 500

Minimum OS Class Required: Kickstart 1.2

Minimum RAM Required: 1 MB

Media Type: 3.5" Floppy Disk

Video Modes Supported: OCS/ECS/AGA

Input Devices Supported: Keyboard, Mouse

Controller Types Supported: Digital Joystick

Number of Players Supported: 1-2 Players

Save Game Methods: Password

Miscellaneous Attributes: Hard Drive Installable

Controls/Joystick/Mouse/Gamepad

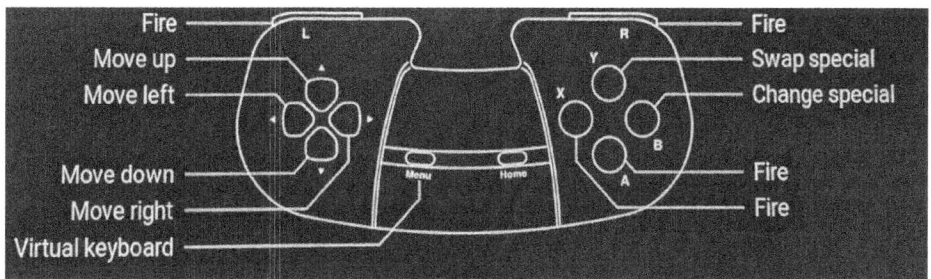

Walkthrough

Longplay: https://www.youtube.com/watch?v=dWrGA-g17qg

Cheats, Hints, Tips & Tricks

Unfortunately all the cheat passwords/tips which were included in the normal version of the game have been taken out of the AGA version. However, try the following passwords thanks to the Renegade help line. They all start you off on World 2-1 and give you lots of lives, money and special weapons etc.

- LQPGMXHF8Y43
- P#M35PK2ZYKN
- 95RL3MBQB2YR

Use these passwords to play the game with 30 lives:

- #P0BK4SNVHP2
- G7#BKWFZBJ#W
- 51TD4M9JGMGT

CHAOS ENGINE LEVEL CODES

- **World 2:** FKH QFM 2BX 6WB
- **World 3:** PFN HH0 #L2 #BX
- **World 4:** 62K BCR #34 9N2

CHEAT MODE

Select a One Player & CPU game and then enter any of the following cheat passwords. They all start you off on World 1-1 with loads of cash, weapons and power-ups.

'JJHHGGFFDDCC'	Navie and Brigand'
HHGGFFDDCCBB'	Thug and Preacher.
'TTTTTTTTTTTT'	Mercenary and Gentleman'
VVVVVVVVVVV'	Brigand and Mercenary.
'XXXXXXXXXXXX'	Gentleman and Navvy'
YYYYYYYYYYYY'	Thug and Gentleman.

MEGA GOLD & PARTY

For starting a single player game with a huge load of gold and different characters:

Type as your single player password:

option 1: TTTTTTTTTTTT (12xT)

option 2: VVVVVVVVVVVV (12xV)

option 3: XXXXXXXXXXXX (12xX)

option 4: YYYYYYYYYYYY (12xY)

Effect Password

Extra Money	TTTTTTTTTT
Level 2	K#SVX7VBBYK
Level 2 (30 extra lives)	#P0BK4SNVHP2
Level 3	086SPKHP1PN
Level 3 (30 extra lives)	G7#BKWFZBJ#W
Level 4 (30 extra lives)	51TD4M9JGMGT

Level passwords (ECS version)

World	Characters	Money	Password
1	Thug, Preacher	50000	HHGGFFDDCCBB
1	Navvie, Brigand	10000	JJHHGGFFDDCC
1	Brigand, Mercenary	30000	VVVVVVVVVVVV
1	Gentleman, Navvie	30000	XXXXXXXXXXXX
1	Thug, Gentleman	20000	YYYYYYYYYYYY
1	Mercenary, Gentleman	45000	TTTTTTTTTTTT
2	Thug, Preacher	40000	LQPBK8JWDNBY
3	Thug, Preacher	30000	8H8BKOSWQY7H
4	Thug, Preacher	30000	P28BKM6XMWWK
4	Brigand, Mercenary	20000	PKJKDL1#DFD4

7.1.10: Dragons Breath

Released: 1990

Other Platforms: Atari ST, MS-DOS

Developed by: Outlaw Productions

Published by: Palace Software, Spotlight Software

Coder/Programmer: Andrew E. Bailey

Graphics: Simon Hunter

Musician/Composer/Sound Effects: David M. Hanlon (Dave Hanlon)

Introduction

Also known as Dragon Lord, is a fantasy-themed strategy game, players control one of three dragon lords competing to find the (game-winning) talisman. This goal is achieved by raising dragons, empowering them via alchemy, and then sending them to conquer towns.

Gameplay

To make or keep your dragons strong, wise, fast and eagle eyed you will need to use magic. Spells are created in an alchemy lab using some combination of many different ingredients, treated in different ways. All having different effects on different targets and often side effects too, possibly making your dragon sick, for example.

Reception

Amiga Format Apr, 1990 94 out of 100

Computer Gaming World stated that "many will find game play painfully slow", but deserved some praise for its novel subject and "innovative game play". The magazine concluded that Dragon Lord would appeal to strategy gamers rather than to adventurers.

Successor

None

Hardware Requirements

Minimum CPU Class Required: Amiga 500

Minimum OS Class Required: Kickstart 1.2

Minimum RAM Required: 512KB

Media Type: 3.5" Floppy Disk

Video Modes Supported: ECS/OCS

Input Devices Supported:

Controller Types Supported: Digital Joystick

Multiplayer Options: No

Number of Players Supported: 1-3 Players

Save Game Methods: Password

Miscellaneous Attributes: Not Hard Drive Installable

Controls/Joystick/Mouse/Gamepad

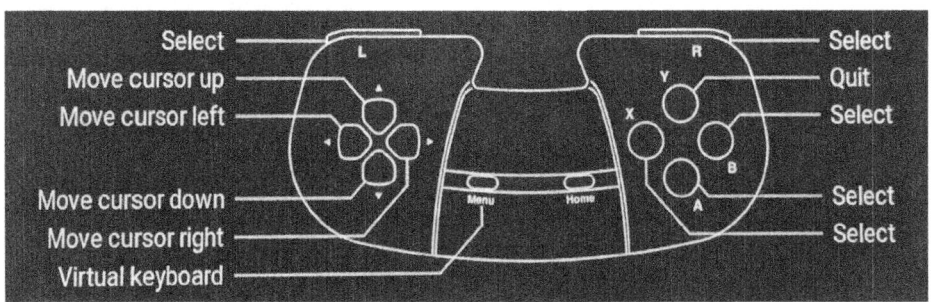

If you have set your dragon on a training mission you will need a Joystick plugged in.

Keys

F1 – toggles sound on/off

F9 – toggles picture fade between normal and fast

7: THE GAMES

Walkthrough

Playthrough: https://www.youtube.com/watch?v=bFhutiR_OI8

Cheats, Hints, Tips & Tricks

The Dragon Spell is a good spell to know

3 Rasgon [grind] [full heat] – 3 Haloros [cut] [full condenser]

3 IGELE [normal] [full heat] [medium condenser] – 2 Rasgon [grind] [full heat]

SPELLS:

(EYESIGHT) 2X RASGON, 2X IGELE 1X ACRUS – (SPEED) 2X RASGON 2X AROLIG 1X ACRUS

(WISDOM) 2X RASGON 2X HALORUS 1X ACRUS – (STRENGTH) 2X RASCON 2X ULIN 1X ACRUS

TRY DIFFERENT WAYS OF PREPARING THESE SPELLS.

7.1.11: F-16 Combat Pilot

Released: 1989

Other Platforms: Atari ST, DOS, Commodore 64, Amstrad Schneider CPC, Sinclair ZX Spectrum, Tandy PC, IBM PCjr

Developed by: Electronics Arts/Black Box/Digital Integration

Published by: Electronics Arts/Digital Integration

Design: David K. Marshall

Coder/Programmer: Colin Boswell, Paul Margrave, Rod Swift

Graphics: Les Doughty, Anthony West

Musician/Composer/Sound Effects: None

Introduction

Created by British software company Digital Integration Ltd. for Amiga as one of the first combat flight simulators to have a dynamic campaign environment. While the graphics, scenery and audio are quite sparse and basic, the instruments and flight dynamics of a F-16C Fighting Falcon are fully featured and modelled. True to the aircraft's flexibility, you pilot the F-16 in assignments as diverse as dogfights, bombing raids or reconnaissance missions. It is up to you to plan your flight route by setting waypoints on the tactical map prior to take-off; you can also (but need not) select the armament of your plane. When you have accumulated enough flight experience, you may command entire squadrons in the fictional Operation Conquest campaign, a simple simulation of an entire war theater that already hinted at what would later become DI's Virtual Battlefield.

Gameplay

Most of the missions start with the player inside a hangar, from which the player enters an IFF code, initiate engine start up, taxi without over-speeding, getting on the runway and takeoff – which adds to the tension if the base is under attack. On the ground, there are tank battalions (which move to different locations as war progresses), radar & missiles installations and Triple-A guns around enemy airfields. It is possible to shoot down friendly aircraft by gunfire, but friendly aircraft cannot be designated or tracked by player's radar.

Reception

F-16 Combat Pilot, although a very good simulator, did not receive much popularity as the DOS version was released a year later than Spectrum Holobyte's Falcon, which was more popular and had much more advanced graphics and audio for its time, and by 1991, the very popular Falcon 3.0 was released. F-16 Combat Pilot was never released with VGA graphics and soon looked very dated. 100% Amiga User International (Nov, 1989)

Hardware Requirements

Minimum CPU Class Required: Amiga 500

Minimum OS Class Required: Kickstart 1.2

Minimum RAM Required: 512KB

Media Type: 3.5" Floppy Disk

Video Modes Supported: OCS/ECS

Input Devices Supported: Keyboard, Mouse

Controller Types Supported: Digital Joystick

Multiplayer Options: Via Modem or null modem serial link cable

Number of Players Supported: 1-2 Player

Save Game Methods: Password

Miscellaneous Attributes: Not Hard Drive Installable

Controls/Joystick/Mouse/Gamepad

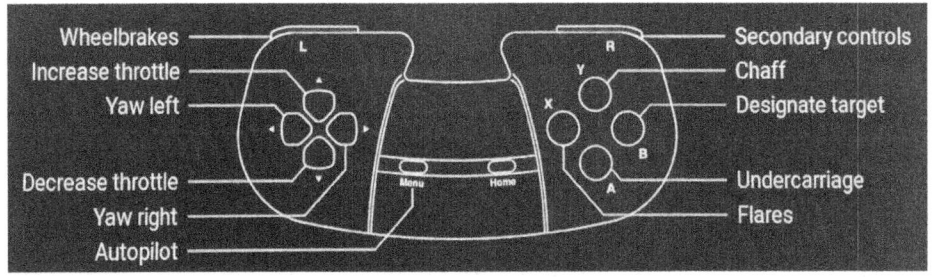

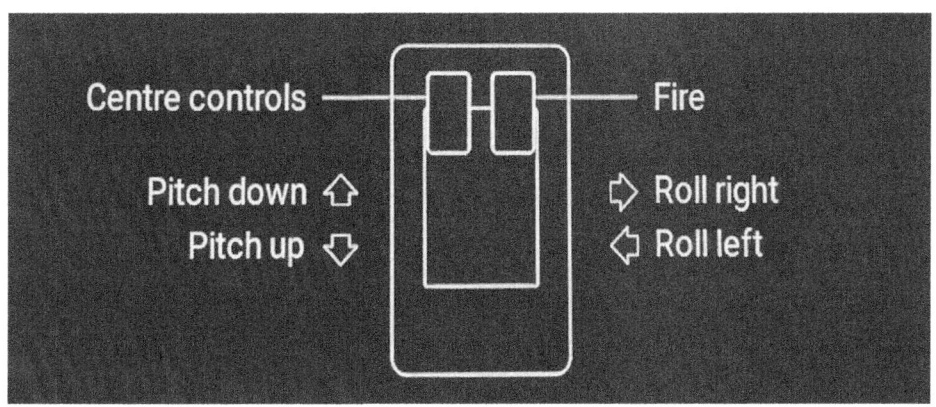

Your aircraft may be flown by using only the Keyboard but you are strongly advised to use a Joystick or Mouse in order to create a sense of "feel" in the controls.

Keys

Roll Right: 6

Roll Left: 4

Pitch Up: 2

Pitch Down: 8

Rudder Left: 1

Rudder Right: 3

Centre Controls: Mouse Left Button

Increase Throttle: +

Decrease Throttle: -

Throttle Slam Open: + and Shift

Throttle Slam Shut: - and Shift

UnderCarriage: U

Airbrakes: Backspace

Wheelbrakes: B

Dogfight Mode: D

Jettison Fuel Tanks: J and F together

Jettison All: J and A together

Eject: Ctrl E

DISPLAYS

F1 Change Left MFD – F2 Change centre MFD

F3 Change right MFD – F9 Radar Target Select

F10 Radar Target Designate

K = HUD pitch bars on/off

H = HUD on/off

WEAPONS SELECTOR

TAB = Weapons select (fwd) – Q = Weapons select (rev)

C = Chaft – F = Flares – SPACE = Pickle Target – SAPCE = Fire Weapons

OTHER KEYS

P = Pause/Continue – Esc = Quit – Ctrl

UP FRONT CONTROL PANEL

F5 = Mode Select – F6 = Channel Select

F7 = Autopilot – F8 = Recce pod on/off

COMMUNICATIONS

T = Transmit Callsign – G = Request GCA

COCKPIT VIEW

Cursor Keys

hold one for a brief look

Shift & cursor key to look

MENU CONTROLS

DEL: Select

HELP or Mouse left or right button: Cancel

Walkthrough

Ingame: https://www.youtube.com/watch?v=x7uY2oAylz0

Cheats, Hints, Tips & Tricks

If you're fed up with landing try the following: Jettison all fuel and weapons and climb to 65000 feet. Stay there until the last of the fuel runs out. Dive towards the ground and at 10 or 11 thousand feet pull up hard. You will then be able to rise about 4000 feet and then start falling towards the ground. Just as you hit the ground the mission will end safely.

7.1.12: Kick Off 2

Released: 1990

Other Platforms: Amstrad CPC, Atari ST, Commodore 64, MS-DOS, Sinclair ZX Spectrum, Sharp 68000, SNES

Developed by: Anco Software Ltd.

Published by: Anco Software Ltd.

Coder/Programmer: Dino Dini

Graphics: Steve Screech

Version: THEA500 Mini: V1.4

Hint! On THEA500 Mini, the "Special Events" are not available.

RGL: Kick off 2 is a single disk game. The Special Events are after-sale supplement disks, not part of the original game.

Introduction

Kick Off 2 retains the pace and accuracy of Kick Off, with a full size multi directional scrolling pitch and the players, markings, goals etc., in correct proportions. Both teams play the game strictly according to tactics. Players move into position to receive passes and gain possession. The ball, as in real game, travels ahead of the player.

Gameplay

With Kick Off the ball did not stick to the player's feet but instead was realistically kicked ahead from the players, in a manner similar to that of Nintendo's Soccer, released in 1985 on the NES. This added a degree of difficulty and skill requirement at the same time. Other attributes, such as action replays, players with different characteristics, different tactics, fouls, yellow cards, red cards, injuries, injury time and various referees with different moods also featured.

Reception

100% Amiga Power (May, 1991), 98% Génération 4 Summer 1990

Predecessor

Kick Off 1989

Successor

Super Kick Off 1991

Hardware Requirements

Minimum CPU Class Required: Amiga 500

Minimum OS Class Required: Kickstart 1.2

Minimum RAM Required: 512KB – Separate enhanced 1 MB version is also available

Media Type: 3.5" Floppy Disk

Video Modes Supported: OCS/ECS

Input Devices Supported: Keyboard, Mouse

Controller Types Supported: Digital Joystick

Multiplayer Options: No

Number of Players Supported: 1-4 Players simultaneous, 8 Player total

Save Game Methods: Password

Miscellaneous Attributes: Not Hard Drive Installable

Controls/Joystick/Mouse/Gamepad

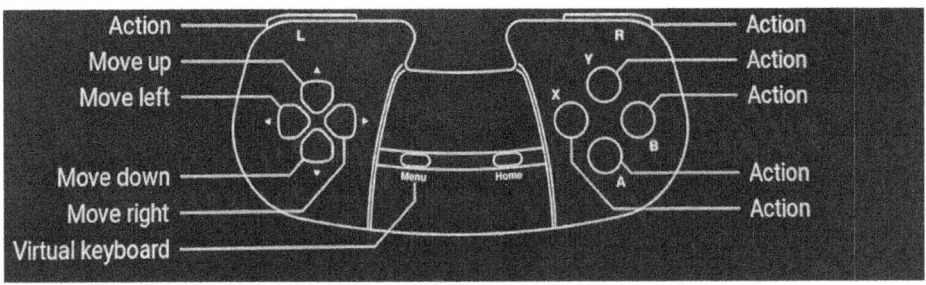

Walkthrough

Longplay: https://www.youtube.com/watch?v=4gILM_z_-1c

Cheats, Hints, Tips & Tricks

cheat #1 <- Switch on autofire, or repeatedly press the fire button and the result will be that your keeper will save the ball every time.

cheat #2 <- In mid-match press all the function keys from left to right (to). "S12" or "S14" should appear in the top right-hand corner. You will now be able to substitute the Computer's keeper and the new guy will be completely useless.

cheat #3 <- During penalties, pushing 'R' will show where the Computer is going to kick the ball to.

cheat #4 <- Substitute the opposing goalkeeper twice and he will not save your shots.

If you press the R key during a penalty kick, you can see exactly where the ball lands. In the game, you press the F1 to F10 keys. Now S12 or S14 should appear in the upper right corner. Now you can replace the opponent's goalkeeper with your own!

BEFORE THE MATCH

\	Pitches
Normal	The standard Kick Off pitch, with good bounce control
Wet	Similar to normal, but with les bounce and roll.
Soggy	Hardly any bounce or roll. After a high kick, the ball will stop dead, so look out for goal mouth scrambles!
Plastic	Extremely bouncy, causing the ball to leave the pitch quite often.

7.1.13: The Lost Patrol

Released: 1990

Other Platforms: Atari ST, DOS

Developed by: Ocean Software Ltd./Shadow Development

Design: Ian Harling, Simon Cooke

Coder/Programmer: Simon Cooke, Nick Byron, Chris Wilson, Kraftwaerk

Graphics: Ian G. Harling

Musician/Composer/Sound Effects: Chris Glaister, Jonathan Dunn

Introduction

Lost Patrol began as an idea to make a game in the style of Cinemaware's ‚interactive movie' titles but with more gameplay, and the designer and artist Ian Harling even sent a game concept to Cinemaware and six other companies but was rejected, until Ocean Software's Gary Bracey accepted it in early 1989 when they decided to move on to the 16-bit market. Lost Patrol was originally intended by Ocean as a follow-up to their 1987's Platoon and was thus initially subtitled Platoon II.

Gameplay

The game is set during the Vietnam War in 1966, when a U.S. helicopter returning troops from a R&R break in Saigon crashes in a remote area of the Central highlands. Seven American survivors of the crash have no radio and face the task of trekking across 58 miles of harsh terrain infested with booby traps and enemies and make their way to the nearest U.S. military outpost at Du Hoc.

Reception

Lost Patrol sold very well and was in the UK's Amiga's top ten chart in late 1990. The game received mostly positive reviews upon its release, including the scores of 85% from The Games Machine. 73% from The One. 79% from Amiga Format, and 83% from CU Amiga. Zero gave the Amiga version of Lost Patrol an overall score of 89%, while the ST version got 88%.

Hardware Requirements

Minimum CPU Class Required: Amiga 500

Minimum OS Class Required: Kickstart 1.2

Minimum RAM Required: 512KB

Media Type: 3.5" Floppy Disk

Video Modes Supported: OCS/ECS

Input Devices Supported: Keyboard, Mouse

Controller Types Supported: Digital Joystick

Multiplayer Options: No

Number of Players Supported: 1 Player

Save Game Methods: Password

Miscellaneous Attributes: Not Hard Drive Installable

Controls/Joystick/Mouse/Gamepad

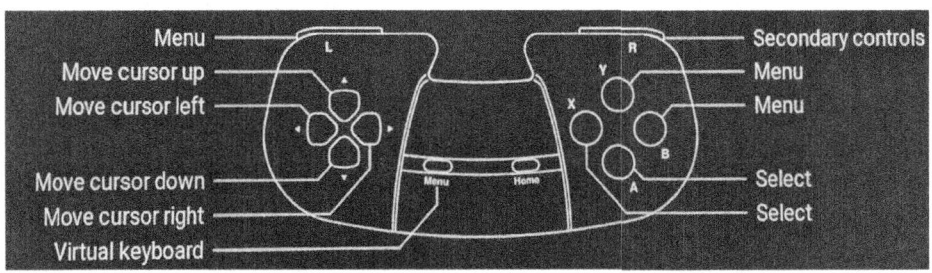

LEFT, RIGHT, DOWN for corresponding movement.

FIRE: Punch

FIRE + LEFT: Kick

Allowing your strength bar in the control panel to fall to zero will count as the death of the designated player.

SNIPER SECTION: (Mouse or Joystick only)

Pinned down by enemy sniper fire you must use the telescopic sights of your rifle to locate the distant enemy then dispose of him. As you and each of your men have different levels of skill as a sharpshooter – and of course you have limited supplies of ammunition – it is important that you choose the man to use the rifle most carefully.

Choosing to retreat from the area will be dangerous under the circumstances. Cycle through your team's names and abilities with the ‚team' icon. Once selected click upon the ‚scope' icon for a magnified view of the terrain which can be searched for the tell-tale flash of sniper rifles.

Remember that the steadiness of the sights corresponds to the ability of the man holding the rifle!

Keys

Cursor RIGHT, LEFT, DOWNWARD for corresponding movement.

X: Punc

Z: Kick

Walkthrough

Playthrough: https://www.youtube.com/watch?v=Gy5bOEF14WM

Cheats, Hints, Tips & Tricks

Rest for 50 minutes and for no loss of food your strength is restored by a few points. This restores all of your remaining men to 99 percent. Keeping up your men's strength and morale is vital. Giving your men 50 minutes' rest a night, or during the day when it's too dark to carry on, will slam your energy and morale levels to max. Even if you don't have much food, you don't have to worry, as your men will not eat it. On reaching the first village (the first white cross on the map), search the area to find a hole in the ground where the villagers appear to be hiding. You then have two options: ENTER TUNNEL or USE GRENADES. Gomez is useful at this point, but if he is dead, go for the USE GRENADES option. Start off questioning the villagers normally by asking them "Where VC?" Once you have an answer, start the hard questioning, or a village boy will get hold of a gun and shoot one of your men.

7.1.14: Paradroid 90

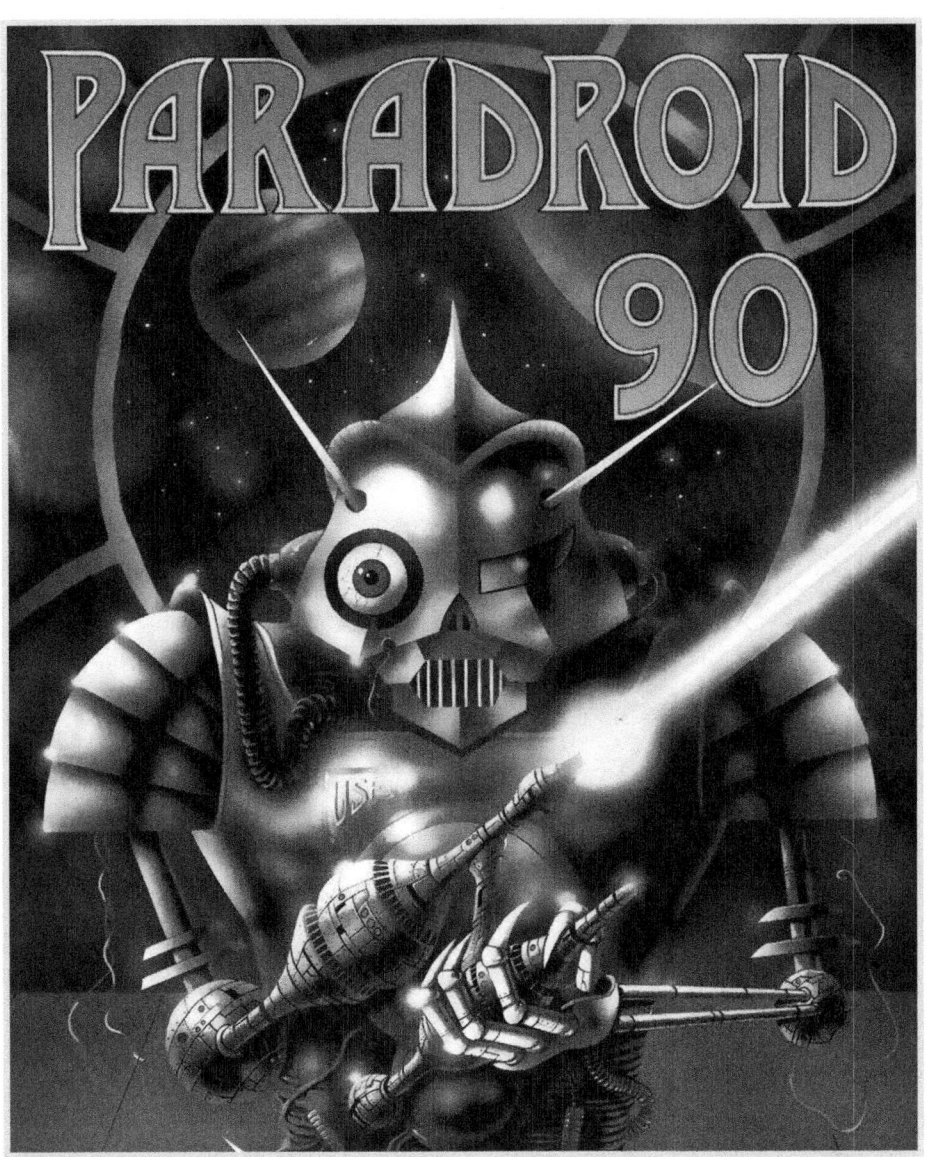

Released: 1990

Other Platforms: Acorn, Atari ST

Developed by: Graftgold Ltd.

Published by: Hewson Consultants, Jester Interactive Publishing

Design: Andrew Braybrook

Coder/Programmer: Andrew Braybrook, Dominic Robinson

Graphics: Michael A. Field, John Cumming, John W. Lilley

Musician/Composer/Sound Effects: Jason Page

Introduction

The game was influenced by several different Computer games and movies, and was built on top of a previous game, "Survive", developed by GEC Marconi. Author Andrew Braybrook said in a Retro Gamer interview that the droid-swapping idea came from an arcade game, Front Line, where the player could enter a tank and had to leave it when it got hit. In another Retro Gamer feature, Braybrook also stated that the cover of the Black Sabbath album Technical Ecstasy influenced him, where two droids "interfacing" can be observed, along with the corridors of the movie Aliens. Development started right after Braybrook finished his previous game Gribbly's Day Out and even shared some code with Gribbly's. Later when Braybrook was working on Morpheus he did another diary for Zzap!64 where he revealed that the then recently released Competition Edition of Paradroid was 50% faster than the original. In the same series he revealed that they had redone the Paradroid graphics in the new (Morpheus) style, which was later released as Heavy Metal Paradroid. Andrew Braybrook did another diary during the development of Paradroid 90 for Amiga Action.

Gameplay

The game is set on a spaceship viewed from a top-down perspective. The ship consists of numerous rooms and levels, each one populated by hostile robots or "androids". The player, in control of a special droid called the "Influence Device", must destroy all the other droids on the ship. Each droid (including the player) is represented as a circle around a three-digit number. The numbers roughly correspond to the droid's "power" or "level", in that higher-numbered droids are tougher to destroy; there are 24 droid types.

Reception

The game has been heralded as one of the best ever original games to appear on the Commodore 64, as can be seen when the readers of Retro Gamer selected it as the best game ever on the platform: Andrew Braybrook's Paradroid is a masterpiece, there's no other way to describe its sheer brilliance.

Predecessor

1985 Paradroid Commodore 64, 1986 Paradroid Competition Edition, 1987 Heavy Metal Paradroid

Successor

Paradroid 2000 (Acorn Archimedes)

Hardware Requirements

Minimum CPU Class Required: Amiga 500

Minimum OS Class Required: Kickstart

Minimum RAM Required: 512KB

Media Type: 3.5" Floppy Disk

Video Modes Supported: OCS/ECS

Input Devices Supported: Keyboard, Mouse

Controller Types Supported: Digital Joystick

Multiplayer Options: No

Number of Players Supported: 1 Player

Save Game Methods: Password

Miscellaneous Attributes: Not Hard Drive Installable

Controls/Joystick/Mouse/Gamepad

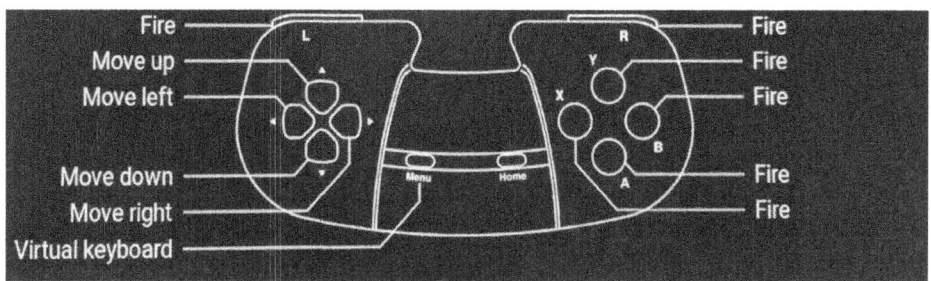

Control is by Keyboard or a Joystick in either port, Mouse control is not supported, select the control mode by pressing F1 to bring up the options screen at any point during the title sequence. Press F1 again to cycle through available modes. Other options shown on this screen are detailed later.

Keys

Up: O P Q W 1 2 0 or the up cursor

Down: L ; A S or the down cursor

Left: M, Z X or the left cursor

Right: ./C V or the right cursor

Fire: ALT, CTRL and either SHIFT key

Pressing the F3 key in the title screen opens an options selection screen.

During the title sequence;

F1: Change controls between Joystick or Keyboard.

F2: Select start ship (any previously visited ship may be started on).

F3: Switch the transfer game on/off.

F4: View previous game statistics.

Convenience Keys

During the game press `Help` to pause, the `Help` or fire to resume game.

During pause mode press `ESC` to quit game. You can pause the game when in the transfer game.

Walkthrough

Playthrough: https://www.youtube.com/watch?v=bRibUjPXUKk

Cheats, Hints, Tips & Tricks

On the title screen, press 'F3' to bring up an option screen.

The extra ship is the pirate mothership. To reach it, collect the grafgold key hidden on every ship. The grafgold keys are usually found under crates and so on. Collecting a key keeps the pirates at bay for a further three minutes. A 5000-point bonus is given for completing a ship with grafgold key. Complete the final ship with every grafgold key to be beamed aboard the pirate mothership for a fight to the death.

7.1.15: Pinball Dreams

Released: 1992

Other Platforms: Atari Falcon, DOS, Game Boy, GBA, Sega Game Gear, GamePark GP32, iOS, OS X, PSN, SNES

Developed by: Digital Illusions

Published by: 21st Century Entertainment, GameTek

Design: Olof Gustafsson

Manager: Fredrik Liliegren: **Producer:** Barry Simpson

Coder/Programmer: Andreas Axelsson

Graphics: Markus Nyström

Musician/Composer/Sound Effects: Olof Gustafsson

Gameplay

The game's four tables each had a theme, as do most real-life pinball & Panchinko machines. The version of Pinball Dreams bundled with the Amiga 1200 had a bug which rendered most of Beat Box's advanced features non-functional.

"Ignition", themed around a rocket launch, planets, and space exploration. The Expert Software's Pinball 2000 port of the game renamed this table "Rocket".

"Steel Wheel", themed around steam trains and the Old West.

"Beat Box", themed around the music industry, charts, bands and tours.

"Nightmare", themed around a graveyard, ghosts, demons, nightmares and generally evil things. Unlike the other tables in the game, the name of the table in the menu did not reflect the name displayed on the table itself—"Graveyard". Some ports of the game (notably the GameTek port to the Game Boy) name this table "Graveyard" in the menu as well.

Reception

Pinball Dreams was overall received positive by press reviews. Electronic Gaming Monthly gave the Game Gear version a 5.8 out of 10, commenting that "Pinball never really worked well on portable systems and Pinball Dreams is no exception. The boards are huge, but the game is a little slow."

Successor

Pinball Dreams 2

Hardware Requirements

Minimum CPU Class Required: Amiga 500

Minimum OS Class Required: Kickstart

Minimum RAM Required: 512KB

Media Type: 3.5" Floppy Disk

Video Modes Supported: OCS/ECS

Input Devices Supported: Keyboard

Controller Types Supported: No

Multiplayer Options: No

Number of Players Supported: 1-8 Players

Save Game Methods:

Miscellaneous Attributes: Not Hard Drive Installable

Controls/Joystick/Mouse/Gamepad

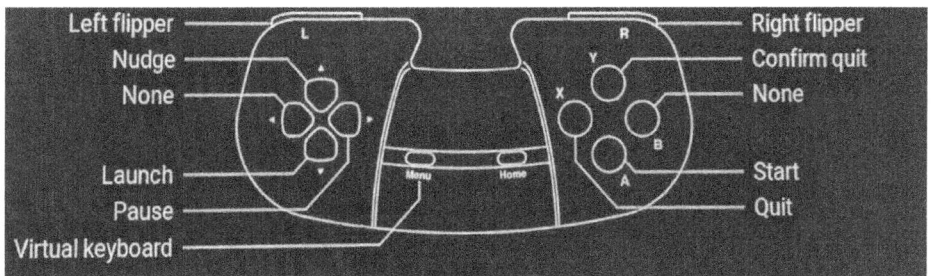

Mouse

Drag downwards – Pull back spring (for shooting ball)

Left Mousebutton – let go of spring (shoot ball)

Keys

To load a table use F-Keys

F1 – IGNITION TABLE (easiest)

F2 – STEEL WHEEL TABLE

F3 – BEAT-BOX TABLE

F4 – NIGHTMARE TABLE (hardest)

In the main screen the space-bar toggles to the hi-score table.

In game:

F1 – F8 = No. of players

Arrow-Down – Pull back spring (release to shoot ball)

P – Pause (any keypress restarts)

ESC – Quit table (after pausing)

ESC – Quit current game (when ball is in chute)

Right SHIFT/ALT/AMIGA – flip right flipper cycle lit/unit lights clockwise

Left SHIFT/ALT/AMIGA – flip left flipper cycle lit/unit lights anti-clock.

SPACE BAR – Tilt the table

M – Toggle Music on/off

If at the end of a game you have made a high-score, simply type in your name (3 letters allowed) when prompted. The delete key can be used to correct mistakes.

Walkthrough

Longplay: https://www.youtube.com/watch?v=6UNGMiPETXo

Cheats, Hints, Tips & Tricks

To get twenty extra balls press Up, Down, Left, Left, Right, Down, Up on the Joystick during game play.

7.1.16: Project-X: Special Edition 93

Released: 1993

Developed by: Team17 Software Limited

Published by: Team17 Software Limited

Design: Andreas Tadic, Rico Holmes

Manager: Martyn J. Brown

Coder/Programmer: Andreas Tadic, Stefan Boberg

Graphics: Rico Holmes

Musician/Composer/Sound Effects: Allister Brimble, Bjørn Lynne, Christopher Brimble

Introduction

The Special Edition is a slightly easier version of the original game from 1992. Taking place many years in the future in colonized space, military scientists have disposed of countless, defective military droids on an uncolonized terrestrial planet called Ryxx. The droids eventually become sentient and, by way of revenge, start an attack against mankind, using a station to continually create more war machines. It is the player's mission to undergo Project X and eliminate the droid forces.

Gameplay

Players control a spacecraft of their choice, battling hundreds of alien ships. Various power-ups, numerous in the first level but increasingly rare afterwards, permit an exponential increase of the spacecraft's seven different weapons (Guns, Buildup, Side Shots, Homing Missiles, Plasma, Magma, and Laserbeam).

Reception

Amiga Computing64 (Sep 1993) 93%. According to Next Generation, Project-X was immensely successful in Europe, but only sold in moderate numbers in the U.S. [2] Amiga Computing called it one of the best shooter games for that platform at the time, both for its technical excellence in graphics and sounds, and for its difficult and interesting gameplay

Successor

The game was followed by a PlayStation-only sequel, X2.

Predecessor

Project-X

Hardware Requirements

Minimum CPU Class Required: Amiga 500

Minimum OS Class Required: Kickstart

Minimum RAM Required: 1 MB

Media Type: 3.5" Floppy Disk

Video Modes Supported: OCS/ECS

Input Devices Supported: No

Controller Types Supported: Digital Joystick

Multiplayer Options: No

Number of Players Supported: 1 or 2 Players

Save Game Methods: Password

Miscellaneous Attributes: No Hard Drive Installable

Controls/Joystick/Mouse/Gamepad

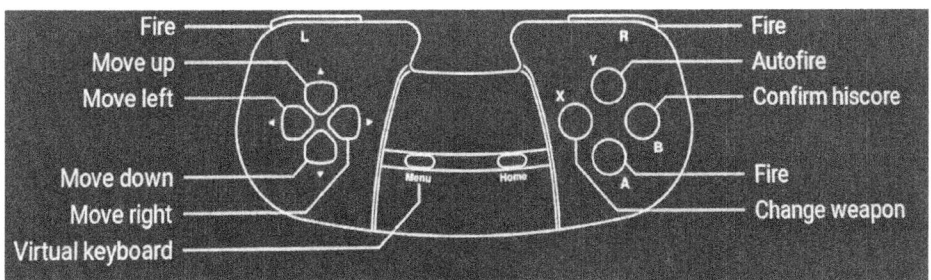

Keys

P – Pause Game

TAB – Toggle status bar on/off

ESC – Quit Current Game

Walkthrough

Longplay: https://www.youtube.com/watch?v=Tih1QIUG2WE

Cheats, Hints, Tips & Tricks

During the game press and hold down the right Mouse button and then hit the [Escape] key, the screen will then turn black. Now with your finger still on the right Mouse button hit the [Return] key and you will be warped to the next level.

7.1.17: Qwak

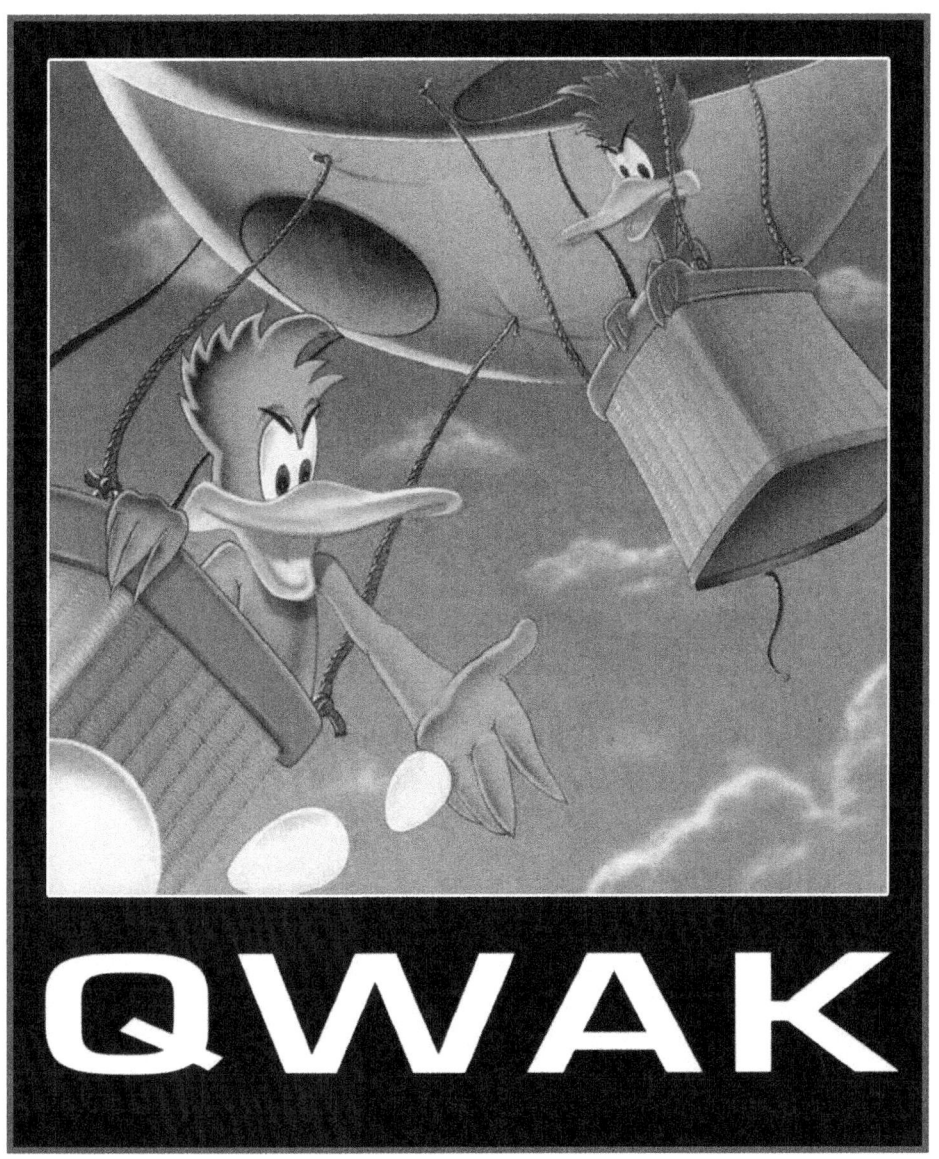

Released: 1993

Other Platforms: BBC Micro, Blackberry, Acorn Electron, Amiga, Amiga CD32, Game Boy Advance, iOS, Mac OS, Windows, Symbian

Developed by: Team17 Software Limited

Published by: Team17 Software Limited

Design: Jamie Woodhouse

Manager: Martyn Brown

Coder/Programmer: Jamie Woodhouse

Graphics: Richard Heasman

Musician/Composer/Sound Effects: Allister Brimble, Bjørn Lynne

Introduction

Qwak is a 2D puzzle-platform game developed by Jamie Woodhouse. It was initially released for the BBC Micro and Acorn Electron in 1989 as part of Superior/Acornsoft's Play It Again Sam 10 compilation. An updated and enhanced Amiga version was given a budget release by Team17 in 1993. This update added several new features, including a two-player mode and additional levels. The game was re-released on the Amiga CD32 later that year in a double-pack with science fiction shooter Alien Breed.

Gameplay

The object of the game is to guide a green duck through eighty levels. Fruit and gems can be collected for points, and enemies are eliminated with projectile egg weapons. Progress through the game is earned by collecting gold and silver keys. There are a variety of power-ups also available, including ‚chocolate egg' weapons and extra shots.

Reception

The Amiga version was awarded 92% and a ‚Gamer Gold' review by Amiga Computing magazine

Official webpage

http://www.qwak.co.uk/

Hardware Requirements

Minimum CPU Class Required: Amiga 500

Minimum OS Class Required: Kickstart 1.2

Minimum RAM Required: 1 MB

Media Type: 3.5" Floppy Disk

Video Modes Supported: OCS/ECS

Input Devices Supported: Keyboard

Controller Types Supported: Digital Joystick

Multiplayer Options: Same/Split-Screen

Number of Players Supported: 1 or 2 Players

Save Game Methods: Password

Miscellaneous Attributes: Not Hard Drive Installable

Controls/Joystick/Mouse/Gamepad

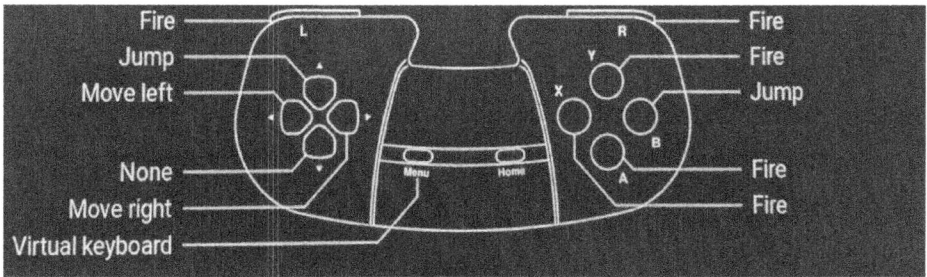

The Joystick controls the direction of your duck.

Press up to jump and fire to throw an egg at the baddies. Player one (Gameport 2) uses the GREEN duck, player two (Gameport 1 or Keyboard) uses the PURPLE duck.

Walkthrough

Longplay: https://www.youtube.com/watch?v=hQNoUJKE-xg

Cheats, Hints, Tips & Tricks

Continue game play: After losing the last life in a one player game, plug the Joystick into the Mouse port and press Fire. The game will resume on the last level played.

Basics: There are eight worlds, and 10 scenes per world. To complete each scene you must collect all the gold keys and make your way through the open door.

Eggs and Baddies: Touching a baddie causes loss of one armour or death. Eggs can be thrown at baddies and it takes one hit to destroy them in World One, two hits in World Two, three hits in World Three, and four hits in World Four upwards. Big baddies take six hits in World One, eight in World Two, 10 in World Three and 12 hits in World Four and above.

Peace Bonus: Completing a scene without throwing and eggs gives a bonus of 10,000 points x double world points, and doubles the egg bonus.

Egg Bonus: Collecting the fruits and completing a scene gives an egg bonus. Each fruit is worth one to six fruit points (red equals one, purple equals six). In World One you need four fruit points for an egg bonus, in World Two, you need six fruit points, in World Three, eight fruit points and in World Four and above you need 10 fruit points for an egg bonus.

Gem Bonus: Collecting all six gems gives a gem bonus which starts at 10,000 points and doubles each time you get it. The gem bonus resets to 10,000 points when you die.

7.1.18: The Sentinel

Released: 1988

Other Platforms: BBC Micro, Commodore 64, Amstrad CPC, ZX Spectrum, Atari ST, DOS

Developed by: Firebird Software

Published by: Geoff Crammond

Coder/Programmer: Steve Bak

Musician/Composer/Sound Effects: David Whittaker

Introduction

The Sentinel, released in the United States as The Sentry, is a puzzle video game created by Geoff Crammond, published by Firebird in 1986 for the BBC Micro and converted to the Commodore 64 (by Crammond himself), Amstrad CPC (with a cross-compiler written by Crammond), ZX Spectrum (by Mike Follin), Atari ST, Amiga (both by Steve Bak) and IBM PC compatibles (by Mark Roll). The Sentinel was among the first games to use solid-filled 3D graphics on home Computers. It won numerous awards upon release and has since appeared on several "best video games of all time" lists.

The IBM PC port supports VGA graphics, with an additional lighting effect: objects and terrain becomes darker the farther away they are from the point of view. The Amiga port has a sampled soundtrack by David Whittaker.

Gameplay

In The Sentinel, the player takes the role of a Synthoid (called just "robot" in the US version), a telepathic robot who has to take control of a number of surreal, checkered landscapes of hills and valleys, by climbing from the lowest spot, where the hunt begins, to the highest platform, over which the Sentinel looms.

The Synthoid itself cannot move across the level; instead it can look around, accumulate energy by absorbing the objects that are scattered across the landscape, create stacks of boulders, generate inert Synthoid shells and transfer its consciousness from one of these clones to another.

Reception

Computer Gaming World called the Commodore 64 version of The Sentinel "outstanding and addictive ... I highly recommend it for many absorbing hours".[3] It received a Gold Medal award by Zzap!64 magazine,[4] describing it as an exceptional piece of software in a class of its own, and refusing to give it a numbered rating as a result.

Successor

Sentinel Returns 1998 (DOS & PlayStation)

Hardware Requirements

Minimum CPU Class Required: Amiga 500

Minimum OS Class Required: Kickstart 1.2

Minimum RAM Required: 512KB

Media Type: 3.5" Floppy Disk

Video Modes Supported: OCS

Input Devices Supported: Keyboard, Mouse

Controller Types Supported: No

Multiplayer Options: No

Number of Players Supported: 1 Player

Save Game Methods: Password

Miscellaneous Attributes: Not Hard Drive Installable

Controls/Joystick/Mouse/Gamepad

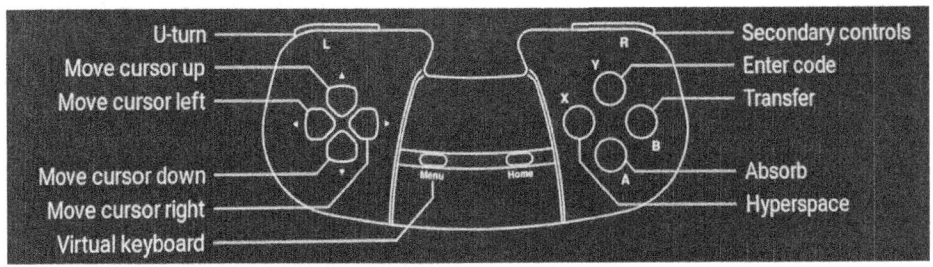

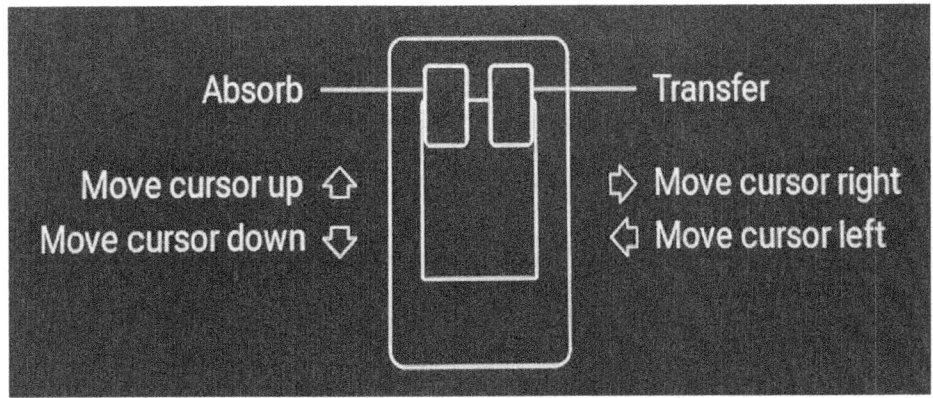

Keys

S: Pan left

D: Pan right

K: Pan up

M: Pan down

T: Create Tree

B: Create Boulder

R: Create Robot

SPACE: Sights on/off

H: Hyperspace

U: U-turn

A: Absorb

Q: Transfer

BREAK: Quit

P: Pause

ENTER: Unpause

Z: Music on/off

Walkthrough

Levelplay https://www.youtube.com/watch?v=Ub6BsT2Gm1c

Cheats, Hints, Tips & Tricks
Some Levelcodes

3: 70511958

8: 16257084

10: 43428170

11: 40556356

18: 68627185

19: 55742564

36: 97578966

50: 61185004

61: 26060764

66: 68657887

80: 18452261

103: 36873128

127: 06567770

150: 92856449

169: 16788555

196: 72957558

205: 78908712

225: 38546570

300: 49703885

400: 82065427

449: 00297522

514: 13679994

610: 39557944

704: 09548849

818: 36852626

906: 42666746

1000: 91569547

1058: 53527981

1102: 76188275

1197: 56217748

1309: 13643654

1400: 79380940

7.1.19: Simon the Sorcerer

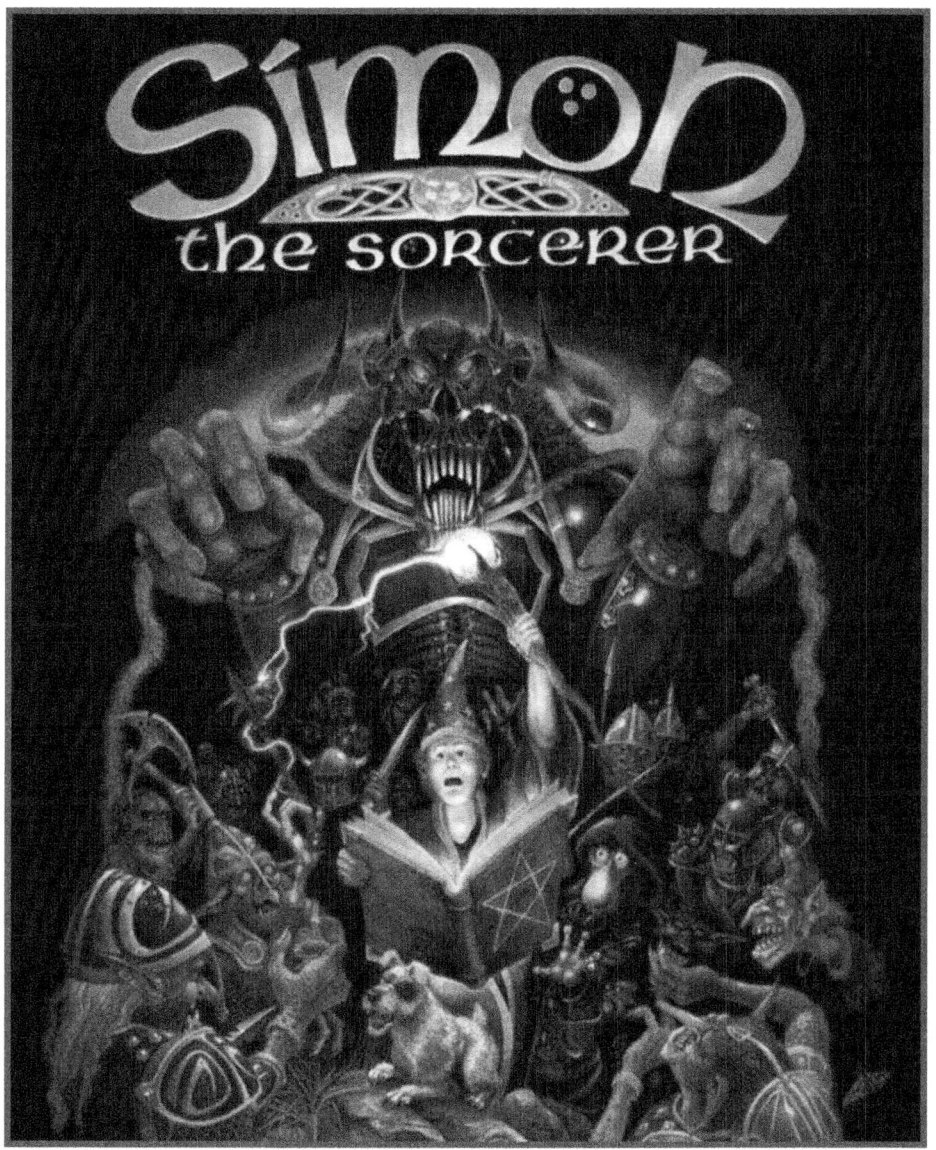

Released: 1994

Other Platforms: Acorn 32, Amiga CD32, MS-DOS, iOS, Android, Microsoft Windows

Developed by: Adventure Soft Ltd.

Published by: Blittersoft/Adventure Soft Ltd.

Design: Simon Woodroffe

Manager: Mike Woodroffe

Producer: Mike Woodroffe, Alan Bridgman

Coder/Programmer: Alan Bridgman

Graphics: Paul Drummond, Maria Drummond, Karen Pinchin, Jeffrey Wall

Writer: Simon Woodroffe

Musician/Composer/Sound Effects: Media Sorcery

Introduction

Simon the Sorcerer is a 1993 point-and-click adventure game developed and published by Adventure Soft, for Amiga and MS-DOS. The game's story focuses on a boy named Simon who is transported into a parallel universe of magic and monsters, where he embarks on a mission to become a wizard and rescue another from an evil sorcerer. The game's setting was inspired by the novels of the Discworld series, and incorporates parodies on fantasy novels and fairy tales, such as The Lord of the Rings and Jack and the Beanstalk. The lead character's design was inspired by that of the fictional British television character Blackadder, with the character voiced by Chris Barrie in the CD re-release.

Reception

Simon the Sorcerer received critical acclaim: across all platforms, the humour and visuals in particular were commended, although criticisms included the controls and the game's linear nature. The game's global sales surpassed 600,000 units by September 1999.[48]

The Amiga version received generally high ratings. CU Amiga praised the high quality graphics and how much fun the game was to play.[46] Amiga

Computing's Simon Clays also praised the graphics and the locations, saying the locations' stylisation made the game resemble a fairy tale. He also enjoyed the puzzles and detail in the game.[32] The One's reviewer said the graphics are "excellent", but believed the music did not take full advantage of the Amiga's sound hardware.[51] A reviewer of Génération 4 thought the Amiga version's graphics are "magnificent".[40]

Hardware Requirements

Minimum CPU Class Required: Amiga 1200

Minimum OS Class Required: Kickstart

Minimum RAM Required: MB

Media Type: 3.5" Floppy Disk

Video Modes Supported: ECS/OCS/ AGA in separate edition

Input Devices Supported: Keyboard, Mouse

Controller Types Supported: Digital Joystick

Multiplayer Options: Null-modem cable

Number of Players Supported: 1-2 Players

Save Game Methods: Password

Miscellaneous Attributes: Hard Drive Installable

Controls/Joystick/Mouse/Gamepad

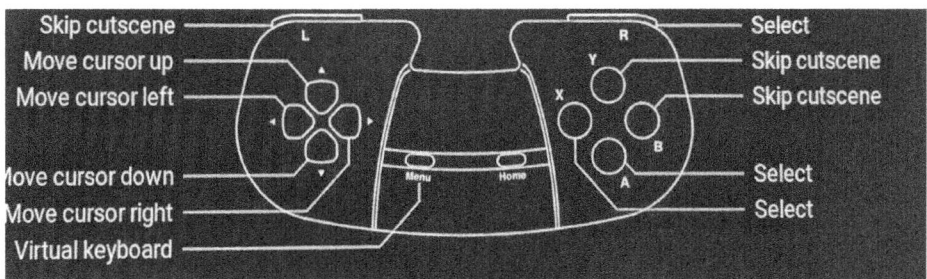

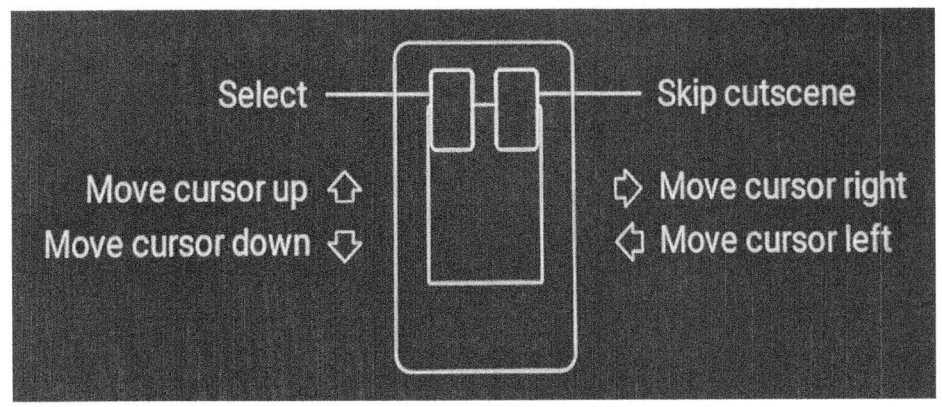

If you don't know by now then there is no hope for you. Feel free to chuck your real Computer out of the window and go back to your games console. We're sure the Queen of the Fungus People (or whatever) would appreciate it.

Seriously though, the Mouse is used to select ICONS on the screen. These will be explained in greater detail later. It is also used to move Simon around the area he is currently in.

Some keys will also be of assistance depending on your musical tastes or reactions.

Keys

Pressing M turns the music off or on (it is a toggle, i.e. pressing it changes to the opposite of its current State).

Pressing S turns the sound effects off or on (it is also a toggle as above).

Pressing Fl will increase the speed of the on—screen text. Pressing F3 will slow down the speed of the on-screen text and pressing F2 will return the text speed to normal.

Walkthrough

Longplay: https://www.youtube.com/watch?v=HGyPtnEQ8gw

7.1.20: Speedball 2: Brutal Deluxe

Released: 1990

Other Platforms: Acorn Archimedes, Atari ST, Amiga CD32, Commodore 64, PC, Sega Master System, Game Boy, Game Boy Advance, Sega Mega Drive/Genesis, Windows Mobile, PlayStation, Xbox 360, iPhone, Symbian (J2ME)

Copyright: Mirrorsoft

Developed by: The Bitmap Brothers

Published by: Image Works, Arena Entertainment, Empire Interactive, Akella, Tower Studios, SOFEL

Distributed by:

Design: Eric Matthews, Steve Kelly, Graeme Boxall, Dan Malone

Coder/Programmer: Robert Trevellyan, Mike Montgomery

Graphics: Daniel Malone

Musician/Composer/Sound Effects: Nation 12; Richard Joseph

Introduction

Speedball 2: Brutal Deluxe is a 1990 video game based on a violent futuristic cyberpunk sport that draws on elements of handball and ice hockey, and rewards violent play as well as goals. The concept of the game is very reminiscent of the 1975 film Rollerball. The original game was developed by Bitmap Brothers, with various remakes for many platforms since being published. It is a sequel to the 1988 game Speedball.

Gameplay

Speedball 2 makes several changes over the original Speedball. Teams have nine players on court rather than five, and targets on the floor and walls can be hit to receive bonus points. The number of points that a team receives for scoring a goal starts at 10 but can be increased to 15 or 20 via the use of score multipliers located on the walls of the pitch. The same number of points for scoring a goal is given for injuring a player from the opposing team. When a player is injured, he is replaced by one of three substitutes. If all three substitutes are injured, the injured player will be forced to return to the game and play on in spite of his injuries. There are five game modes: knockout, cup, league, practice and multiplayer. Each game lasts for 180 seconds.

Reception

Speedball 2 is one of Bitmap Brothers' most successful titles. Zzap, CU Amiga and Computer and Video Games scored the game highly. The music, written by Simon Rogers and remixed and coded by Richard Joseph, won the 1991 Golden Joystick Award for Best Soundtrack.[2] The voices, including the ‚Ice Cream' salesman, were voiced by sometime Richard Joseph collaborator Michael Burdett working under the pseudonym Jams O'Donnell. The game was voted the 3rd best game of all time in Amiga Power.

Predecessor

Speedball

Hardware Requirements

Minimum CPU Class Required: Amiga 1200

Minimum OS Class Required: Kickstart 1.1

Minimum RAM Required: 512KB

Media Type: 3.5" Floppy Disk

Video Modes Supported: OCS/ECS

Input Devices Supported: Keyboard, Mouse

Controller Types Supported: Digital Joystick

Multiplayer Options: Simultaneous/Split-Screen

Number of Players Supported: 1-2 Players

Save Game Methods: Password

Miscellaneous Attributes: Not Hard Drive Installable

Controls/Joystick/Mouse/Gamepad

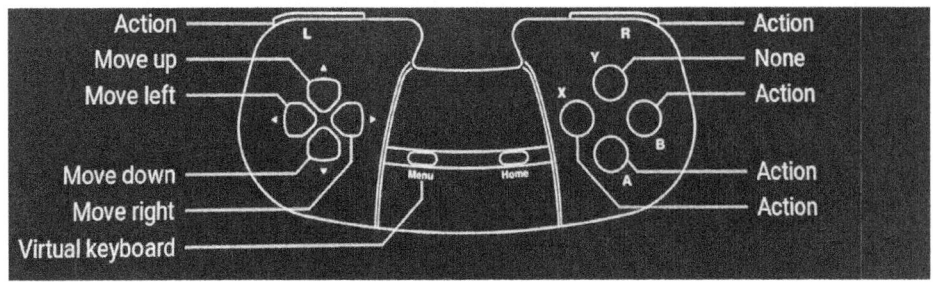

Keys

ESC: ESCAPE TO THE MAIN MENU

F: FAST MODE (TEAM MANAGER)

ANY OTHER KEY: PAUSES THE GAME (ANY KEY AGAIN TO START)

Walkthrough

Longplay: https://www.youtube.com/watch?v=iyX4BPU-Bao

Cheats, Hints, Tips & Tricks

The original version was not compatible with accelerated Amigas. The first compatible one came from a pirate team.

Rather than spending cash on increasing your entire team attributes, make your centre forward and goalie as powerful as possible. Then save up your cash and buy star players as soon as they are offered.

Put the first player as centre forward where he should be able to outrun all other players and also kill a few opponents every game. Just with your centre forward strong, you should be able to win the second division. Keep buying players and replace your current ones.

Always go for the score multipliers first, and if you need a few quick points, hit the stars and bounce domes. If you position yourself a few pixels away from a bounce dome, you should be able to throw the ball to hit the dome twice with each throw. If you throw the ball quick enough, the opposition will often get beaten up at the same time so you can amass some quick points.

7.1.21: Stunt Car Racer

Released: 1989

Other Platforms: Amstrad CPC, Atari ST, Commodore 64, MS-DOS, ZX Spectrum

Developed by: MicroStyle

Published by: MicroProse, MicroStyle, MicroPlay

Design: Geoffrey J. Crammond, Julie Burness

Coder/Programmer: Geoffrey J. Crammond, Norah Crammond

Graphics: John Cumming

Musician/Composer/Sound Effects:

Introduction

Stunt Car Racer (published as Stunt Track Racer in the United States) is a racing video game developed by Geoff Crammond.[1] It was published in 1989 by MicroProse, under their MicroStyle and MicroPlay labels in the United Kingdom and in the United States, respectively.

Gameplay

The game differs from other racing games in that the races take place on an elevated race track, with nothing to stop the player from accidentally driving off the side. Most race tracks in the game have gaps in them, which players can fall into. If this occurs then the player's vehicle is hoisted back onto the track (by a nearby crane), costing valuable time. Turbo can be used to make a car go faster, but it can only be used for a limited amount of time in each race.

Reception

The game received critical acclaim. Amstrad Action gave the game 96/100, defining it a "truly stunning racing sim" and one of the best ever on Amstrad CPC. Crash gave the game 87/100, praising the graphics and the entertainment, but criticizing the limiting number of tracks.

Amiga Power and Your Sinclair ranked Stunt Car Racer respectively the 10th and the 85th best game of all time.

Hardware Requirements

Minimum CPU Class Required: Amiga 500

Minimum OS Class Required: Kickstart 1.2

Minimum RAM Required: 512KB

Media Type: 3.5" Floppy Disk

Video Modes Supported: OCS/ECS

Input Devices Supported: Keyboard

Controller Types Supported: Digital Joystick

Multiplayer Options: Null-modem cable

Number of Players Supported: 1-8 Players

Save Game Methods: Password

Miscellaneous Attributes: Not Hard Drive Installable

Controls/Joystick/Mouse/Gamepad

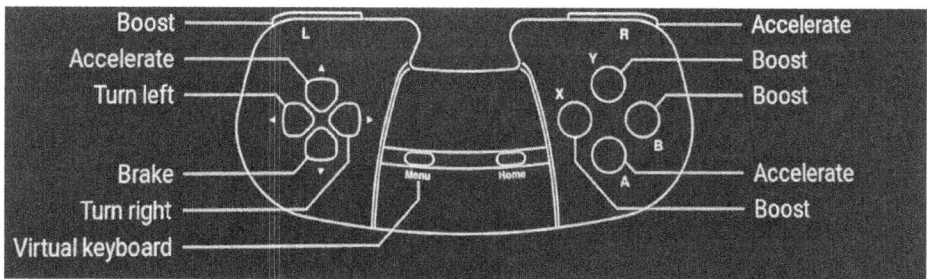

Steering – Joystick left/right

Accelerate forwards – Push Joystick forward

Brake/reverse – Pull Joystick back

Boost (limited supply) – Press the button

Note: Once acceleration is selected by pushing the Joystick forward, you can return the Joystick to its central position as the car will continue to accelerate until you brake or freewheel the car. This avoids the need for constant forward pressure to be applied to the Joystick. Pulling the stick back cancels the acceleration, and returning the stick to its central position allows the car to free wheel.

Keys

The key controls differ slightly form the Joystick in order to avoid the need to press more than two keys at any one time. With the "Boost and Accelerator" key depressed, your car will be accelerating with boost. Once the key is released, the car will continue to accelerate, but without the boost. Therefore, the key does not need to be held down continuously unless boost is required.

Forward acceleration is turned off by pressing either of the two brake/reverse keys. The car will then freewheel until another key is pressed. Two brake/reverse keys provide two braking/reversing rates, i.e. with and without boost.

Steering

S = Left

D = Right

Boost + accelerator forward: "RETURN" Key

Boost + brake/reverse: SPACEBAR

Brake/Reverse: "=" Key

The car control keys are redefined from the cockpit. First of all, PAUSE the game (see item 4 of further controls). Then press the F1 key.

The "PAUSED" message on screen will be replaced by a "DEFINE KEYS" message.

The Computer then asks for the keys that you wish to use for the relevant controls. It then requests that you verify the keys that have been pressed. Enter the same keys again and the Computer will not return to the MAIN game. If the second entry does not match the first, the Computer will ask for another set of keys to be pressed and verified. You must then unpause the game to continue.

In multiplayer mode, each player can redefine the keys at any time during a race (preferably before the start). These settings are stored for each individual player and are automatically re-installed in subsequent races involving that player.

Walkthrough

Longplay: https://www.youtube.com/watch?v=q7w_0yP5RwU

Cheats, Hints, Tips & Tricks

If you get stuck in a hole or at the bottom of a jump, drive slowly up to the wall and accelerate with boost. This will minimise your damage.

7.1.22: Super Cars II

Released: 1991

Other Platforms: Amstrad/Schneider CPC464/664/6128, Atari ST/E, Sinclair ZX Spectrum 128/+2/+3

Developed by: Magnetic Fields (Software Design) Ltd.

Published by: Gremlin Graphics

Coder/Programmer: Shaun Southern

Graphics: Andrew Morris, Jeremy C. Smith

Musician/Composer/Sound Effects: Barry Leitch, Ian Howe (Howie)

Introduction

Super Cars II is a 1991 top-view racing game developed by Magnetic Fields, and published by Gremlin Graphics Software Ltd. The game was available for the Amiga and the Atari ST. It is the sequel to the 1990 game Super Cars.

Gameplay

Supercars 2 is an overhead racing game loosely. The actual race track is larger than the screen, so the track scrolls in all directions as you progress. Your aim as the driver of the red car (or the green car in the two-player mode) is to finish the race in one of the top five positions, preferably first. Fail to achieve this and you'll be thrown out of the championship and have to start from scratch on track one. Instead of just three cars, you must now take on 10 Computer controlled cars. Being a good driver is not the only skill required to win a race. Various weapons are available and can be used to bring a spectacular halt to your fellow competitors.

Reception

Amiga Action 20 (May 1991) 93%

Carsten Borgmeier wrote in Amiga Joker magazine, "Super Cars II is the stuff Computer runabouts dream of.

Hardware Requirements

Minimum CPU Class Required: Amiga 500

Minimum OS Class Required: Kickstart

Minimum RAM Required: 512KB

Media Type: 3.5" Floppy Disk

Video Modes Supported: OCS/ECS, AGA as extra edition

Input Devices Supported: Keyboard

Controller Types Supported: Digital Joystick

Multiplayer Options: Same/Spilt-Screen

Number of Players Supported: 1-2 Players

Save Game Methods: Password

Miscellaneous Attributes: Not Hard Drive Installable

Controls/Joystick/Mouse/Gamepad

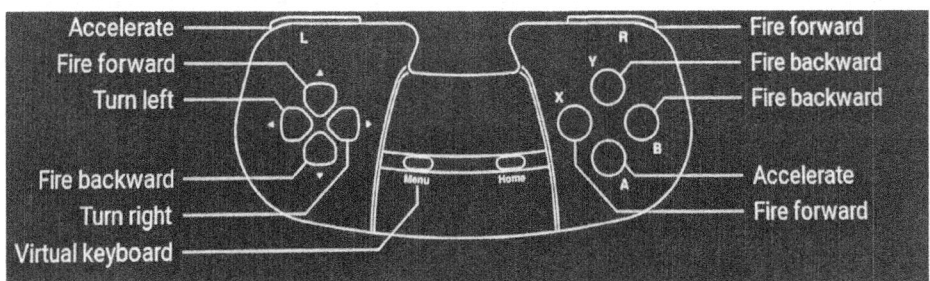

Left = Turn left.

Right = Turn right.

Forward = Activate front weapon.

Backwards = Activate rear weapon.

Fire = Accelerate or brake, depending on mode

Keys

The following keys correspond to the appropriate Joystick controls

Z = Turn left.

X = Turn right.

Space = Fire.

L = Forward.

Comma = Backwards.

Walkthrough

Longplay: https://www.youtube.com/watch?v=F3gvfxHBiWc

Cheats, Hints, Tips & Tricks

Enter for Player One "Wonderland" and for Player Two "The Seer". Now you have a car with all the extras and full armament.

Always qualify and have 99% of all weapons:

Enter "I WALK THE HILL" as a name for Player One and "INWARDS" as a name for Player Two.

Unlimited money:

Type "HARD DRIVING" before starting game play.

7.1.23: Titus The Fox: To Marrakech and Back

Released: 1992

Other Platforms: Amstrad CPC, Atari ST, DOS, Game Boy, Game Boy Color

Developed by: Titus France SA

Published by: Titus France AS

Design: Florent Moreau

Coder/Programmer: Carlo Perconti

Graphics: Francis Fournier, Stephan Beaufils

Musician/Composer/Sound Effects: Unknown

Introduction

Titus the Fox: To Marrakech and Back is a side-scrolling platform game developed by Titus France for the Amiga, Amstrad CPC, Atari ST, and MS-DOS. The game was originally released in 1991 under the name Lagaf': Les Aventures de Moktar—Vol 1: La Zoubida, featuring French comedian Lagaf' as a tie-in with his song "La Zoubida". For the international edition, Titus retooled the game to feature its mascot and released the game as Titus the Fox: To Marrakech and Back in 1992.

Gameplay

Titus the Fox is a fairly basic platforming game, with more emphasis on exploration throughout the levels than straight-up fighting enemies. Titus the Fox can pick up and throw boxes at enemies, however.

Reception

CU Amiga (Apr, 1992) Fox hunting may not be very fashionable at the moment, but that hasn't stopped Titus constructing an entire game around it. Titus the Fox is easily their best platform yet. It's a joy to play and offers more of a challenge than the usual jump'n'run games due its cunning puzzles and the sheer variety of enemy sprites on the prowl. There are more than 900 screens in total which will keep even the most experienced games player engrossed for weeks.

Hardware Requirements

Minimum CPU Class Required: Amiga 500

Minimum OS Class Required: Kickstart 1.2

Minimum RAM Required: 512 KB

Media Type: 3.5" Floppy Disk

Video Modes Supported: OCS/ECS

Input Devices Supported: Keyboard

Controller Types Supported: Digital Joystick

Multiplayer Options: No

Number of Players Supported: 1 Player

Save Game Methods: Password

Miscellaneous Attributes: Hard Drive Installable

Controls/Joystick/Mouse/Gamepad

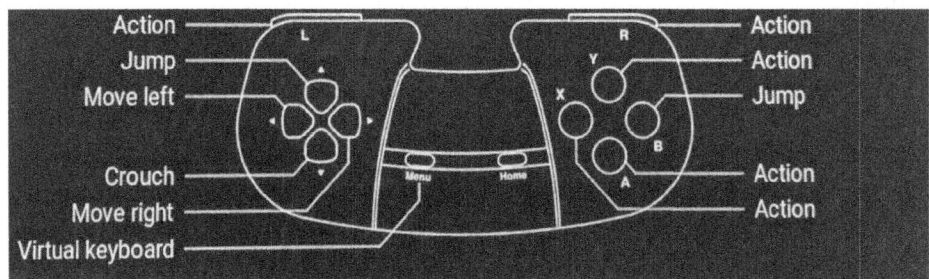

Up = Go up/Jump

Down = Go down/Duck/Crouch

Left = Go left

Right = Go right

Fire = Throw an object

Down + Fire = Pick up an object/Place an object

Down (after a few seconds) = Enter secret passages

Keys

F1 = Lose a life

F2 = Game Over

F4 = Status Screen

F5 = Music On/Off

F6 = Sounds Effects On/Off

F7 = Sounds Filter On/Off

F10 = Toggles the games speed divided by 2

4 & 6 = Scrolls the screen

P = Pause

Cursor Up/Q = Go up/Jump

Cursor Down/A = Go down/Duck/Crouch

Cursor Left/L = Go left

Cursor Right/M = Go right

Space/Enter = Throw an object

Cursor Down + Space/Enter = Pick up an object/Place an object

Cursor Down (after a few seconds) = Enter secret passages

Walkthrough

Playthrough Video: https://www.youtube.com/watch?v=8dCR77lf_iM

Difficulty

There does not appear to be any difference in the level structure between the difficulties. Rather, the speed of the game appears to double if you choose Hard Mode – while Titus can move faster, the enemies also jump up in speed in lockstep, so you will have less time to react to dodging enemies and projectiles.

Jumping

In Titus the Fox, there are some odd physics here and there. For example, if you stand on the side of a windowsill instead of the centre, and jump, you can hop higher from the side. This is especially important when carrying items, as jumping from the side will allow you to make the jump, but not if you are on the centre.

If you find a balloon, hop on it. On the fourth hop and every hop thereafter, you will jump especially high, which is useful for reaching otherwise inaccessible high ledges.

Cheats, Hints, Tips & Tricks

During the game press both the [Amiga] keys [C] and [F4]. You'll then receive a message presenting you with 99 lives.

Codes and Starting Level

- 01: 2625 – On The Foxy Trail
- 02: 8455 – Looking For Clues
- 03: 2974 – Road Works Ahead
- 04: 4916 – Going Underground
- 05: 1933 – Flaming Catacombes
- 06: 0738 – Coming To Town
- 07: 2237 – Foxys Den
- 08: 5648 – On The Road To Marrakesh
- 09: 6390 – Home Of The Pharaohs
- 10: 8612 – Desert Experience
- 11: 4187 – Walls Of Sand
- 12: 1350 – A Beacon Of Hope
- 13: 9813 – A Pipe Dream
- 14: 5052 – Going Home
- 15: 2045 – Just Married

7.1.24: Worms: The Director's Cut

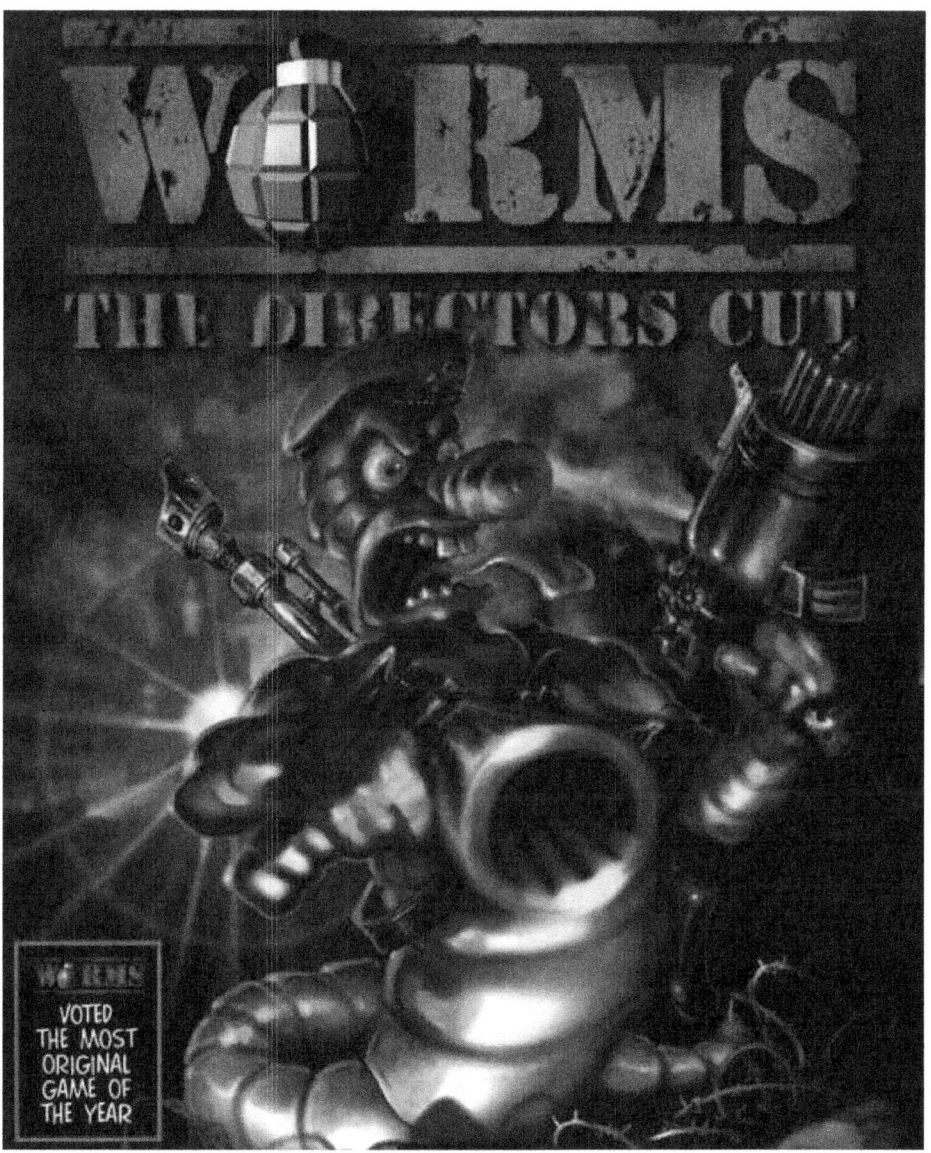

Released: 1997

Other Platforms: Amiga CD 32

Developed by: Team17 Software Limited

Published by: Ocean Software Ltd.

Design: Andy Davidson

Manager: Martyn Brown

Coder/Programmer: Andy Davidson, Mark Fitt

Graphics: Andy Davidson, Rico Holmes, Kenny Magnusson, P-A Gustafsson, Chris Blyth, Tony Senghore, John Allardice, Wiggz, Boby Little, Pete Lyon

Musician/Composer/Sound Effects: Bjørn Lynne

Introduction

It is an artillery strategy game, a sequel to Worms, developed by Team17 and published by Ocean Software. It was programmed by Andy Davidson and released in 1997 for the Amiga platform only.

The player has control of a team of worms and takes turns at attacking either Computer or human opponents controlling other teams. The game builds upon Worms (1995) and adds various graphical and gameplay developments. The Director's Cut received positive reviews, but only sold 5,000 copies worldwide – primarily due to the game being sold at the extreme end of the Amiga's lifespan.

Gameplay

The Director's Cut features turn based combat in the same style as its predecessor, Worms. The game has a 2D side-on view of the battlefield where players fight worms against each other. The game can be played against the Computer, or with multiple players taking control of teams of four worms. The worms can use various weapons, some of which are limited in quantity. Each worm has a life meter and the team with the last surviving worm(s) is the winner.

Reception

Worms: The Director's Cut was received well by critics, with Amiga Format and CU Amiga awarding the game 90% and 91% respectively. The game was seen as an improvement over the features of Worms, with many gameplay elements praised. The developments in the presentation also received positive criticism, in particular the added graphical layers was highlighted as an example of a "cosmetic correction". Despite the positive reviews, The Director's Cut only sold 5,000 copies worldwide.

Predecessor

Worms (1995)

Hardware Requirements

Minimum CPU Class Required: Amiga 1200

Minimum OS Class Required: Kickstart 3.0

Minimum RAM Required: 2 MB

Media Type: 3.5" Floppy Disk

Video Modes Supported: AGA

Input Devices Supported: Keyboard, Mouse

Controller Types Supported: Digital Joystick, Joypad

Multiplayer Options: No

Number of Players Supported: 1 Player

Save Game Methods: Password

Miscellaneous Attributes: Hard Drive Installable

Controls/Joystick/Mouse/Gamepad

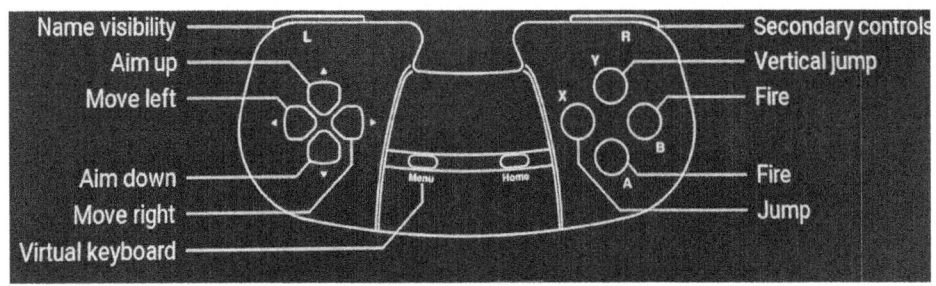

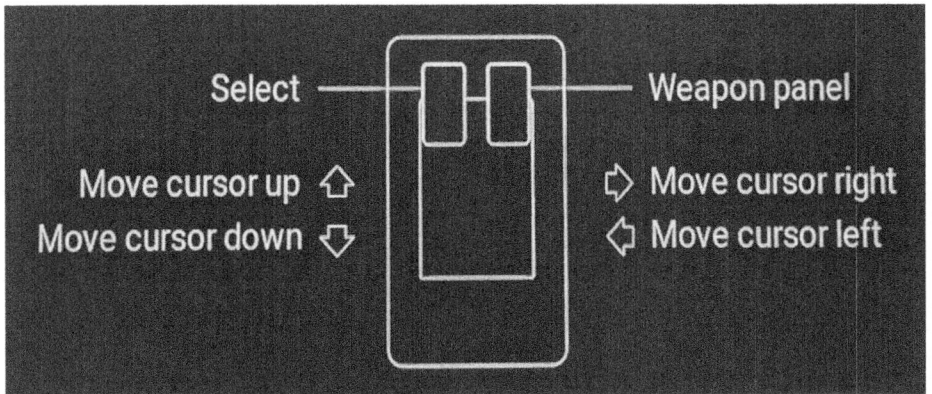

Use the Mouse

Keys

The Standard Weapons

[F1]BAZOOKA – [F1 X 2] HOMING MISSILE

[F2] GRENADE – [F2 X 2] CLUSTER BOMB – [F2 X 3] GRENADE LAUNCHER

[F3] SHOTGUN – [F3 X 2] UZI – [F3 X 3] HANDGUN

[F4] FIRE/PUNCH – [F4 X 2] DRAGONBALL

[F5] DYNAMITE – [F5 X 2] SHEEP

[F6] AIRSTRIKE – [F6 X 2] TELEPORT – [F6 X 3] PETROL BOMB

[F7] BLOWTORCH – [F7 X 2] DRILL – [F7 X 3] LANDMINE

[F8] NINJA ROPE – [F8 X 2] BUNGEE

[F9] GIRDERS – [F9 X 2] SKIP GO

[F10] KAMIKAZE – [F10 X 2] SURRENDER

THE SPECIAL WEAPONS

[6] HOMING PIGEONS – [6 TWICE] MAD COWS

[7] HOLY HAND GRENADES – [7 TWICE] BANANA BOMB

[8] MINIGUN – [8 TWICE] BASEBALL BAT

[9] SUPER SHEEP – [9 X 2] SHEEP ON A ROPE – [9 X 3] SHEEP STRIKE

[0] OLD WOMEN – [0 X 2] PRICELESS MING VASE

Additional Controls

Help = Centre on current Worm

/ ---------[numeric keypad only] Toggles through remaining Worms

R = Force Action Replay

P = Pause Game[Indicates current worm and landscape code]

DEL = Toggles between all worm – names visible, your worm names visible, no worm – names visible

ESC = Quit Options

BACKSPACE = Vertical Jump

RETURN = [pressed twice quickly] Backjump

* = Toggle in game WormCam on/off. [a camera that follows the action as opposed to a static camera that stays centred where you have specified.

ENTER = [numeric keypad] Toggles KO bar behind/in front of scenery

CUSTOMISED LANDSCAPES

As with the first Worms, it is possible to create your own Custom Levels.

You can now also produce 2-layer level by producing two 16 colour IFF pictures, one for the background and one for the foreground.

The background layer can be walked in front of, and as the foreground is blown up the background is revealed – allowing you to create levels like the inside of a house which you can walk into and climb up the stairs! To create your own, you need to draw the following in a paint package such as Electronic Arts excellent Dpaint series;

Lo – Res,16 colour, Page size of 960 x 350

Colour 0 Transparent

Colour 1 White/Near White for TEXT

Colour 2 Pink/Near Pink for WORM COLOUR 1

Colour 3 Can be anything

Colour 4 Lighter shade of Colour 3

Colour 5 Can be anything [mine colour]

Colour 6 Lighter shade of Colour 3

Colours 7 – 15 Can be anything

Once you have your level either save it directly into the TWCUSTOM draw as FILENAME.WRM16 or use the WormPrefs program on disk 3 to create 2 – layer levels and specify other things like mountain set, gravity, friction etc.

If you have saved your levels on a separate disk, you will need to select the NEW CUSTOM DISK option from the RECORDS section, with the disk in the internal drive.

WormPrefs also lets you create your own landscape types [like forest] or [arctic] etc using a template, and your own mountain sets.

Walkthrough

Longplay: https://www.youtube.com/watch?v=IVY7hJgdUmI

Cheats, Hints, Tips & Tricks

Type in on the title screen before Game Start:

Amiga	Unknown
Andy	Unknown
Artillery	All worms can't move
Ben hutchings	Unknown
Betong asna	Concrete Donkey on title screen
Boing	Transform title ball into Amiga ball
Cheat	Unknown
Chipram	Display free Chip RAM
Chorlton and the wheelers (wheelies)	All secret weapons on third panel
Fisk	Unknown
Gravity	Title ball is affected by gravity
Jamie and his magic torch	All extra weapons
Kartong apa	Swedish weapon names
Kilburn	Unknown
La cienda honduras	Unknown
Little fluffy sheep	Exploding crates release sheep
Magicla mystery tour	Names of worms are not displayed
Magnet	Magnetized title ball follows the Mouse
Music	Music on/off.
Nutter	All weapons are more powerful
Omnipotent blue worm	Invulnerable, worms can run over water
Pestilence	Worms burn on death
Pong	Disable bouncy title ball
Red Bull	Worms jump higher and hit harder

Supa shoppa	Mines become weapon boxes
Tbl	Unknown
Tony	Unknown
Total Wormage	The spinning grenade on the title screen can be bounced around using the Mouse; Original Total Wormage logo on panel and original weapon names
Version	Display version number
Weirded	Strange title screen colors

Land generator codes:

Enter one of the following codes to generate the corresponding type of land.

Land type	Code
Low water level	LOW
Medium water level	MEDIUM
High water level	high
Strange landscape	WEIRDED
Normal landscapes	NORMAL
Play last level again	1471
Select random custom level	CUSTOM
Select random graffiti level	GRAFFITI
Only generate forest levels	FOREST
Only generate cavern levels	CAVERN
Only generate forest/cavern levels	FOREST CAVERN
Generate all levels	ALL

7.1.25: Zool: Ninja Of The "Nth" Dimension

Released: 1993

OtherPlatforms: Acorn Archimedes, Amiga, Atari ST, Amiga CD32, MS-DOS, Game Boy, Game Gear, Master System, Genesis, SNES

Developed by: Gremlin Graphics

Published by: Gremlin Graphics

Design: George Allen

Coder/Programmer:

Graphics: Adrian Carless (Ade Carliss)

Musician/Composer/Sound Effects: Patrick Phelan

Introduction

In Zool you play the interstellar cosmos dweller from the Nth dimension. You must guide Zool through thousands of screens of surreal and bizarre action in a bid to bring the intergalactic Ninja back to the Nth dimension. You must take Zool to the limits of the Universe, to the outer limits of the known universe, through quite a bit of unknown universe, and beyond the fairly well known but it wouldn't want to walk through it at night on my own universe. Before reaching home Zool has to successfully work through all manner of bizarre situations, worlds and enemies. The only way to do this is by exploring each world until the exit is found, and progressing onto the next one. It sounds fairly straightforward, sure, but when you add in the enemies, strange features and surreal events, this is one journey that's going to be, well, weird.

Gameplay

The game is a platform game, relying on smooth, fast-moving gameplay. Its protagonist is Zool, a gremlin "Ninja of the Nth Dimension" who is forced to land on Earth; in order to gain ninja ranking, he has to pass seven lands, beating a boss at the end of each of them. The game contains a number of embedded minigames, including several arcade games, a scrolling space shooter and a game accessible only by making Zool play a certain tune on an in-game piano or finding certain invisible warp points.

Reception

The original Amiga game was released to critical acclaim, receiving scores of 97%, 96%, 95% from Amiga Computing, Amiga Action and Amiga Format respectively. Electronic Gaming Monthly claimed, "Zool sports great graphics, but ends up with a case of Super Trolland's disease: your character moves much too fast and with little control!" GamePro gave a positive review of the Game Gear version, praising its "great graphics and sound abound", as well as its "crisp" gameplay.

Retrospectively, Virgin Media included Zool on their list of top ten video game ninja heroes. In 2011, Wirtualna Polska ranked it as the 22nd best game for the Amiga, noting its "absurdly" high difficulty

Successor

Zool 2

Hardware Requirements

Minimum CPU Class Required: Amiga 500

Minimum OS Class Required: Kickstart 1.2

Minimum RAM Required: 1 MB

Media Type: 3.5" Floppy Disk

Video Modes Supported: AGA, OCS/ECS in another edition

Input Devices Supported: Keyboard, Mouse

Controller Types Supported: Digital Joystick

Multiplayer Options: No

Number of Players Supported: 1 Player

Save Game Methods: Password

Miscellaneous Attributes: Not Hard Drive Installable

Controls/Joystick/Mouse/Gamepad

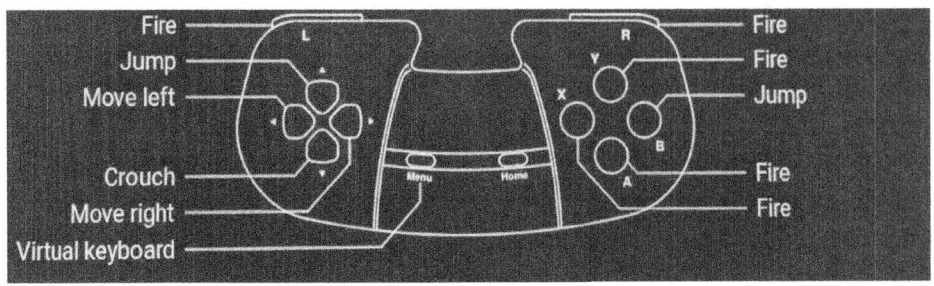

Up: Jump Vertically.

Note: Zool will spin in the air if fire is pressed again while he is in the air allowing him to kill airborne enemies.

Down: Crouch.

Left: Run Left.

Right: Run Right.

Up+Left: Jump Diagonally Left.

Up+Right: Jump Diagonally right.

Down+Left: Slide left, allowing Zool to crash into some enemies and kill them.

Down+Right: Slide Right, allowing Zool to crash into some enemies and kill them.

Keys

None yet.

Walkthrough

Gameplay https://www.youtube.com/watch?v=DcMIYpyBHI4

Cheats, Hints, Tips & Tricks

There is a hidden bonus room with plenty of points and some extra lives in Level 1.3. How you can find it is shown here:

https://youtu.be/285JB0h0QxY?t=20

For a bonus zone on level 2-2, play these notes on the first piano; Brown, Yellow, Red, Orange, Green.

Before starting the game, type "GOLDFISH", the screen will flash and activate these Keys

1: Invulnerable

2: next sublevel

3: Next main level

4: Self-destruction!

5: Jump warp to level 6.1

[F1] to [F6] Level select

[F7] Extra life on bonus level

[F8] to [F10] Normal game without restart points

Cheat mode (alternate):

Type "streetlamp" at the options menu for following functions:

Effect Key

1: Invincibility

2: Lose one life

Numpad [Plus]: Level skip

Numpad [Minus]: Go to previous level

4: Restart current level

Programmer messages.

Type one of the following codes during game play.

ADE – PAT – GREGGS – TONY – BERNI – GEORGE – MARK – PAUL – CASSON – SHORTIE – MICK – DONKIN – ASH – HILEY – SYD – SIZ – RICHIE

7.2: Bonus USB Games: Citadel

Right before THEA500 Mini was delivered already a huge bonus was added in form of another Amiga game classic Citadel.

First published in 1995 by Virtual Design, and offered here as an enhanced 2022 release.

- Download the bonus games zip file: https://bit.ly/THEA500-Bonus-Games-1_0_0
- Unzip the file to your USB stick
- Make sure the WHDLoad package is also installed to the USB stick

Game details: https://retrogames.biz/games/thea500-mini/

Released: 1995

Other Platforms: Amiga CD32

Developed by: Virtual Design, Arrakis Software

Published by: Black Legend

Design: Paweł Matusz (Kane/Suspect), Artur Bardowski (ArtB/Suypect), Jakub Bardowski, Jan Rózycki, Artur Opala (Kalosz/Suspect), Marcin Stangel

Coder/Programmer: Paweł Matusz

Graphics: Artur Bardowski, Radek Czeczotka

Musician/Composer/Sound Effects: Artur Opala

Cytadela Project Homepage: http://cytadela.sourceforge.net/

Introduction

A revolt on a distant prison island must be foiled by you in this first-person shoot 'em up. Reaching the control room will suffice, but a further challenge of finding the six pieces of a hidden bomb can be undertaken if you're brave.

The game features texture-mapped visuals and a variable screen size, making it suited to anything from a humble A500 (most Doom-style games needed at least an A1200) or a well-accelerated machine.

The prison complex is on several levels, with teleporters linking different sections, and the chance to reach the final control room via several different paths. You don't get a weapon at the start of the game, and ammunition is in shorter supply than usual, meaning that you can't just shoot randomly and hope for the best. Another way of killing people off is to set them on fire.

Gameplay

At first you find yourself at the emergency entrance to the Citadel, in the underground part of it which had originally been constructed by the now extinct alien race once inhabiting B104-GS12. You have nothing with you as you did not expect having to leave the Scout. Your first task is to therefore find some means of defence and then start exploring the Citadel in order to unravel its mysteries.

The aim of the game is to escape from the Citadel. As you quickly realise you cannot single-handedly restore order in the base, therefore you must also destroy it following the orders received while still on the X16.

Reception

The most important thing, however, is what happens on the screen. And it happens, as usual, a lot. The graphics are detailed and juicy – apart from the usual subtitles, "No Tuxedo" plaques on the walls, I noticed excellent details, such as wobbly chains, hooks hanging from the ceiling, corpses nailed to the walls, lamps, etc. The exchange of gunfire is extremely impressive. The exchange of gunfire is amazingly impressive. I haven't seen such a bloody and cruel slaughter even in the tasty "Rise of the Triad". Here, not only do brains fly and splatter on corners, ceilings and windowsills – when you press the trigger of a flamethrower, you can admire "living torches". Something like this has never been seen before...

Hardware Requirements

Minimum CPU Class Required: Amiga 500

Minimum OS Class Required: Kickstart 1.3

Minimum RAM Required: 1 MB

Media Type: 3.5" Floppy Disk

Video Modes Supported: OCS/ECS

Input Devices Supported: Keyboard, Mouse

Controller Types Supported: Digital Joystick, Joypad

Number of Players Supported: 1 Player

Miscellaneous Attributes: Hard Drive Installable

Controls/Joystick/Mouse/Gamepad

Mouse: move the Mouse to turn left or right; click the first (left) Mouse button to move forwards; click the second (right) Mouse button to use selected weapon/item.

Joystick: move the Joystick to move forwards, move backwards, turn left, turn right; press the first button to use selected weapon/item.

Keys

In the menu

'enter' – selects the highlighted menu position

'space' – selects the highlighted menu position; in the INFO submenu it turns on/off text scrolling

'esc' – in main menu exits the game; gets back to the main menu (which results in quitting the gameplay) when pressed in 'level summary' and in 'choose complex' menus

arrows – move the selection cursor

In the game

'enter', 'shift' – use the selected weapon/card or use the hand

'esc' – exits to the menu (quits the game)

'space' – use the hand

up arrow, 8 on numpad, W – move forwards

down arrow, 5 on numpad, S – move backwards

left arrow, 7 on numpad – turn left

right arrow, 9 on numpad – turn right

4 on numpad, A – strafe left

6 on numpad, D – strafe right

'tab' – map on/off

p – pause on/off

z – vision noise on/off

F1 – select hand

F2 – select handgun

F3 – select shotgun

F4 – select machinegun

F5 – select flame thrower

F6 – select blaster

F7 – select rocket launcher

F8 – select red card

F9 – select green card

F10 – select blue card

[– increase the Mouse speed

] – decrease the Mouse speed

Walkthrough

Video https://www.youtube.com/watch?v=0QkhuBMunvU&list=PLCbFe3KgvvbulkJ-ftsze1OlVPidAB8T6

or search for: Cytadela – Citadel – Walkthrough – Amiga Game

Cheats, Hints, Tips & Tricks

During the game type:

kbbmorms – Energy to 666

lorien – Full map

hotkiss – Max weapons and ammo

hotkiwi – Unlimited health

kitiara – Skip to next level

idaho – Jump one field

alibaba – All parts of the bomb

7: THEGAMES

7.3: Adding games & WHDLoad

THEA500 was of course designed so that you can easily play more games than the built-in ones.

It is not enough to simply plug a USB drive with games into THEA500, because they would not be recognized. Not even if they were already available as WHDLoad archives.

If you just plug in a USB drive, the "USB Media Access" icon appears, but when you select it, the following message appears:

You have to download the WHDLoad tool first.

Go on by reading the next chapter Install and Update WHDLoad.

The WHDLoad A500 archive contains a collection of settings for all supported games. These settings are necessary for the emulator, the hardware and the games to work together. Data like which CPU is required, how much and what kind of RAM is needed, what is the minimum requirement for the graphics (ECS/OCS/AGA) etc. are stored here.

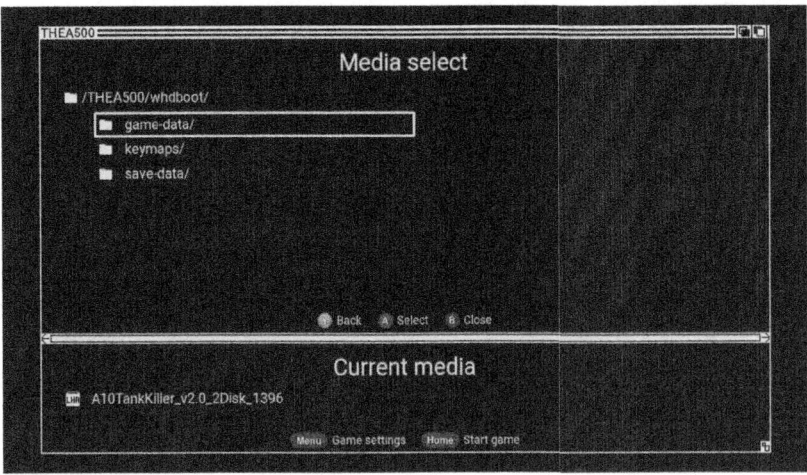

WHDLoad was developed back in 19xx and since then it has been improved and expanded by many users with many games and demos. Constantly new ones are added.

Here are a few facts about WHDLoad:

WHDLoad Supports CD32 and CDTV titles.

Native support for CD32 is being investigated.

Hint! In order to play the WHDLoad game, the WHDLoad package must be present on each USB drive that you plug into THEA500.

Important notes about WHDLoad

If you pull out the USB-Drive while you are in the load screen, the WHDLoad screen is closed and you automatically end up back in the carousel.

If you have not made a state save, everything is gone than!

Question to RGL: Why appears THEA500 logo sometimes before a WHDLoad game starts?

Answer RGL: It appears when the LHA archive has no configuration in the WHDLoad package. The console then tries to guess the correct setup, which is when you see the logo.

Q: Sometimes a green, red, tuquoise or a blue colored THEA500 logo appears before a WHDLoad game is starting.

A: The colour change is random.

Q: Some WHDLoad games have loading screen where some tweaks could be chosen before the game is starting. Very often based on a Workbench like screen with toggle buttons, that only can be toggled by Mouse. I did not get it always to work.

A: You need to make sure you configure Port 1 to be a Mouse if you want to access these options.

7: THEGAMES

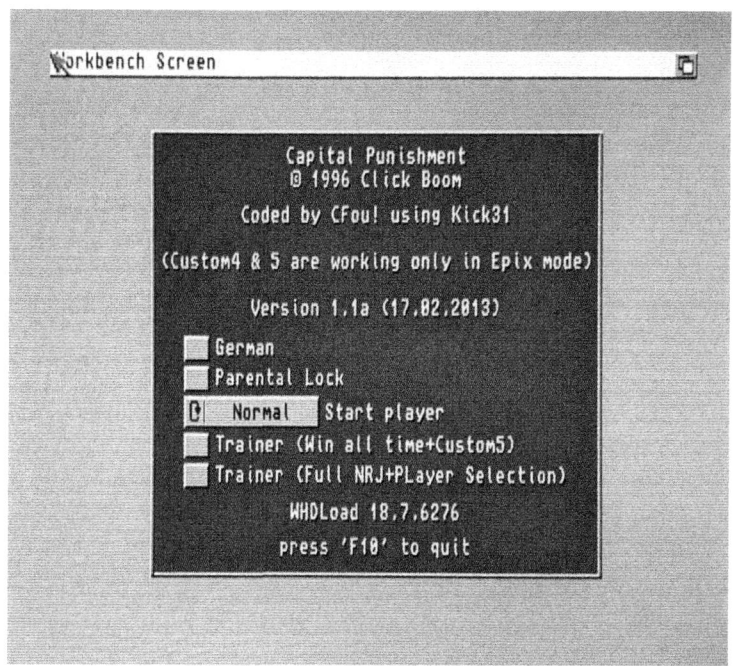

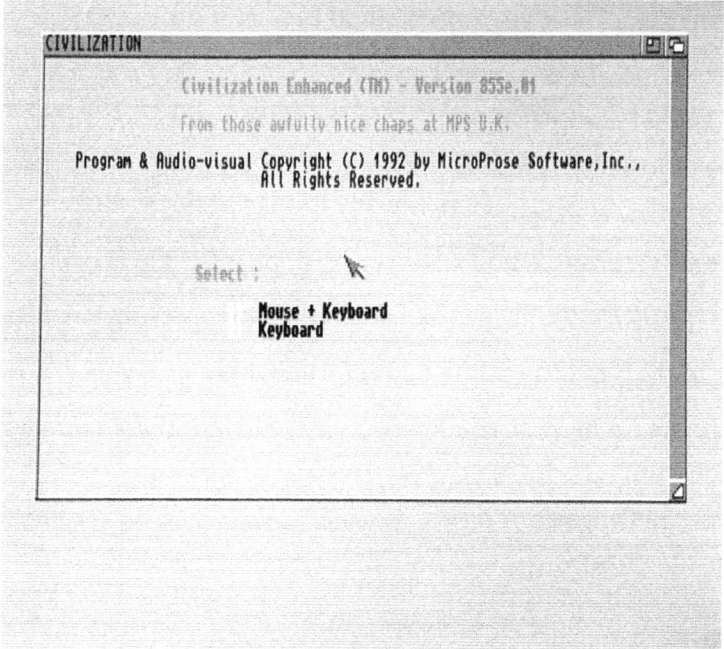

7.3.1: Install and Update WHDLoad

See also: "5: THEUpdates & Firmware" on page 79

Unlike the firmware update, you don't have to install anything, but the WHDLoad directory with the latest version has to be in the main folder of each USB-Drive (sticks and hard drives) from which you want to launch games.

The update process is very easy. All you need is the newest file, and a USB-Drive.

1. Download the newest file THEA500-WHDLoad-package-1.x.x.zip from https://retrogames.biz/support/thea500-mini/whdload/ by clicking on Download under the most recent file.

2. Insert a FAT32 formatted USB-drive.

3. Extract the contents of the file to the root of the USB-Drive where then the directory "THEA500" must be. Don't place the file inside a folder on the stick or rename the file. If you do, the file will not be recognised. If that folder already exist, either delete it first or overwrite all files with the new ones!

4. Plug the USB-Drive into THEA500 Mini and start your games.

Hint! On the download page you will find a link to Bonus Game(s) section! With the release of the first WHDLOad package as Bonus the game Citadel.

Note that differently to the firmware update you can use earlier editions than the version currently used. Usually this is not necessary.

The best way is to watch and subscribe the YouTube and Facebook pages.

Facebook: https://www.facebook.com/THEC64andMoreByRetroGamesLtd

YouTube: https://www.youtube.com/c/THEC64/

If a new firmware or WHDLoad-version is launched, there you will find the announcement.

The newest file together with a change history, will be available on the official support page:

WHDLoad for THEA500 Mini: https://retrogames.biz/support/whdload

7.3.2: Making a WHDLoad archive

WHDLoad is a very useful but unfortunately not very easy to learn tool!

If you want to play a game that is not on THEA500 Mini, then I recommend you to use an internet search engine and with some luck find an already finished Sleeve.

The best place to start is the official WHDLoad webpage: http://www.whdload.de/download.html

Loads of Amiga games and goodies ready to go https://www.whdownload.com

Note! It should go without saying that you should only download games you own or legally allowed to be shared.

However, it is certainly worth reading through the following instructions so that you understand the work that has gone into making WHDLoad work at all.

Here is the official manual, kindly provided by Bert Jahn. Many thanks Bert!

http://www.whdload.de/docs/en/

7.4: Transfer original Amiga disks

See also: "9.4: Disk Images & File Formats" on page 306

Question to RGL: Will it be possible to read original disks in any way via a USB-Solution?

Answer RGL: If you mean IPF files, this will be possibly in the future.

If you want to play your original game disks, you need to have transfer method of getting the data on an USB drive.

The following chapters explain some different ways to do so.

7.4.1: Transfer by Nullmodem cable

Here is described how you can the transfer original Amiga disks to a PC.

1: What is needed

Hardware and programs on the Amiga:

- null modem cable (not a normal serial cable)
- a (few) Amiga formatted floppy disks
- Workbench 1.3 and WB Extras 1.3
- Programs and files on the PC:
- ADF Sender Terminal r3
    - https://amigaland.de/wp-content/uploads/2018/10/adf_sender_terminal_13r3_full.zip
- German help for ADF Sender Terminal
    - https://amigaland.de/wp-content/uploads/2018/10/adf_sender_terminal_help_13_ger.zip
- Transdisk or Transdisklog
    - https://amigaland.de/wp-content/uploads/2018/10/transdisk.zip
- Receive.bas
    - https://amigaland.de/wp-content/uploads/2018/10/receive.zip

2: Preparations

Start AmigaBasic, (you can find it on the Extras 1.3) now you have to write a small basic program to send the file transdisk from the PC to the Amiga or so the Amiga can receive and save the file. (Another hint, you should check all adf's and floppies for viruses, very important). So type the following into the Amiga Basic Written by Wolfgang Stoeggl (1998):

```
INPUT "filename? ",file$
INPUT "size (bytes)? ", size&
PRINT "Now send the file!"
OPEN "ser:" FOR INPUT AS #1
OPEN file$ FOR OUTPUT AS #2
n% = 1024
WHILE LOF(2) < size&
diff&=size&-LOF(2)
IF diff&<1024 THEN n%=diff&
t$=INPUT$(n%,#1):PRINT #2,t$;
LOCATE 5,1
PRINT LOF(2)
WEND
PRINT "Received file: ",file$
PRINT "filelength =", LOF(2), "bytes"
CLOSE
END
```

After you have been so diligent save the program as receive.bas. So the first step is done. Now connect the Amiga and the PC with the null modem cable now start the ADF Sender Terminal on the PC and under CommPort | Port Open = activate then under CommPort | Properties set the following: maximum Speed=19200, Data Bits=8, Parity=none, Stop Bits=1, Echo=off, Flow Control=RTS/CTS. You should use these settings otherwise the files will be transferred but most of the time they are faulty, if the transfer should fail anyway just lower the build rate until it works. Now start the Workbench and under Prefs | Serial | make the same settings as in the ADF Sender Terminal, mostly only the Baud Rate and the Handshaking (Flow Control) must be adjusted, besides you can also set the Buffer Size to the maximum of 16000, then save the whole thing.

The best thing to do now is to boot the Amiga again and start the Workbench, insert the disk with the reseive.bas and AmigaBasic and start the program receive.bas now it wants to know a filename, enter here transdisklog then it wants to know the size of the file, here you should enter 11092 and now the Amiga waits for the said file. So in the ADF Sender Terminal click on Send, open the transdisklog and the PC sends the file to the Amiga. If everything went smoothly you should hear the Amiga writing the file to the floppy, also the program shows the bytes transferred. To avoid confusion later I would rename the transdisklog to transdisk. Activate write protection and test the file transdisk, start the AmigaShell and change into the directory with transdisk (e.g. cd df0: or cd df1: depending on whether you have one or two drives) and enter transdisk, if the file is error free a list with parameters should appear which can be used by transdisk. If nothing happens there just do the whole process again, but this time with a lower build rate (don't forget – the settings must be the same on the Amiga and ADF Sender Terminal). If you succeeded, you can copy the transdisk file to the Workbench (saves the annoying disk change and logically on the backup copy of the Workbench).

3: Send and/or receive

Amiga – PC

PC: start ADF Sender Terminal, click on Receive and create an adf file, now the program waits for the data from the Amiga. AMIGA: switch to AmigaShell and enter the following:

    transdisk >ser: +

or

    transdisk >ser: -d trackdisk 0 +
    (here transdisk waits to be able to insert a new disk)

or

    transdisk >ser: -d trackdisk 1 +
    (not tested, but should transfer the disc to DF1)

With this option you send the disc in DF0 to the PC, now just insert the desired disc and the files will be transferred. This process can take up to 20 min. depending on the build rate, if the transfer fails or the adf file is not readable just select a lower build rate (on Amiga and PC).

PC – Amiga

Now first format a few disks then switch back to the AmigaShell and enter the following:

    transdisk -w ser: -d trackdisk 0

With this option the adf file will be sent to drive DF0: and of course converted.

If you have two floppy drives you can enter the following:

    transdisk -w ser: -d trackdisk 1

With this option the adf file will be sent to drive DF1: and of course converted.

This process can take up to 20 min. or longer, depending on the build rate, if the transfer fails or the ADF file is not readable, simply select a lower build rate and transfer again.

4: Tips & Tricks

With transdisk you can convert and transfer adf, but it takes too long with a max. baud rate of 19200, better and faster with transwarp, here baud rates of 115200 are possible, that means a disk is converted in about 3 minutes. Instead of using the transdisklog as described above you should transfer the transwarp file, important is that you transfer the file twice (directly one after the other) and of course you have to specify a different file size (transwarp with right click on properties and read the number of bytes). More info about transdisk can be found in the zip directories of WarTrans and TransWarp, info about transferring files with receive.bas can be found in the German help of Adf Sender Terminal.

Other transfer programs:

- Transwarp 1.1
    - https://amigaland.de/wp-content/uploads/2018/10/transwarp11.zip
- WarTrans 1.0
    - https://amigaland.de/wp-content/uploads/2018/10/wartrans10.zip

Have fun trying them out. Of course I am not responsible for any damage caused by the use of the programs and this text.

7.4.2: Greaseweazle

Greaseweazle is a USB device and host tools allowing versatile floppy drive control. By extracting the raw flux transitions from a drive, any disk format can be captured and analysed: PC, Amiga, Amstrad, PDP-11, musical instruments, industrial equipment, and more. Greaseweazle also supports writing to floppy disks, from a range of image file formats including those commonly used for online preservation (ADF, IPF, DSK, IMG, HFE, ...)

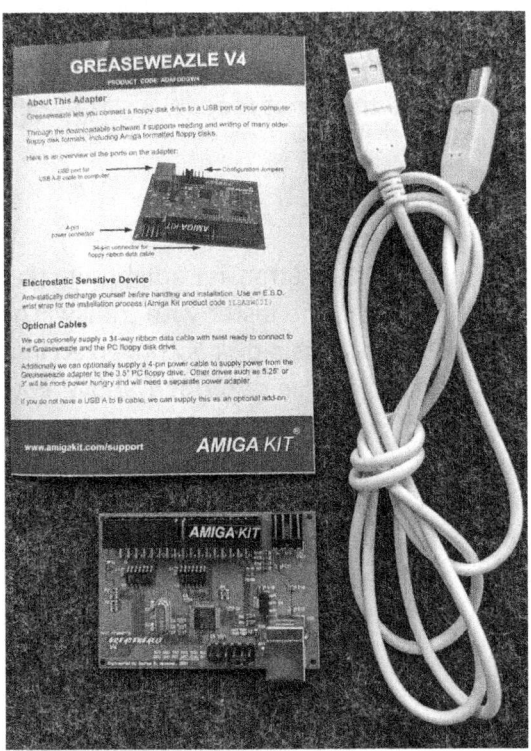

I bought a Greaseweazle and it worked flawlessly like a charm.

Purchase a Greaseweazle

https://github.com/keirf/Greaseweazle/wiki/Purchase-a-Greaseweazle

Download Host Tools

https://github.com/keirf/Greaseweazle/wiki/Download-Host-Tools

There are other solutions, just do a search.

7.4.3: External drives

Unfortunately by now it is not possible to use an USB-Drive which emulates a real Disk Drive to read and write original Disks.

Perifractics very cool self-made USB-Drives 1541 mini & Macro, unfortunately didn't work either. https://www.perifractic.com/takeout-shop/1541-mini/

8: Rebuild to a Maxi

Before you read the next chapters and you immediately want to open up your Amiga 500 case, you should need these:

- A RetroPi installation mount kit (this is by now the best option that I found, even though you can't just mount the Mini mainboard on it without some rebuild.
- A Torx screwdriver and a Phillips screwdriver.
- A thin knife.

- Some panel adapter cables. I took 2 for USB and one for HDMI.
- A short USB-Mini to USB-A cable for the leonardo power.
- A USB-C panel mount cable
- The protective plate of the Amiga 500 is secured with Torx screws and with some brackets that can be lifted well with a thin knife tip.

8: Rebuild to a Maxi

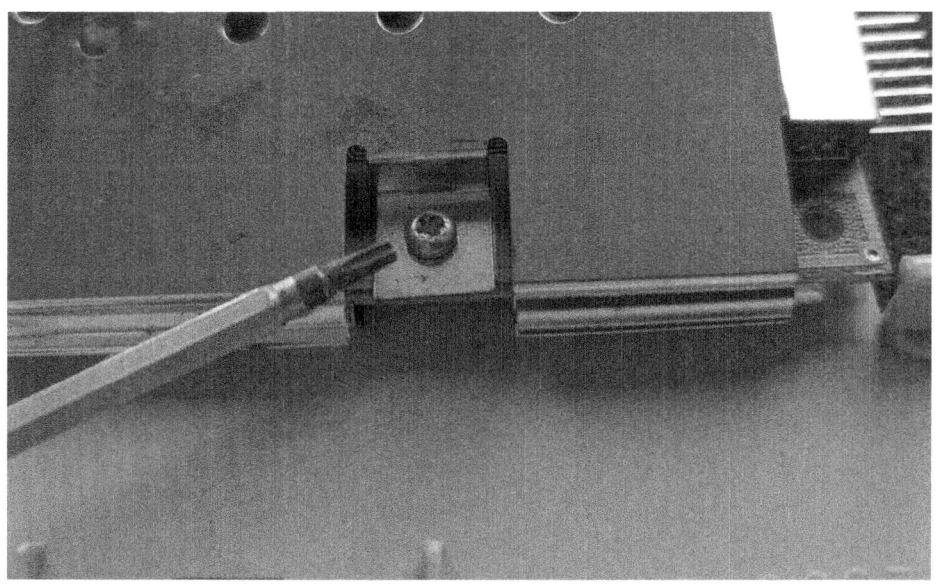

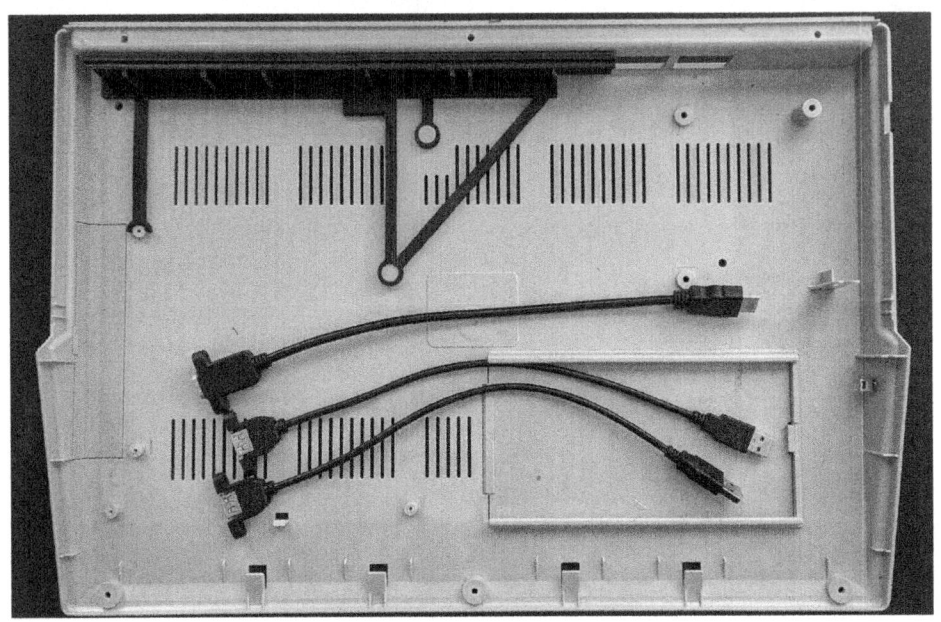

Here you can watch how to build the Maxi: https://www.youtube.com/channel/UChjTe7l8hkqmaV6z--YsRSw/videos

Or search in YouTube for: Tentelain Retro THEA500.

Have fun building the THEA500 Maxi :)

Ps. The full description with pictures will be available in the THEA500 Big Book.

8.1: Keyboard

On building the Mini into the original Amiga 500 case, you likely want to add the original Keyboard. There are not too many, but several ways to connect the Keyboard via USB to the Mini.

Keyrah, which is an well-known adapter for the Commodore 64, isn't one of them! All versions of Keyrah do not support the Amiga 500 Keyboard. Only Amiga 1200 and 600!

https://icomp.de/shop-icomp/en/produkt-details/product/keyrah-v2.html#filter=*

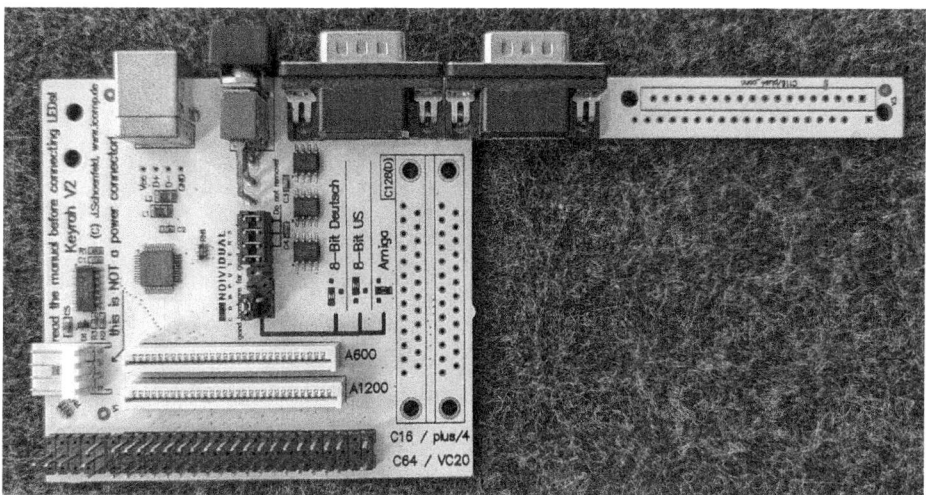

This is the best working and available solution today:

Amiga 500 Keyboard USB Interface – Arduino/Amibian/Amiberry

In this article, we will show you how you can turn your humble Amiga Keyboard into a USB Keyboard for use on your PC or raspberry pi. It's a very tactile board that outperforms my Logitech Keyboard with ease! (We wrote this guide using it!).

Why?

Being able to repurpose an Amiga case and Keyboard for use with Amibian makes the "virtual" Amiga experience just that much more authentic. Whilst solutions such as the Tynemouth Amiga interface board are great, it's not the cheapest solution (£50). Why not employ some DIY and make your very own Arduino solution for less than £20.

Note: *No "real" Amigas were hurt in this project. The Amiga 500 case and Keyboard used were "saved" from a completely dead machine with an unrepairable motherboard.*

I tested it by myself with this components:

- Amiga 500 Keyboard
- Leonardo R3 ATMEGA32U4-AU
- Cabling & Crimp kit (if you want to make it reliable)
- Soldering Iron + solder (optional)

And this software:

Arduino IDE: https://www.arduino.cc/en/Main.Software

Arduino Amiga Keyboard script/code (Sketch for the board) Arduino IDE from https://github.com/tkoecker/amigakb

And finally the howto:

https://www.retro32.com/gaming/amiga/030120212092-staff-project-amiga-500-Keyboard-usb-interface-arduino-amibian-amiberry

For me everything worked out fine and once I had all components together, the adapter was done in under 20 minutes.

Amiga 500 Keyboard stands brackets

Want to use your Amiga 500 Keyboard on your PC? Look no further than these stunning Amiga 500 Keyboard stands.

They have been expertly crafted to allow your Amiga 500 Keyboard to stand proudly on your desk whilst connected via USB to the device of your choice. This exclusive 3D printed item features the iconic Amiga A and are available in Amiga 500 beige, black, grey white and purple.

Includes: 2 x Amiga Keyboard side panel stand adapter

Does not include the Arduino Keyboard adapter – they can be made to order so get in touch.

Fitting: The sides of the Keyboard will slide directly into the side brackets. We'd recommend using hot glue to hold them in place and to prevent damage to the Keyboard itself. Depending on the desk surface you may also want to source some non-slip self-adhesive feet.

These are made to order – please allow 2 working days for them to be produced!

https://www.retro32.com/product/amiga-500-Keyboard-stands-brackets-side-standalone?attribute_colour=Black

Keyboard connectors and pinouts

Here all pin and socket assignments of the Amiga Keyboards/Computers are summarized.

https://www.amigawiki.org/doku.php?id=de:signals:Keyboard_pinouts

Arduino based AMIGA 500/1000/2000 Keyboard Interface

This turns your Arduino Leonardo into an AMIGA 500/1000/2000 Keyboard Interface which means that you can use your Amiga Keyboard as an HID Keyboard on your PC/Mac/PS3/Raspberry Pi or whatever. (like keyrah)

All you need is the Amiga Keyboard and the Arduino without any shield or additional hardware. It does not work with Amiga 600/1200 Keyboards since they have no serial interface.

It's also possible to hook up 2 digital Joysticks (e.g. competition pro) with db9 connector.

See http://arduino.cc/forum/index.php?topic=134108.0 48

Based on Thomas Radtkes project http://www.raspberrypi.org/phpBB3/viewtopic.php?f=40&t=10990 37 I rewrote the code to make it faster and smaller. I also changed the behaviour a little bit to match my own preferences.

The Keyboard must be connected to digital inputs 8, 9, 10, GND and 5V. The Power LED can be directly connected to 5V.

Read more at https://forum.arduino.cc/t/amiga-500-1000-2000-Keyboard-interface/136052

Arduino based adapter to connect an Amiga 2000, 3000 or 500 Keyboard as an USB HID Keyboard.

This board allows to connect an Amiga Keyboard as an USB HID Keyboard (for example on a PC, Raspberry Pi, or Vampire V4SA). It uses a "pro micro" Arduino clone for the USB communication, and connects it to the Amiga specific Keyboard connectors

https://www.pcbway.com/project/shareproject/Amiga_2000___3000___500_Keyboard_USB_adapter.html

LL530 – Amiga Keyboard and Controller USB widget (seems unavailable)

This allows you to connect Commodore and Atari Controllers, and Amiga Keyboards to your RasPi or Desktop Computer, for emulation & gaming.

https://www.tindie.com/products/BleuLlama/ll530-amiga-Keyboard-and-Controller-usb-widget/

Amiga 500 USB Keyboard Controller kit (seems unavailable)

This is a kit which will allow you to convert a (preferably non-functional) Commodore Amiga 500 or Commodore Amiga 500+ into a USB Keyboard which can be used just like any other USB Keyboard. It also includes two Joystick ports which allow you to use standard 9 pin Commodore/Atari style Joysticks as USB Joysticks (for Joysticks only, they do not support the Amiga Mouse), and two audio jacks to connect to provide rear audio output from a Raspberry Pi or other single board Computer.

https://www.thefuturewas8bit.com/tms-a500-key.html

The Kipper2k A500 replacement Keyboard (Out of stock and seem to stay unavailable)

Cherry MX Brown Switches

PC Board with custom Keyboard Controller for the A500 model

USB on all Keyboards for use with Raspberry Pi's for example

Full set of key caps with the closest to original colors as possible or black key caps as an option

Extra key caps for PAL/North America, included

All Cables necessary for use out of the box

New A500 LED's Included for power and floppy indicators

Support plate with stabilizers for the larger keys

Future enhancements are planned

https://amigaonthelake.com/new-a500-replacement-Keyboard-with-full-set-of-amiga-keycaps/

8.2: New Amiga 500 Cases

Maybe you want your new THEA500 Mini in a new maxi case too :)

Then you definitely should have a closer look at the A1200NET webpage.

The new A500 cases are made from a set of custom and newly designed Injection Molds.

There are three molds for the whole case plus an optional unit for Tank Mouse shells.

The first mold is for the case top shell, the second for the bottom and the third for all trapdoors and parts.

Specifications

The new A500 case is a perfect replica of Commodore design.

Some areas of the case are enhanced to support the installation of modern hardware.

A few differences are:

- The plastic used in production is more UV resistant.
- Screw threaded inserts all the place. No more broken plastic clips.
- The bottom trapdoor offers additional cooling.
- A New right-side trapdoor is available with extra I/O slots. Plus one plain door.
- A set of metal threaded mounting points to supports Raspberry Pi© & Apollo Vampire V4 Standalone.
- Multiple colors available

https://www.a1200.net/amiga-500-case/

9: Amiga Operation System

"AmigaDOS", "Amiga OS", "AmigaOS", "Workbench", "Kickstart"... What is the correct name of the Amiga operating system?

Overview

In modern Computers the operating system consists of the system software that "makes the hardware usable" and provides shared components to application software. The operating system normally "comes with" the Computer. In the Amiga, like on other Computers, the operating system consists of a part that is loaded from disk (floppy disk or hard disk), and a part which is stored in higher speed and/or read only memory (e.g. ROM or PROM chips on the Computer motherboard).

CAOS, Tripos, AmigaDOS and Intuition

According to the original plans, the Amiga hardware was to be accompanied by CAOS, which stood for "Commodore Amiga Operating System", and was to be built on top of lower-level components like the Exec kernel. Instead of the complete CAOS, of which the intended "DOS" library was running late and thus never made it into a shipping version, the DOS portion (but not the kernel) of a British research project known as Tripos (named after the chair where Cambridge University exam candidates had to sit), was ported and merged into the rest of the Amiga operating system.

When the Tripos manual was edited, renaming instances of "Tripos" to "AmigaDOS" and removing references to the Tripos kernel, some parts were left in place with the result that the (renamed) "AmigaDOS" was still referenced as an operating system (which Tripos originally was), leading to some confusion about the name of the Amiga operating system. This search and replace operation is the reason why at Cloanto we have both original "AmigaDOS" documentation from 1985 and 1986 stating that "AmigaDOS is a multi-processing operating system designed for the Amiga", and written developer's documentation by Commodore saying that "AmigaDOS" should not be used to refer to the name of the Amiga operating system.

When the Amiga was launched, in 1985, operating systems, and the word "operating system" itself, while well known to Computer science students, did not have as strong an identity and recognition to the broad audience as they would have in the following decades. "OS" was beginning to be used in engineering and academic environments, as can be guessed from the "OS" in Commodore's "CAOS" project naming, its British "Tripos" friend, and even the "GEOS" software for the C64. But for the public at large, and even for the 1985 Byte Magazine Amiga article (included in Amiga Forever), which introduced the Amiga to the masses, the Amiga and its operating system were simply… the "Amiga". (The article also uses terms like "disk operating system" and "desktop", but not "AmigaDOS" or "operating system".)

By the 1985 launch event the Amiga code was still unfinished. The then-current ROM ("Kickstart") version was 0.7, and did not include a desktop user interface, but rather booted into a command line window titled "AmigaDOS", while the screen title bar displayed the capitalized name "INTUITION". "Intuition" was also a part of the 1985 New York Amiga launch presentations. Later it was repositioned into a more technical role, not exposed in the screen title, but remaining documented for developers as the Amiga component providing user interface functionality (windows features and user interface elements like menus, buttons and other controls).

Amiga OS

As Computer users became more aware of what an "operating system" was, and recognized "OS" as its abbreviation, it was also clear that the "DOS" part of "AmigaDOS" was somewhat of an understatement for an operating system which comprised not only a "disk" part, but also substantial multitasking, multimedia and other components. Also, "DOS" brought to mind IBM and Microsoft's much less sophisticated "DOS".

Slowly, "Amiga OS" became used to refer to the Amiga operating system as a whole, while "AmigaDOS" and "DOS" retained the intended focus on the disk and file subsystem. In spite of Commodore's demise in 1994, in that same year version 3.1 of the operating system was officially released as "Amiga OS 3.1".

In light of the historical roots of the Amiga operating system and of subsequent official company decisions and popular use, we consider "Amiga OS", which is both generic and formally correct, to be a better name for the

9: Amiga Operation System

Amiga operating system than the more narrow "Kickstart" and "AmigaDOS" names.

From Amiga OS to AmigaOS

While other companies too used "OS" as a stand-alone word in their operating system names (e.g. Apple, for its original "Mac OS" series), somebody possibly decided that "OS" in itself, meaning "operating system", was too generic.

Sun Microsystems, whose Sun 2 and Sun 3 workstations had been in use at Amiga first, and Commodore later, to build parts of the Amiga operating systems, had been branding its own operating system as "SunOS" (without the space) at least since SunOS 3.5 and 4.0 in 1988.

It too much longer for Apple to drop the space in its "Mac OS", which became "macOS" only in 2016.

While the Amiga operating system was still marketed as "Amiga OS" (with the space) in 1994, under ESCOM's ownership in 1995 the name "AmigaOS" (without the space) started being used.

By the year 2000, the "AmigaOS" name was being used quite pervasively by Amiga, Inc. both in the updated copyright notices and in the official operating system file set, e.g. as an "AmigaOS ROM Update" item which was part of version 44.13 of the SetPatch command. It was only natural then for AmigaOS 4.0 to follow without the space.

Workbench

The name "Workbench" was originally not meant to express the concept of an "operating system" as in "OS" or "DOS". Neither Commodore-Amiga nor any of its successors ever used the word "Workbench" to refer to an operating system. Nevertheless, perhaps also because of the lack of branding clarity about what ought to have been the "real" name of the Amiga operating system, and because of Cloanto's increasing use of this word in Amiga Forever, "Workbench" kept receiving an increasing preference by the public.

One of the many unique points of the Amiga Forever project is its consistent use of the name "Workbench" for the operating system, which as such has become a Cloanto "trademark".

Cloanto's use of the "Workbench" name for the operating system also helps avoid confusion with projects like AmigaOS 4.0, as Amiga Forever focuses entirely on "Classic" Amiga systems.

Historically, there are two other uses of the name "Workbench" within the Amiga family:

One of the floppy disks that shipped with early Amiga Computers was called "Workbench", while other disks in the same set were named "Kickstart", "Extras", "Fonts", etc.

"Workbench" was also a name used for the desktop user interface

Never, however, was the operating system itself called "Workbench", or did Commodore try to use the term "Workbench" as a broader operating system brand.

Kickstart

The first Amiga, i.e. the Amiga 1000, had an additional floppy disk, named "Kickstart". The Kickstart disk was needed because when the Amiga 1000 shipped, the ROM-based part of the operating system was not stable enough, so the machine was manufactured with only enough code to boot into the operating system from the Kickstart disk. After that, the Amiga 1000, like other Amiga models (which had a "real" ROM chip on their motherboard), could continue loading from other floppy disks (e.g. games), or from hard disk. Interestingly enough, the Amiga 3000 had a similar problem (i.e. the hardware was finished before the new operating system was ready), so that early versions of it loaded their operating system ROM code from a "kickstart" file (located on hard disk).

Interviewed by Cloanto in 2015, Intuition developer RJ Mical described the names used by the Amiga team in the early development days. While individual Amiga OS components had prominent recognition and were referred to by name, e.g. "Exec" or "Intuition", the set as a whole, and as such what was seen as the Amiga operating system, was referred to as "Kickstart" for a long time.

Related Links

ROM and Operating System Files in Amiga Forever
https://www.amigaforever.com/kb/13-114

Preinstalled Workbench 3.X Files
https://www.amigaforever.com/kb/15-107

Downloading Amiga Kickstart ROMs
http://www.amigakickstart.com/

Thanks goes to Amiga Forever for this chapter

9.1: Kickstart

Kickstart is the name given to the essential parts of the AmigaOS operating system, usually located in ROM. Kickstart contains among others the exec.library (the kernel), the dos.library (the DOS), the graphics.library and the intuition.library (the system libraries for the Amiga GUI).

Build in THEA500 Mini, is Kickstart 1.3 and 3.1. The reason is simple, since the vast majority of games are compatible with these Kickstarts.

To play games that require a Kickstart ROM that is not available in the A500 Mini, you would have to buy it. Since a long time there is the possibility to buy Kickstart ROMs as a file, download it and put it on a USB-Drive.

The Kickstart chips contain the "fixed" part of the Amiga operating system. Depending on the type of Computer, this is either a 256 KB ROM, a 512 KB ROM or two 256 KB ROMs. A few Amiga models require the Kickstart on floppy disk, for example the Amiga 1000 and a few variants of the Amiga 3000.

9.2: Operation Systems & Workbench

How to start the Amiga Workbench on THEA500 Mini:

What you need:

- A USB-Keyboard connected to the Mini
- Load the free game Citadel from Retro Games Ltd.: *https://bit.ly/THEA500-Bonus-Games-1_0_0* and unpack it to yout FAT32 formatted USB-drive.
- You should have a folder named "THEA500 Bonus Games", and in this the files of Citadel 1.3.
- Get an HDF file with a working workbench installed (search via google J) and put it on the USB-drive.
- Prepare an uae-configuration file:
- Get an HDF file with a working workbench installed (search via google J) and put it on the USB-drive .
- Prepare an uae-configuration file:
- Open the file Citadel_v1.3_ol.uae with the Windows-Notepad or any other text editor (not Word) and add anywhere:
    - use_gui=yes
    - amiberry.open_gui=F12
- Save the file with the name Citadel_v1.3_ol.uae in the folder THEA500 Bonus Games (make sure that the file does not have .txt as file extension).
- Additionally but only necessary if you want to play a hdf based game, a CD-game or a game from an adf-file:
- A HDF File with a game
- A ADF file with a game
- A game ISO image (the .cue file is not needed)

Make a folder on the same USB-drive called "Config". Hint! Whenever you make a change to the Workbench, such as the resolution, it is best to immediately save the configuration file.

Running the Workbench

Select Cital from the USB drive with A and start it with Home.

Then the user interface of AmiBerry which is the emulator of the mini will show up.

Go to the menu "Path" and select the path of the config directory with the three dots on the right and click OK (the folder is in the root directory of the drive under "mnt").

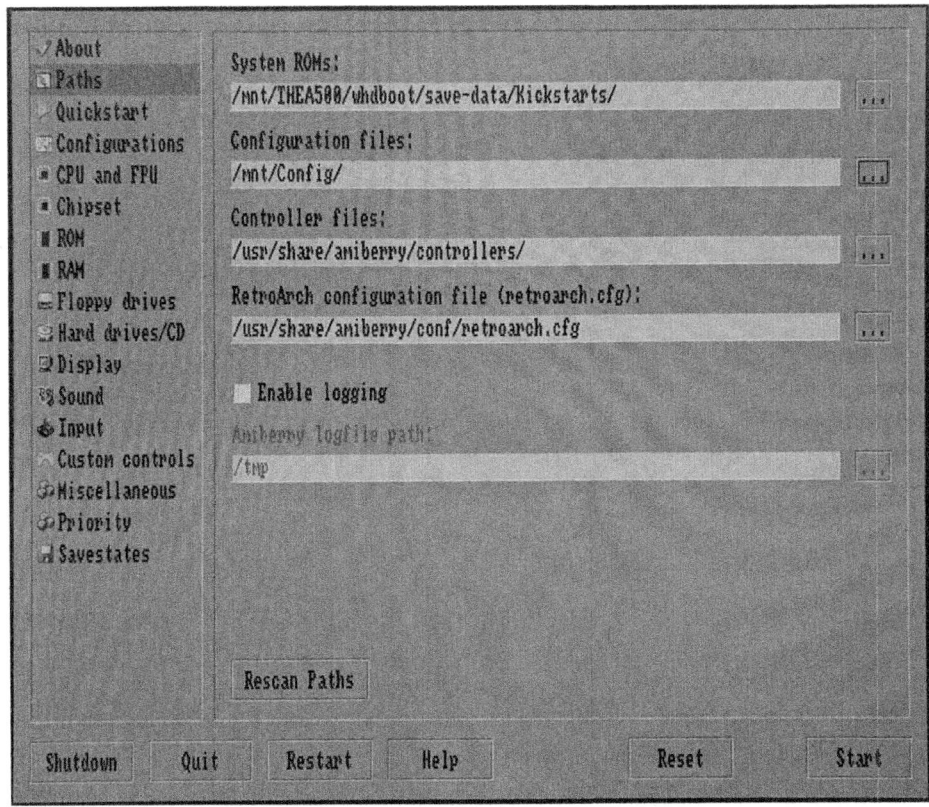

Then go to the menu "Hard drives/CD" and delete all entries there. Add then with "Add Hardfile" again over the three points the hdf with the Workbench.

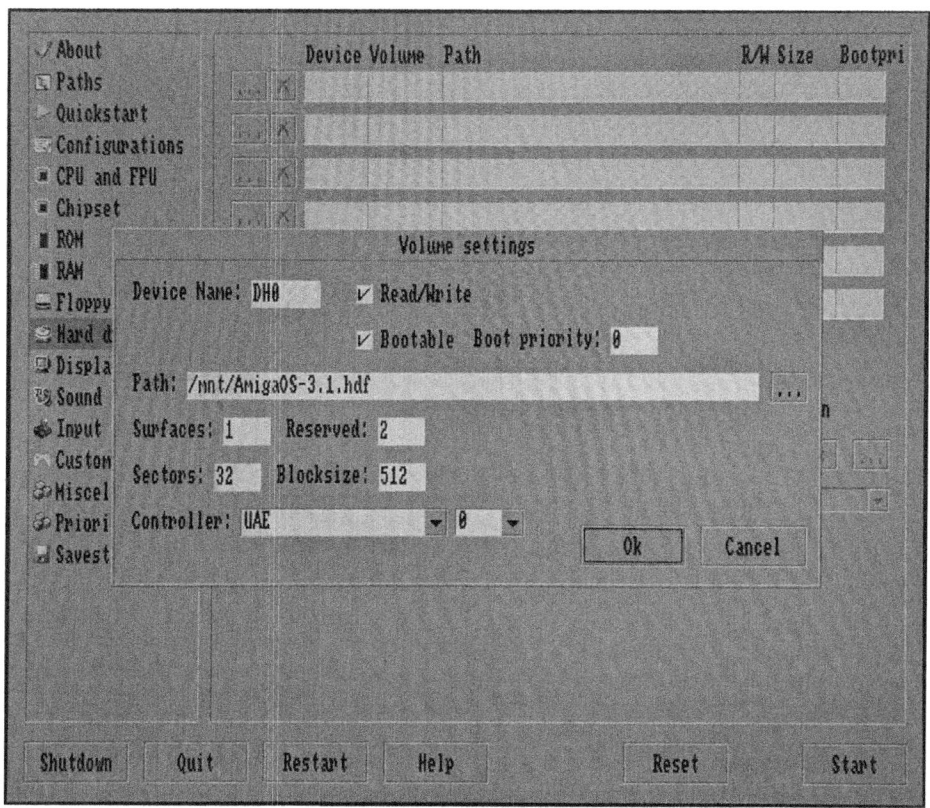

Go to the menu "Configurations" and save the config with the name of your choice.

Now you can run the Workbench for the first time with choosing "Start".

You can always press "F12" to return to the AmiBerry settings menu and make changes. Don't forget to save the configuration from time to time.

PS. The savestates in AmiBerry can only be saved on floppy disk files and does not work with .hdf/hard disks.

If you like to try out how the look and feel of different Workbenches is, visit the Chapter AMIGA 30 – The Commodore Events.

Introduction to the Amiga Workbench

The story of Amiga begins in 1982 when (primarily) David Morse and Jay Miner found the company "Hi Toro", which shortly after is renamed "Amiga Inc.". They want to develop a general-purpose Computer for everyone. The backers wanted primarily a game console, but especially Miner, who (or rather his dog) is considered the father of the Amiga, wanted to build a full-fledged personal Computer. He was very right about that, as the games market suffered a collapse shortly after the company was founded. In 1984, Commodore bought Amiga Inc. for 27.1 million dollars, which saved the project from failure for the first time (several more times were to follow).

The first Amiga version, the "Lorraine" (rel. 1985), later christened Amiga 1000, ran with a Motorola-68000-CPU, had 128KB memory and a connector for a color or b/w Monitor or a TV. The 4096 selected colors were exactly those, which did not fray when changing from foreground to background color in NTSC.

After AmigaOS 0.7 Beta and 0.9 Beta were only equipped with CLI (Command Line Interface) in August 1985, AmigaOS 1.0 was released for sale in October 1985. This had a graphical user interface for the first time, the Amiga Workbench. However, it was already introduced in July of that year in the Lincoln Center in New York in a specially scheduled large event and not as usual at the American home electronics fair CES. Andy Warhol uses the Amiga during the show of Debbie Harry ("Blondie") to create a picture of her.

At this event, the Amiga's multitasking capability was already demonstrated: word processing, data sorting, animation, business graphics and spreadsheets in their own windows at the same time. Apart from gaming, the Amiga was mainly used for editing videos. Other important applications were music and 3D animation. Software like Cinema 4D and Lightwave were for the first time only available on the Amiga (with hardware extension "Toaster") and the special – effects of various Hollywood flicks (e.g. "Death suits her") were created with these Computers. It was also the first Computer with speech synthesis capability, due to its 8bit analog/digital converter. It also had AUTOCONFIG, a kind of plug&play, starting with version 1.3.

For more information, versions and downloads you should visit the Workbench Nostalgia http://www.gregdonner.org/workbench/

Amiga Workbench – 1st generation: OS 1.x.

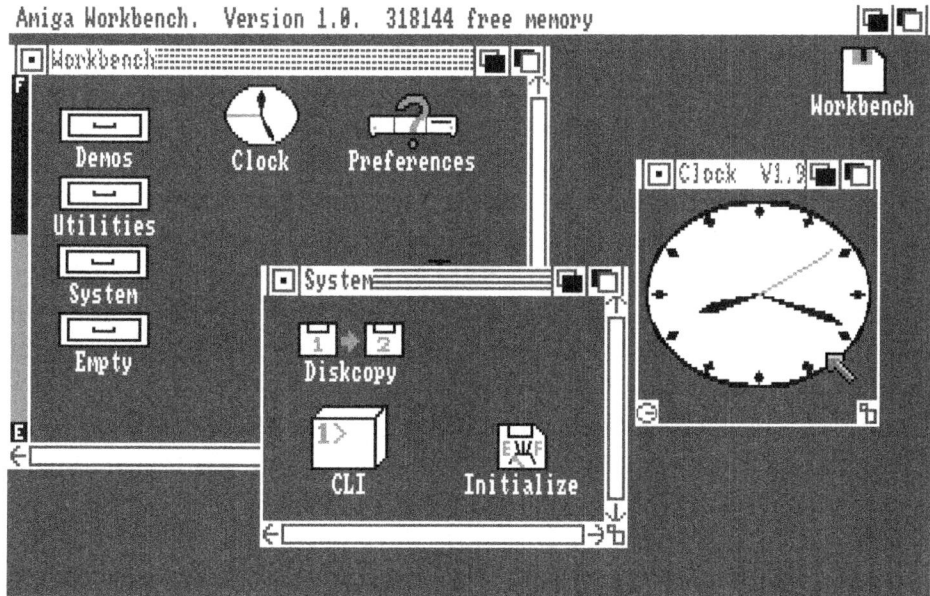

With the first Amiga, later christened Amiga 1000, version 1.0 of the Amiga operating system was shipped in 1985. Even this very first version set standards that remained unmatched for a long time: Pre-emptive multi-tasking allowed an optimal distribution of CPU computing time to different processes. The user interface could be operated intuitively with the Mouse, but at the same time it was possible to perform more complicated operations with the Keyboard via the CLI (the predecessor of the shell). At the same time, this OS was one of the smallest and most effective on the market – a plus point that has remained with it to this day.

There were no Kickstart ROMs on the Amiga 1000: This was delivered on a disk and loaded first at startup. After switching on, the user was only greeted by a screen asking to insert the corresponding floppy disk.

The first version of the operating system was still quite buggy and crashed frequently, nevertheless it inspired the Amiga fans of the first hour.OS 1.0 supported for the screen output only the American NTSC system. Like the nowadays better-known Workbench 1.3, it had a blue background. However, the pictograms were still very simple and two-dimensional. When dragging pictograms, only the Mouse pointer changed to a circle with an X in it. ABasic as programming language and a tutorial were also included on disk.

Already in the same year, 1985, there was the first update: 1.1. There were two versions: one for NTSC (V 31.x), another one for PAL (V32.x) for the European market. The only really visible difference to version 1.0 were three small demos: "Lines", "Boxes" and "Dots". For the rest, it was probably mostly a siipmiung of bugfixes. With the Amiga 500 resp. 2000 the version 1.2 was released in 1987. This was the first version with Kickstart-ROMs, which the Amiga 1000 didn't have yet. Some Amiga-typical features were introduced with 1.2, especially the RAM disk and Auto-Config – which was "invented" almost a decade later as "Plug and Play" by competitors. On the newly added "Extras" floppy disk, among other things, the program "AmigaBASIC" was found – developed by none other than the then relatively small company Microsoft developed. Apart from that, there were minor optical improvements: The Trashcan pictogram was renewed, and pictograms remained visible when dragged with the Mouse. AmigaOS 1.3 is still in use on an astonishing number of systems today. It was shipped in 1988, together with new ROMs. Now additional memory was included automatically, and booting from media like hard disks was possible. The new "FastFileSystem" was faster and could store a bit more data. However,

9: Amiga Operation System

automatic booting was only possible from "old" hard disk partitions, since the FFS was not yet stored in ROM. The pictograms were completely revised and now had a more appealing 3D look. Internally a lot of changes were made: Some DOS commands were added, others were revised. The mount command and the mountlist were introduced. Various handlers (like aux handler and speak handler) were added. In the following years there were smaller updates (1.3.2, 1.3.3 and 1.3.4), in which especially bugs were eliminated. Apparently Commodore saw AmigaBASIC as one big bug: It was removed completely from 1.3.3 because it crashed too often. Considering who the program came from, this was certainly a wise decision. Apart from these minor revisions, the only thing worth mentioning is that the RAM disk was given the name RAMBO: in version 1.3.2, but this was later changed again. Possibly this was also a forgery, though.

In this first version 1.0 it was already possible to drag, but the icon was not displayed during dragging, only the pointer changed to a red crosshair. Only NTSC was supported.

Version 1.1, released in December 85, already supported PAL, but it was only introduced in Europe in February 1986. Several demos (Boxes, Lines, Dots) already tried to show something of the graphics capabilities of the Computer.

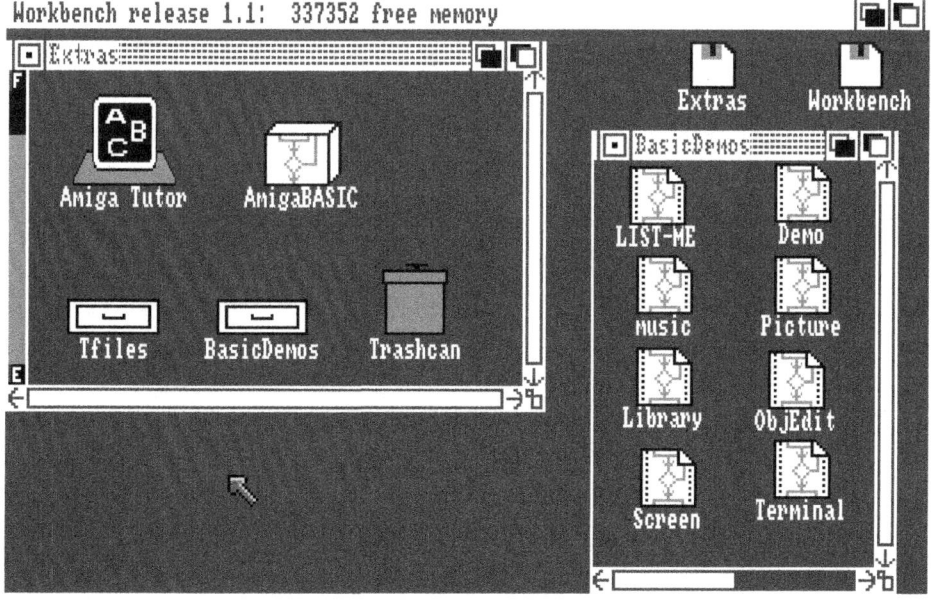

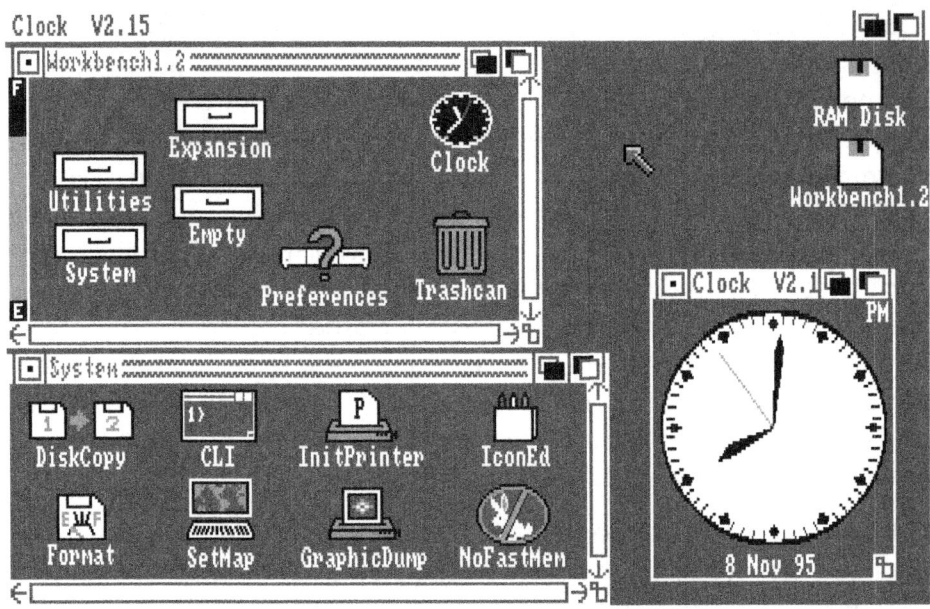

Version 1.2 (already Amiga 500 and 2000) made it possible for the first time to select several icons at the same time and to print the screen contents (GraphicDump). Icons were now also visible during dragging. Furthermore an extra icon for the RAM (temporary memory) was added.

In the 1988 released version 1.3 there was a more comfortable CLI, the shell and several other useful programs like PIPE (cf. UNIX), More (text viewer) and SAY (speech output). All icons got a "3D look" and the preferences had a new graphical interface. A permanent memory with icon named RAMB0 was added.

9: Amiga Operation System

Amiga Workbench – 2nd generation: OS 2.x.

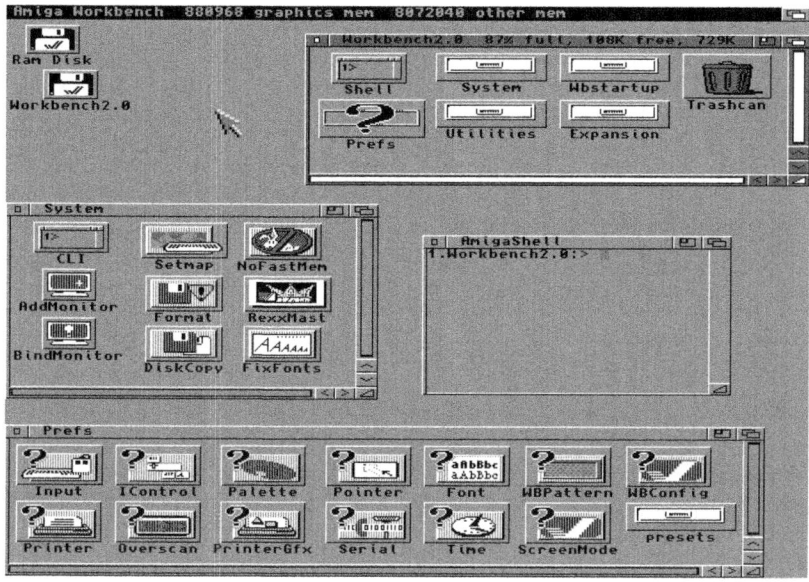

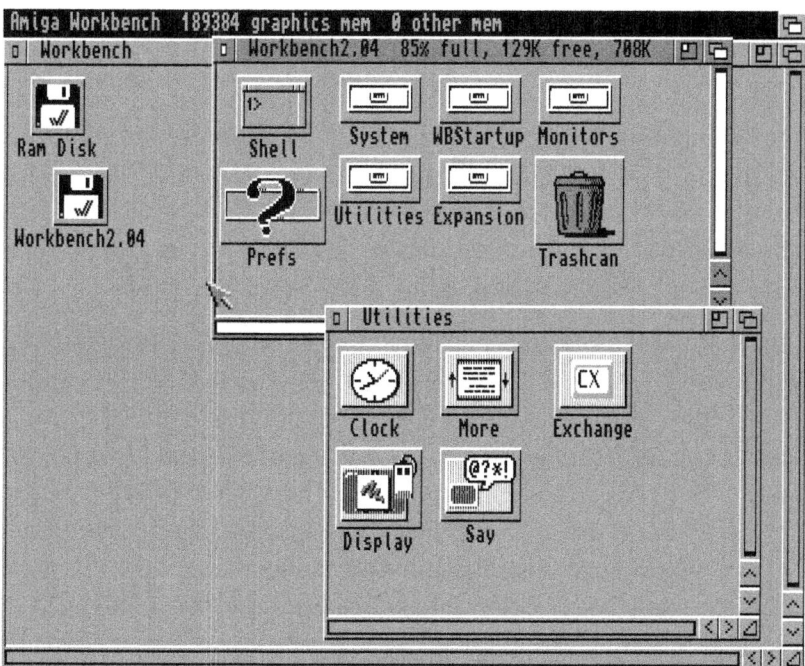

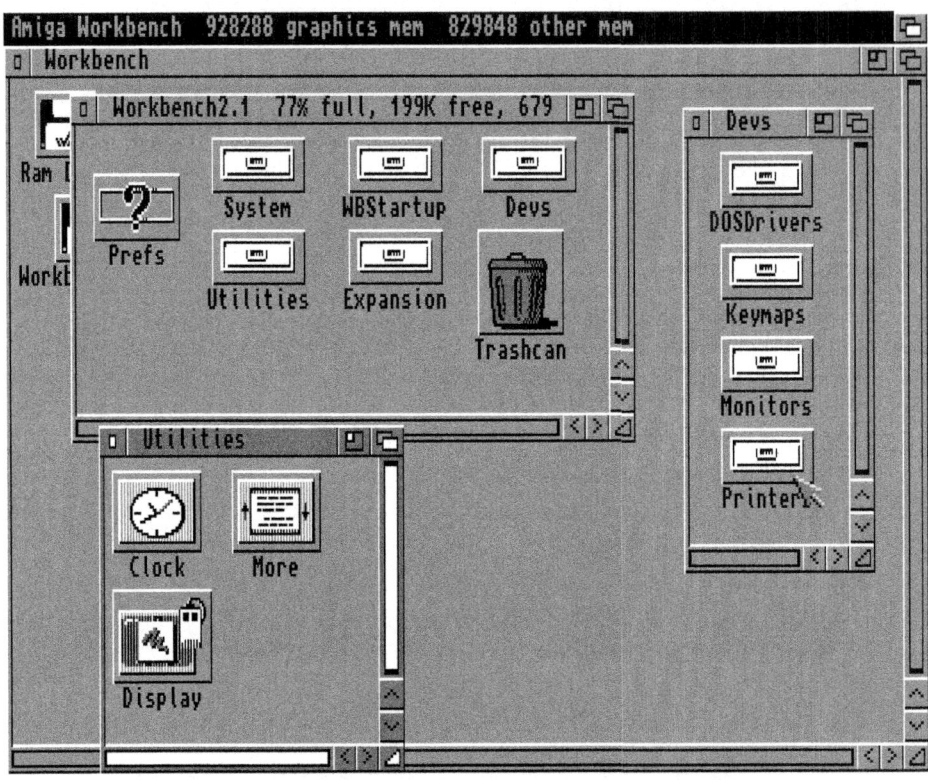

With the first Amiga 3000, the Amiga OS 2.0 was delivered in 1990. There were no roms at the beginning, instead a "superstart disk". OS 2.0 already had the appearance of all following versions: The background was gray, the pictograms redrawn and three-dimensional. The disk pictograms were now placed on the left instead of the right side of the screen.

Internally, a lot had already been done compared to 1.3, but the really big step came with OS 2.04. This was available with the Amiga 500+ in October 1991. Now, there were also new ROMs. The menu system was completely reworked compared to versions 1 .x. The list of changes is long: A boot menu was added, so it became possible to boot from different partitions. GadTools was integrated into the ROM, where now also for speed reasons some of the most important DOS commands were built in. The file system was completely reworked. The OS supported scalable fonts for the first time with the Agfa Compugraphic Fonts. The "Preferences" were split up into many small programs. The operating system provided standard file and font requesters for the first time. ARexx was introduced as a new cross-program programming language and replaced AmigaBASIC.

The Amiga 600 was shipped with OS 2.05. A new ROM allowed access to the internal IDE Controller and the PCMCIA port. Externally, there were practically no differences to OS 2.04. By the way, the first A600s are said to have been manufactured with the ROMs of the A500+, so that they could neither access the IDE Controller nor the PCMCIA port. If you got one of these, you had no choice but to upgrade your new Computer if you wanted to use these Controllers. Unfortunately, in retrospect, one can only say: Typical Commodore.

At the end of 1992, OS 2.1 was released, which was only available as an update and without new ROMs. It was more stable than the 2.0 versions. It also had a new, standardized screen mode requester. It also offered the possibility to read and write PC and Atari floppies via CrossDOS. The mount command was changed, the mountlist was abolished (but still supported) and the structure that is still valid today was introduced: The directories "Devs" and "Storage", each with the same subdirectories "DosDrivers", "Keymaps", "Monitors" and "Printers". This structure meant a revolution in the integration of peripherals: Device drivers could be (de)activated permanently by simply moving them back and forth with the Mouse or could be started with a double click.

A further innovation was the locale.library, which made it possible to adapt programs flexibly to the respective national language. However, the speech output was no longer included, since the license fees were obviously out of proportion to the benefits. Sometime during this period, the AmigaGuide was also developed, which was not part of an OS package, but was available separately for commercial packages before OS 3.0.

Bigger changes in design and (less) in operation came only in 1990 with Workbench 2.0, whose look & feel was very gray, but more spatial. This version was available for the first time with the Amiga 3000, V2.04 (`91) then also for the A500+. The menu was completely reworked and there was the possibility to select bootdevices at startup.

Version 2.1 (`92) brought mainly hardware related improvements like compatibility to Motorola 68040, less memory consumption and support for 40MB harddisks. The very popular speech output program SAY was for the first time no longer included in the distribution, probably due to a dispute with its programmers.

Amiga Workbench – 3rd generation: OS3.x

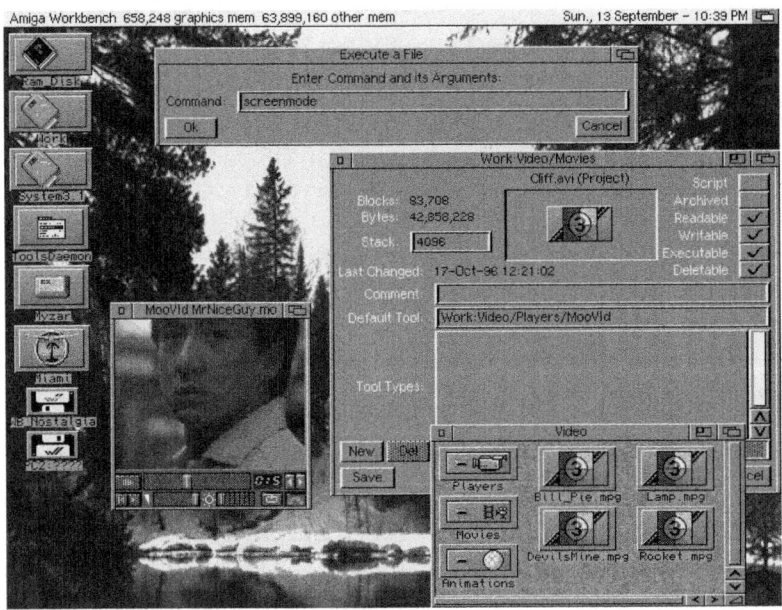

9: AMIGA OPERATION SYSTEM

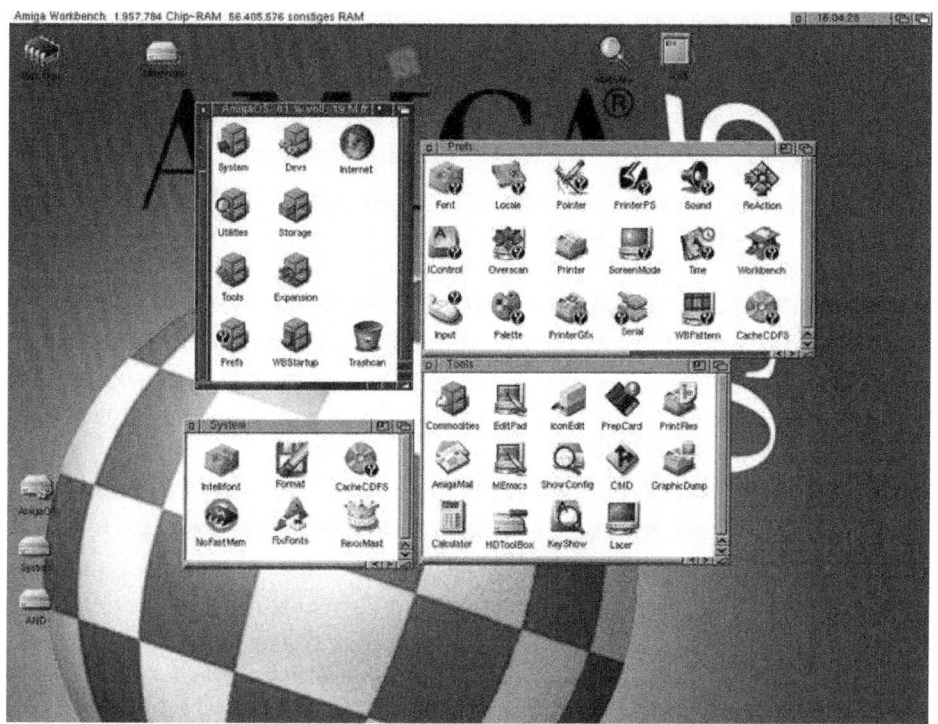

Also in 1992 AmigaOS 3.0 appeared, which was initially reserved for the AGA Amigas, A1200 and A4000. One of the most important innovations were certainly the datatypes, which guaranteed a flexible use of all possible data types. Multiview immediately showed how it works: Whether graphics or AmigaGuide — almost everything could be displayed or played. The AmigaGuide was officially represented here for the first time, in a strongly modified and extended version compared to the previously distributed version — but unfortunately also with more errors. Of course there was also a new version of the file system. In the graphical area, cosmetics were done once again: The menus, now black on white, also appeared in the §-D look. The color palette was slightly revised. In addition, it was possible to define backgrounds for the Workbench and individual windows and to adapt the appearance of the Workbench to a large extent to one's own wishes. In addition, the graphics output routines had been thoroughly reworked, so that many things ran faster and considerably more windows could be opened at the same time without the system becoming noticeably slower. Visually, not too much had changed – but "under the hood" a lot had changed, especially with the datatypes.

The last revision was released in 1994. OS 3.1 was first released with the corresponding new ROMs by VillageTronic, which had the license to distribute it for its Picasso-II users. Official deliveries by Commodore followed a bit later. OS 3.1 mainly removed a number of bugs from OS 3.0.RTG support was improved; now it was also possible for graphics card users to run the Workbench in 256 (previously only 16) colors. New datatypes for animations and CDXL were added. For the CD32, the built-in Akiko chip for fast graphics operations and the non-volatile RAM were supported. Furthermore, the Amiga finally got a proper CD-ROM file system, even if it was still buggy. Today, there will probably be only a few systems that still look exactly as the developers had imagined at that time. The open structure of the operating system makes it easy to insert patches of all kinds. This starts with purely optical improvements like the MagicWB or the new icons and continues with commodities, the small auxiliary programs. Numerous tools make working with the Workbench easier, but also increase the risk of crashes, since not all extensions are always compatible with each other. After five years of development break with two bankruptcies of the respective parent company, it is time for an update that removes some of the limitations.

A bigger jump was not felt again until 1992 with Workbench V3.0. Support for the AGA chipset and a much-improved design, background images and Multi View, a display window mode that could recognize and display different media types (images, sounds, text and even video, which could be played directly from CD for the first time). The recycle bin was no longer on the workbench and the scrollbars got arrows added.

Version 3.5 (1999) was already shipped on CD, had support for 4 GB hard disks and had a very modern GUI with animated icons and support for long file names. Also supported was TCP/IP and thus web – browsing and email.

In 2001 the Amiga became very multimedia capable with V3.9, had a player for AVI and QuickTime videos and one for MP3/WAV/AIFF. The browser and the email support were further improved (e.g. JavaScript capability). AmiDOCK, a new start bar, very similar to the MacOS start bar, packer and unpacker and an improved file search program.

Amiga Workbench – 4th generation: OS4.x

In 2001 Amiga Inc. signed a contract with Hyperion Entertainment to develop the PowerPC native AmigaOS 4 from their earlier release AmigaOS 3.1. Unlike the earlier versions, which were based on the Motorola 68k central processor, OS4 runs only on PowerPC computer systems. The distribution policies of Amiga, Inc. (current Amiga brand owners) for AmigaOS 4.0 and all later versions required that OS4 be bundled with the new third-party "Amigas" hardware, with the sole exception of Amigas with Phase5 PowerPC accelerator cards, for which OS4 is available separately. This requirement was removed in the agreement between Amiga, Inc. and Hyperion in settling a dispute over ownership of AmigaOS 4. In 2014, Hyperion introduced AmigaOS 4.1 Final Edition with all previous downloadable updates and some new features such as Unified Graphics Library with a RTG support and support for more than 2 GB RAM.

The last release was version 4.0 in October 2004.

The system no longer runs with the Motorola 68000 series, but with its PowerPC. The "Guru" (see next section) was replaced by the "Grim Reaper", a program similar to Task Manager in Windows. Also new is support for TrueType and PostScript fonts with optional anti-aliasing. Improved CD support also allows writing and booting from CD without having to be mounted first. Disk size is unlimited and there is a partitioning wizard.

The little specials

The Amiga has always been something special, and the respective developer team was proud of their work. No wonder that the developers somehow immortalized themselves in practically every version, even if Commodore didn't like that. Therefore, the corresponding messages were hidden better and better. OS 1.3 reveals information about the developers in the title bar if you press both Alt and both Shift keys together with one of the F keys. If you insert a floppy disk instead of pressing an F key, you get the message: "The Amiga, born a Champion." You may have to go to "Last Message" in the menu to read the message. OS 2.x already made it more difficult to get the information: A program must be started from the Workbench, then Ctrl, both Alt and both Shift keys must be pressed, one of the Workbench menu items must be selected, the right Mouse button must be released again, and only then the other keys must be pressed. After this orgy, you will get the following messages in the Workbench title bar:

- "Quit" We made it....
- "Backdrop" Better than ever!
- "Execute" OS Group: Bryce, Michael, Peter, Darren, Randeil
- "Update GFX: Allan, Bart, Spencer, Steve, Chris, Ray
- "Redraw" SP: Eric, Martin H, Bill, Martin T, Brian, Kevin
- "Last Message" Others: Andy, Dale, jimm, Kodiak, Ned, Porter, Carolyn, David, CATS, QA
- "About" Thanks to: Bill Hawes, Software Distillery

It is a bit easier to get the signatures of all developers: They can be found in a directory on the installation disk of OS 2.04: 2.0Install:Tools/Test/Who. info

In OS 3.x you also have to press all Shift, Alt and Ctrl keys and then take the Mouse with the third "free" hand and call "About" from the menu several times, leaving the open windows each time. However, this only works if you have no more than 16 tasks running.

A review by Marc Breisinger – Thank you Marc!

9.2.1: The Command Line Interface – CLI

AmigaOS has two primary interfaces user facing interfaces: Graphical User Interface (GUI) and Command Line Interface (CLI).

The CLI is better known as the Shell which provides a mechanism for the user to enter commands to the operating system or user programs. It is a low-level version of the GUI also known as the Workbench. Some commands are unique to the Shell, just as some are unique to the Workbench. In practice, the two user interfaces complement each other with a large amount of overlap. The choice is left to personal taste.

The Shell, its user-supplied commands and responses from the Shell and other programs can be displayed in a Console text window on the screen. Alternatively, the user interface may be via a remote mechanism such as a terminal program running on another Computer. Such a remote machine might be connected via a serial interface, a network connection or other means.

Shell Components

There are four components that make up the user's visible Shell console:

- Shell,
- con-handler,
- console.device and
- Console preferences editor

Shell

The Shell is the heart of the group. It is the Shell that writes the command prompt, reads the user input, runs any programs that the user requests on the command line and passes the user's command line options to the program. The Shell passes Read and Write requests (among others) to the con-handler for distribution to the user interface.

con-handler

The con-handler directs the Read and Write requests at a device level, to the Console window, to a serial AUX: device or any other supported interface. The con-handler also performs command and file name completion ("tab-completion"). If the user requests a text window on the screen ("CON:"), the con-handler requests the console device to open and maintain a suitable text window.

console.device

The console device is a device driver like any hardware driver. However, it has no hardware to control, it opens a screen window and reads/writes text to and from that window. It is common to refer to the text window as the Console. The console device translates ANSI standard text and embedded commands into text in the window, including embedded cursor movement and editing commands.

When requested by the user, the console creates and maintains a history of all text displayed in the Console Window. The user can retrieve this history after the Console window has been closed.

The Console supports a menu which can be used to modify some attributes of the screen text, e.g. text colour, font size, etc.

Console Preferences

The Console preferences editor allows the user to set some default attributes of the Console text. These default values can be over-ridden by console menu or application programs. Like any other Preferences editor, changes can be made temporarily or permanently.

The commands in this chapter are executed from the Shell window. On the following webpage are they described in alphabetic order; however, some commands reserved for system use appear together at the end of the chapter.

https://wiki.amigaos.net/wiki/AmigaOS_Manual:_AmigaDOS_Command_Reference

And here is a short overview:

addbuffers	Expands the system cache for a drive
adddatatypes	Creates a list of data types
alias	Sets shortcuts to other files
ask	Creates a yes/no query during a shell script
Assign	Creates shortcuts to drives and folders
avail	Displays the available RAM
binddrivers	Activates device drivers from the expansion folder
break	Cancels the (mentioned) process
cd	Changes the current folder
changetaskpri	Changes the priority of the shell task
conclip	Exchanges data between console and clipboard
copy	Copies files and folders
cpu	Shows the installed processor and/or turns the cache on or off
date	Shows or changes the system date
delete	Deletes files or directories
dir	Displays the file contents of a folder. More information is shown by the list command
diskchange	Notifies the system of a disk change
echo	Prints a string
ed	Starts the editor ED
edit	Edits text line by line
else	Part of an IF query in a shell script
endcli	Ends the current shell process and closes the console window
endif	Ends an IF query in a shell script

endshell	Terminates a shell process
endskip	Ends a SKIP block in a shell script
eval	Compares integer or boolean expressions
execute	Starts a script
failat	Defines at which error value a command sequence terminates
fault	Displays the error description of a DOS error number
filenote	Appends a comment to a file
get	Fetches the value of a local variable
getenv	Fetches the value of a global variable
iconx	Starts a shell script via an icon
if	IF queries can be used to define decisions in a shell script
info	Displays information about mounted drives
install	Writes or checks a disk boot block
iprefs	Displays the system settings
join	Merges multiple files into a new file
lab	Defines a label for a script file
list	Shows an exact file overview of a folder (see also 'dir')
loadresource	Loads a system resource into RAM
loadwb	Starts the Workbench
lock	Makes a drive read-only
magtape	Rewinds or forwards SCSI streamers tapes
makedir	Creates a new folder
makelink	Creates shortcuts between file names
mount	Makes a device available (e.g. CD drives have to be mounted)

9: Amiga Operation System

newcli	Opens a new shell window
newshell	Opens a new shell window
path	Controls the list of directories that are searched for commands by the shell
prompt	Changes the appearance of the prompt of the current shell window
protect	Changes the protection bit of files or folders
quit	Terminates a shell script
relabel	Renames the media in the current drive
remrad	Removes the reboot protected RAM disk 'RAD'.
rename	Changes the name of files and folders, can also be used to move them
requestchoice	Allows the use of standard system query windows under DOS
requestfile	Allows the use of the standard file selector
resident	Shows and changes the list of system commands in memory
run	Starts a program as a background process
search	Searches files for pieces of text
set	Fills a local variable with a value
SetClock	Reads or changes the system clock
setdate	Changes the date of a file
setenv	Fills a global variable
setfont	Changes the character set of the shell
setKeyboard	Changes the Keyboard layout
setpatch	Starts a patch for the installed ROM
skip	Jumps to a label within a shell script
sort	Sorts the lines of a file alphabetically

stack	Shows or changes the stack size of the shell
status	Lists information about the current shell processes
type	Displays the file contents
unalias	Removes a shortcut
unset	Deletes a local variable
unsetenv	Deletes a global variable
version	Shows the version number of the selected file (without specifying the operating system version)
wait	Stops a shell script for a certain time
which	Searches the command path of an object
why	Shows the detailed error message with which the previous command was aborted]]

9.2.2: Startup Sequence

```
Ed 2.00
;$VER: Startup-Sequence_LD 40.3 (31.8.93)
; Startup-Sequence for low-density floppies

C:SetPatch QUIET
C:Version >NIL:
C:AddBuffers >NIL: DF0: 15
FailAt 21

C:MakeDir RAM:T RAM:Clipboards RAM:ENV RAM:ENV/Sys
C:Copy >NIL: ENVARC: RAM:ENV ALL NOREQ

Resident >NIL: C:Assign PURE
Resident >NIL: C:Execute PURE

Assign >NIL: ENV: RAM:ENV
Assign >NIL: T: RAM:T
Assign >NIL: CLIPS: RAM:Clipboards
Assign >NIL: REXX: S:
Assign >NIL: PRINTERS: DEVS:Printers
Assign >NIL: KEYMAPS: DEVS:Keymaps
Assign >NIL: LOCALE: SYS:Locale
Assign >NIL: LIBS: SYS:Classes ADD
```

Each time your Amiga is booted, it executes the Startup-sequence script file Startup-sequence script file located in the S: directory. The Startup-sequence file allocates disk buffers, makes device assignments, reads saved Preferences settings, and performs other functions that configure the Amiga for use.

Because any errors introduced into the Startup-sequence file can cause a fatal disruption of the normal system startup, we strongly recommend that you do not alter your Startup-sequence file. Instead, we recommend that you create a file called User-startup in the S:directory. Creating a User-startup file allows you to customize your system at startup while preventing any disruption of the normal booting process. This file is automatically executed by the Startup-sequence before opening Workbench.

Note

Do not modify the original Startup-sequence file. Altering your Startup-sequence file can cause fatal system startup errors.

The User-startup and other startup files in the S:directory can be modified to run programs at startup, print special introductory messages, or automatically open a Shell window on the Workbench screen. Any AmigaDOS command can appear in a startup script, including commands to execute other scripts.

9.3: BASIC

BASIC – the Beginners All Purpose Instruction Code, is one of the oldest most simple programming languages.

Like the Commodore ViC20 and C64, Commodore wanted to have the option to use BASIC-Programs, and so Amiga Basic came into place.

9.3.1: What is Amiga Basic?

AmigaBASIC was a BASIC version for the Commodore Amiga developed by Microsoft, which was part of the AmigaOS versions 1.1 to 1.3. It replaced the ABasiC (from MetaComCo) of version 1.0 and was in turn replaced by ARexx with AmigaOS version 2.0. Since the Amiga was shipped in Germany only some months later than in the USA, it was shipped there from the beginning with AmigaBASIC instead of ABasiC. AmigaBASIC remained the only software Microsoft produced for the Amiga.

If you want to learn Amiga Basic with Videos, I suggest this production:

AMIGA BASIC Welcome to the first of my Amiga series with many videos on the Amiga personal Computer to come. Covering Amiga games, Amiga Demoscene and utilities. All Things Amiga.

https://www.youtube.com/watch?v=fsOO5wlGl70

Structure

AmigaBASIC belonged to the first BASIC versions, which got along without line numbers and made a structured programming possible in rudiments and was derived from the somewhat older Macintosh BASIC of Microsoft. For changeovers, which knew so far other BASIC dialects, the integrated development environment as well as the structure of the language were trend-setting. Problematic however was the assumption of existing BASIC programs. It turned out however very fast that the extensive possibilities of the Commodore Amiga could be used only insufficiently – although Microsoft supplied AmigaBASIC with a library particularly co-ordinated with the Amiga. It was possible to access the system libraries from BASIC – but working with them from AmigaBASIC proved to be very awkward and error-prone. For example, the HAM mode could only be accessed under AmigaBASIC with the help of the system libraries.

Possibilities

On this BASIC implementation it was noticeable that the interpreter was no longer an integral part of the operating system as on the previously designed home Computers. In the context of the multitasking system, it ran as an equal program in the window system of the user interface and consequently had to be started first before it was available as a runtime environment or development system for programs.

AmigaBASIC broke new ground by abandoning line numbers and allowed the definition of SUB routines and even function calls with arguments and return values. Thus AmigaBASIC programs became clearer than those for example of GW-BASIC. The BASIC dialect was at least partly adapted to the possibilities of the Amiga. So there was the possibility to query the Mouse and a rudimentary possibility of event-driven program control was implemented. The graphic and sound possibilities of the Amiga could also be used – even if only incompletely. With the "say" command the output of synthetic English language was possible.

Limitations and problems

AmigaBASIC was considered to be incomplete in its development, buggy and above all very slow. In some cases the difference to a C or assembler implementation was a factor of 1000. If – which was common at that time – an empty loop with 1000 runs was measured as a short performance test, the value of 800 ms was only slightly below its direct competitor C64 with about 1000 ms. Considering the fact that the underlying CPU was about a factor of 10 faster, this was a more than disappointing result. It was also irritating that the interpreter initially offered no more than 10,000 or 25,000 bytes of available BASIC memory – significantly less than on a C64 in basic configuration. An Amiga 1000 offered 256 kB or (extended) 512 kB, four to eight times the memory of its competitor, so one would have expected much more.

When Amigas with memory beyond the megabyte limit became available, the BASIC memory could be successively increased with the "clear" command. However, it turned out that AmigaBASIC was limited to an address space of 24 bits – corresponding to 16 MB of memory – due to its Mac origin. AmigaBASIC programs which used RAM beyond this "artificial" limit were therefore not executable.

In addition, AmigaBASIC suffered from the very bad reputation of the BASIC programming language at that time. Most users therefore quickly turned to C, Assembler or Modula-2, since powerful compiler packages for these languages were available for the Amiga and it was only possible to fully exploit the capabilities of the hardware and the operating system in this way. Several times third party manufacturers tried to enhance the importance of the BASIC language by a compiler (e.g. HiSoft Basic Compiler, GFA-BASIC or MaxonBASIC), but always only with moderate success. The final "death sentence" for AmigaBASIC were however license cost problems with the manufacturer Microsoft.

Meaning

Even if some impressive programs were developed with AmigaBASIC, this BASIC dialect never played a commercial role. Nevertheless AmigaBASIC is also a symbol for a time, in which listings were still typed from magazines, in order to get so at small programs or simple games. Old, possibly beloved, AmigaBASIC programs can be ported to QBasic or with a little more effort to FreeBASIC.

Further development to the freeware compiler "ACE-Basic

ACE is an extended AmigaBASIC compiler, which together with the freeware tools A68K (assembler) and Blink (linker) can create executable programs on its own. Based on the syntax of AmigaBASIC, it is possible to create programs which fully exploit the capabilities of the Intuition programming environment under AmigaOS and which can beat the interpreted AmigaBASIC in execution speed by far. This compiler was created by the Australian David Benn, Launceston, Tasmania. It is published under the GNU General Public License. The current version 2.4 (September 17, 1996) is available on Aminet as a download, see this Weblink http://aminet.net/package/dev/basic/ace24dist

Literature

The AmigaOS versions which came with AmigaBASIC had a manual included which explained the functionality in form of a reference. Remarkably, it contained the only ASCII table published by the manufacturer which represented the complete character set (modified ISO 8859-1), which was otherwise missing in the official book series "The Amiga ROM Kernel

Manual". Especially in the years between 1986 and 1991 a lot of literature about programming in this language was published, some of which is still available in retro bookshops today.

9.3.2: Beginners guide to Amiga Basic

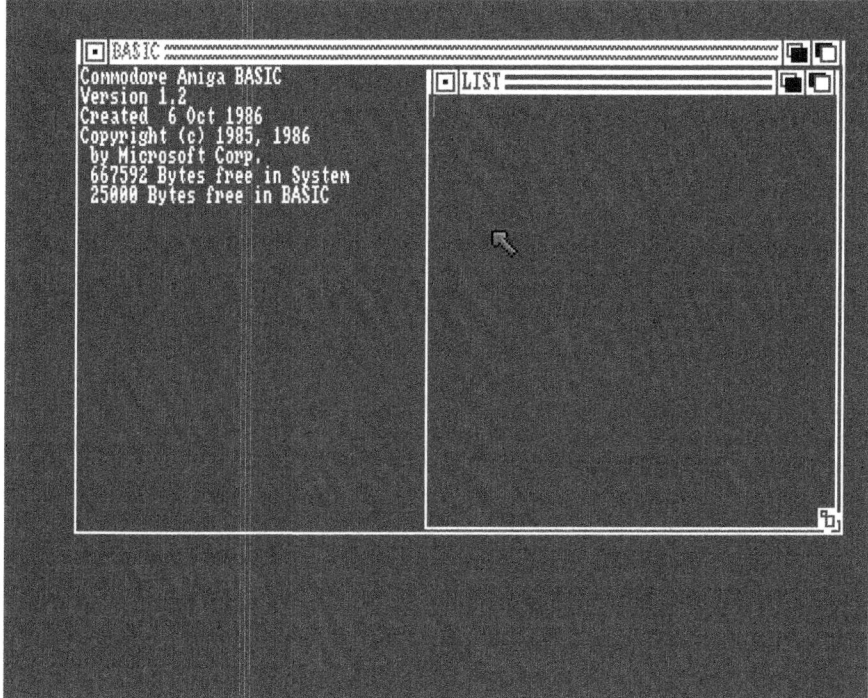

There is a very good tutorial the "Beginners guide to Amiga Basic" written by my friend Mikael Lundin.

https://blog.mikaellundin.name/2016/02/03/beginners-guide-to-amiga-basic.html

It learns you step by step to program in Amiga Basic.

The full text with pictures will be available in the THEA500 Big Book.

Here you will find another very good source that is more for advanced programming: http://www.pjhutchison.org/basic/basic.html

9.4: Disk Images & File Formats

See also: "7.4: Transfer original Amiga disks" on page 258

.adf: Amiga Disk File (ADF) is a file format used by Amiga Computers and emulators to store images of floppy disks. It has been around almost as long as the Amiga itself, although it was not initially called by any particular name. Before it was known as ADF, it was used in commercial game production, backup and disk virtualization. ADF is a track-by-track dump of the disk data as read by the Amiga operating system, and so the "format" is really fixed-width AmigaDOS data tracks appended one after another and held in a file. This file would, typically, be formatted, like the disk, in Amiga Old File System (OFS).

ADF-Files are directly supported till Firmware 1.1.1.

.adz: An ADZ file is an ADF file that has been compressed with gzip. The typical file extension is .adz, derived from .adf.gz

.dms: the DISK-Masher (SDS Software). The Disk Masher System was a method used on the Amiga to create a compressed image of a floppy disk. The floppy disks were read in block by block, retaining their data structure. The DMS was especially popular in the demoscene and the warez-scene, because with this system disk images could be easily distributed in mailbox networks or generally via dial-up.

.fdi: FDI (from Formatted Disk Image) is a universal disk image file format specification originally published by Vincent Joguin in 2000. The FDI format is publicly documented, and accompanied by open source access tools. Because the format can store raw low-level data, as is for example required to support copy protection schemes and other non-standard formats, FDI files can be larger than disk image files in other formats. The typical file extension is .fdi. Because of the universal design of the FDI format, files in other disk image formats, such as ADF, ADZ and DMS, can in theory be converted to FDI.

.ipf: The ADF file format can only store disks that have legal AmigaDOS format tracks. Disks with non-standard tracks may be available in ADF format, albeit cracked in order to create a regular AmigaDOS volume. However, the Amiga itself was not limited to storing data in these standard tracks. The Amiga's floppy disk Controller was very basic but transparent, and for that reason very flexible allowing disks of other and custom formats to be read and written as well. Disk handling is not locked down like the one in a modern PC, and so most of the work to read and write disks is done by the operating system itself. However, because programmers did not have to use the operating system routines, it was quite normal for games developers to create their own disk formats and also apply many different sorts of copy protection. As it was, most full-price commercial Amiga games had some form of custom disk format and/or copy protection on them. For this reason, most commercial Amiga games cannot be stored in ADF files unaltered, but there is an alternative called Interchangeable Preservation Format (IPF) which was specifically designed for this purpose.

The Software Preservation Society Interchangeable Preservation Format (.IPF) is an open format for which the source code of the official library is available.

.jst: This is some sort of archive file for a tool that installs any NONDOS games just as WHDLoad, but is older. Jst normally require only ORGINAL versions of the games to work.

.whd file is a WinUAEX WHDLoad Settings. WinUAEX is an Amiga 500/1200/CD32 emulator ported from WinUAE.

9.5: Archive Files

Tip: With the first Firmware 1.0 the Mini supports only .lha file, and with the update to 1.1.1 additional the .lzh archives.

.pp: Powerpacker (Nico François). Power Packer is a well-known and powerful compression program. The clear graphical interface allows you to quickly select and compress files using the Mouse. The compressed file can then be executed directly without having to unpack it first. In addition, files that have already been compressed with other compression tools can be unpacked and compressed again in Power Packer format (repack).

.lha/.lhz: lha (Stephan Boberg). LHa designates a compression program family for file archiving. The associated file format LZH is based on the LZHUFF procedure, in which first with the Lempel-Ziv-Storer-Szymanski algorithm (LZSS) repeating sections of a data stream are deduplicated and in the second step with an entropy coding after Huffman still more strongly compressed. The widely used Deflate algorithm was derived from the LHa sources.

.lzx: LZX is an LZ77 family compression algorithm. It is also the name of a file archiver with the same name. Both were invented by Jonathan Forbes and Tomi Poutanen in 1990s.

9.6: Picture Files

Even though THEA500 Mini cannot display images, the most popular image formats are presented here.

.iff: The Interchange File Format (IFF) was introduced in 1985 by the Electronic Arts company as a standard file format in their products. It is actually a whole family of file formats characterized by the common TLV structure (abbreviation for Type-Length-Value).

Know types:

- IFF-ILBM InterLeaved BitMap: IFF-ACBM Amiga Continuous BitMap: HAM6/HAM8, EHB, IFF24
- IFF-DEEP : XiPaint
- IFF-RGB8/RGBN : TurboSilver (Impulse)
- IFF-SHAM, IFF-DHAM/DHIRES
- IFF-YUVN : VLab (Macrosystems Computer GMBH)
- IFF-DCOL : Direct color
- IFF-PCHG : Palette change.
- IFF-PBM : Deluxe-PaintIle (PC version)
- IFF-RGFX : Retargetable Graphics

.lbm: is an image file format that conforms to the IFF (Interchange File Format) standard. The format originated on the Amiga platform and on IBM-compatible systems. Files in this format or the associated PBM (Planar Bitmap) format usually appear in games of the late 1980s and early 1990s that were either Amiga ports or whose graphical elements were designed on Amiga machines.

A characteristic feature of the format is that it stores bitmaps in the form of nested bitplanes, which gives the format its name. This reflects the way Amiga graphics hardware reads graphics data natively from memory. A simple form of compression is supported to make ILBM files more compact.

On the Amiga, these files are not associated with any particular file extension. However, when used on PC systems where extensions are used systematically, they used a .lbm or occasionally a .bbm extension.

.svg: SGX (SGX Graphics File Format) is a raster graphics format associated with the SView line of Amiga graphics software (SuperView, SView, SViewNG, SViewII, SViewIV, SView5) developed by Andreas Kleinert. Older versions of the format are also known as SVG, or SuperView Graphics.

9.7: Animation Files

If you ever will come across a file with the ending .anim, here is the explanation:

.anim: This is a file format, used to store digital movies and Computer generated animations (hence the ANIM name), and is a variation of the ILBM format, which is a subformat of Interchange File Format.

Known Types:
- ANIM-1 (xor)
- ANIM-2 (long delta)
- ANIM-3 (short delta
- ANIM-4 (general delta)
- ANIM-5 (byte vertical compression)
- ANIM-6 Stereo glasses (Cryogenic Software)
- ANIM-J (Eric Graham's compression)
- ANIM-I (Eric Graham's compression)

9.8: Amiga Filesystems

OFS: Old/Original File System: used with AmigaOS up to and including version 1.3, originally Amiga File System

AFS: The Amiga Fast File System (AFFS, sometimes just FFS or AFS) is the file system of AmigaOS greater than 1.3. This file system is a further development of the original Amiga file system (OFS), which became necessary because the original file system was designed for use on floppy disks and with the spread of hard disks or larger data carriers problems arose with both speed and capacity utilization.

Variants and versions

- AmigaOS knows six different variants or versions of the file system. These can use a block size between 512 bytes and 32 kilobytes, as well as exist as multi-user file system (muFS) called equivalent to AFFS.
- DOS\0 - The original Amiga file system ("OFS," original file system) for floppy disks. It is also called "old" Amiga file system ("OFS," old file system).
- DOS\1 – The first Amiga "Fast File System" (FFS or AFFS). This first version cannot correctly convert diacritical characters in file names between upper and lower case.
- DOS\2 – Bugfix for the first AFFS (DOS\1) to handle accented (diacritical) characters correctly, and thus first international version.
- DOS\3 – The international "Amiga Fast File System."
- DOS\4 – Amiga FFS with directory cache, which however only worked well on floppy disks.
- DOS\5 – Amiga FFS with directory cache also for hard disks.[1]

IceFS: Optional freeware file system for MorphOS

JXFS: File system under AmigaOS as of version 4.1

PFS (Professional File System): An AmigaOS file system originally developed commercially for the Amiga in 1995 by Michiel Pelt. It is available today on Aminet under BSD license. PFS shows good performance due to the simplicity of its design and is a compatible successor to Ami-Filesafe.

Divided into two main sections, metadata is stored at the beginning, consisting of a root block and a generic set of blocks. The rest is another contiguous generic array of blocks where the actual data is stored.

The metadata is stored in a tree structure of individual blocks. The entire data structure is stored in the metadata, so the data part contains only "real" data. The metadata describes the location of the data (in files) with the associated addresses of blocks, which makes the metadata very compact.

When a metadata update occurs, the system copies the metadata block to be changed into a newly allocated block in the metadata section with the changes made, and then recursively changes the metadata in the original block in the same way. Finally, if the root block must also be changed, this results in an "atomic" metadata update.

The degree of file fragmentation is comparatively small.

As the first Amiga file system where the concept of the "recycle bin" was natively integrated on file system level, it keeps the last deleted files in a hidden directory of the (root) hard disk. PFS V5.3 was developed in C and a small amount of assembler code.

SFS (Amiga Smart File System): Applicable from AmigaOS 3.x, standard file system under MorphOS. It is a journaling filesystem used on Amiga Computers and AmigaOS-derived operating systems (though some support also exists for IBM PC compatibles). It is designed for performance, scalability and integrity, offering improvements over standard Amiga filesystems as well as some special or unique features.

SFS is written in C and was originally created and released as freeware in 1998 by John Hendrikx. After the original author left the Amiga scene in 2000, the source code to SFS was released and its development continued by Ralph Schmidt in MorphOS.

Since May 2005 SFSobjec and SFSconfig are available under the GPL license. SFS development has now forked; as well as the original Amiga version, there are now versions for MorphOS, AROS, AmigaOS 3, and a version for AmigaOS 4, which have different feature sets but remain compatible to each other. In addition, there is a driver for Linux to read (experimental to write) Amiga SFS volumes, GRUB natively supports it, and there are free drivers to use it from UEFI.

As of 2008, SFS was one of the independent filesystems still being used on Amiga Computers.

Versions for AROS, AmigaOS and MorphOS are based on different branches. The Linux version is independent code.

RDB: In computing, a rigid disk block (RDB) is the block on a hard disk where the Amiga series of Computers store the disk's partition and filesystem information. The IBM's PC equivalent of the Amiga's RDB is the master boot record (MBR).

Unlike its PC equivalent, the RDB doesn't directly contain metadata for each partition. Instead, it points to a linked list of partition blocks, which contain the actual partition data. The partition data includes the start, length, filesystem, boot priority, buffer memory type and "flavor", though the latter was never used. Because there is no limitation in partition block count, there is no need to distinguish primary and extended types and all partitions are equal in stature and architecture.

Additionally, it may point to additional filesystem drivers, allowing the Amiga to boot from filesystems not directly supported by the ROM, such as PFS or SFS.

The data in the rigid disk block must start with the ASCII bytes "RDSK". Furthermore, its position is not restricted to the very first block of a volume, instead it could be located anywhere within its first 16 blocks. Thus, it could safely coexist with a master boot record, which is forced to be found at block 0.

Nearly all Amiga hard disk Controllers support the RDB standard, enabling the user to exchange disks between Controllers.

9.9: Amiga DOS – The Disk Operation System

AmigaDOS is the disk operating system of the AmigaOS, which includes file systems, file and directory manipulation, the command-line interface, and file redirection.

In AmigaOS 1.x, AmigaDOS is based on a TRIPOS port by MetaComCo, written in BCPL. BCPL does not use native pointers, so the more advanced functionality of the operating system was difficult to use and error-prone. The third-party AmigaDOS Resource Project (ARP, formerly the AmigaDOS Replacement Project), a project begun by Amiga developer Charlie Heath, replaced many of the BCPL utilities with smaller, more sophisticated equivalents written in C and assembler, and provided a wrapper library, arp.library. This eliminated the interfacing problems in applications by automatically performing conversions from native pointers (such as those used by C or assembler) to BCPL equivalents and vice versa for all AmigaDOS functions.

From AmigaOS 2.x onwards, AmigaDOS was rewritten in C, retaining 1.x compatibility where possible. Starting with AmigaOS 4, AmigaDOS abandoned its legacy with BCPL. Starting from AmigaOS 4.1, AmigaDOS has been extended with 64-bit file-access support.

Console

The Amiga console is a standard Amiga virtual device, normally assigned to CON: and driven by console.handler. It was developed from a primitive interface in AmigaOS 1.1, and became stable with versions 1.2 and 1.3, when it started to be known as AmigaShell and its original handler was replaced by newconsole.handler (NEWCON:).

The console has various features that were considered up to date when it was created in 1985, like command template help, redirection to null ("NIL:"), and ANSI color terminal. The new console handler – which was implemented in release 1.2 – allows many more features, such as command history, pipelines, and automatic creation of files when output is redirected. When TCP/IP stacks like AmiTCP were released in the early 1990s, the console could also receive redirection from Internet-enabled Amiga device handlers (e.g., TCP:, copy file TO TCP:Site/Port).

Unlike other systems originally launched in the mid-1980s, AmigaDOS does not implement a proprietary character set; the developers chose to use the ANSI–ISO standard ISO-8859-1 (Latin 1), which includes the ASCII character set. As in Unix systems, the Amiga console accepts only linefeed ("LF") as an end-of-line ("EOL") character. The Amiga console has support for accented characters as well as for characters created by combinations of ‚dead keys' on the Keyboard.

Case sensitivity

AmigaDOS is in general case-insensitive.[7] Indicating a device as "Dh0:", "DH0:" or "dh0:" always refers to the same partition; however, for file and directory names, this is filesystem-dependent, and some filesystems allow case sensitivity as a flag upon formatting. An example of such a file system is Smart File System. This is very convenient when dealing with software ported over from the mostly case-sensitive Un*x world, but causes much confusion for native Amiga applications, which assume case insensitivity. Advanced users will hence typically only use the case sensitivity flag for file systems used for software originating from Un*x.

Re-casing of file, directory and volume names is allowed using ordinary methods; the commands "rename foo Foo" and "relabel Bar: bAr:" are valid and do exactly what is expected, in contrast to for example on Linux, where "mv foo Foo" results in the error message "mv: `foo' and `Foo' are the same file" on case-insensitive filesystems like VFAT.

Volume naming conventions

Partitions and physical drives are typically referred to as DF0: (floppy drive 0), DH0: (hard drive 0), etc. However, unlike many operating systems, outside of built-in physical hardware devices like DF0: or HD0:, the names of the single disks, volumes and partitions are totally arbitrary: for example a hard disk partition could be named Work or System, or anything else at the time of its creation. Volume names can be used in place of the corresponding device names, so a disk partition on device DH0: called Workbench could be accessed either with the name DH0: or Workbench:. Users must indicate to the system that "Workbench" is the volume "Workbench:" by always typing the colon ":" when they are entering information in a requester form or into AmigaShell.

If an accessed volume name cannot be found, the operating system will prompt the user to insert the disk with the given volume name, or allow the user to cancel the operation.

In addition, logical device names can be set with the "assign" command to any directory or device; programs often assigned a virtual volume name to their installation directory (for instance, a fictional word processor called Writer might assign **Writer:** to DH0:Productivity/Writer). This allows for easy relocation of installed programs. The default name SYS: is used to refer to the volume that the system was booted from. Various other default names are provided to refer to important system locations. e.g. S: for startup scripts, C: for AmigaDOS commands, FONTS: for installed fonts, etc.

Assignment of volume labels can also be set on multiple directories, which will be treated as a union of their contents. For example, FONTS: might be assigned to SYS:Fonts, then extended to include, for example, Work:UserFonts using the add option of the AmigaDos assign command. The system would then permit use of fonts installed in either directory. Listing FONTS: would show the files from both locations.

Conventions of names and typical behaviour of virtual devices

The physical device DF0: shares the same floppy drive mechanics with PC0:, which is the CrossDOS virtual device capable of reading PC formatted floppy disks. When any PC formatted floppy disk is inserted into the floppy drive, then the DF0: floppy Amiga icon will change to indicate that the disk is unknown to the normal Amiga device, and it will show four question marks ???? as the standard "unknown" volume name, while the PC0: icon will appear revealing the name of the PC formatted disk. Any disk change with Amiga formatted disks will invert this behaviour.

File systems

AmigaDOS supports various filesystems and variants. The first filesystem was simply called Amiga FileSystem, and was suitable mainly for floppy disks, because it did not support automatic booting from hard disks (on floppy, booting was done using code from the bootblock). It was soon replaced by FastFileSystem (FFS), and hence the original filesystem was known by the name of "Old" FileSystem (OFS). FFS was more efficient on space and quite measurably faster than OFS, hence the name.

With AmigaOS 2.x, FFS became an official part of the OS and was soon expanded to recognise cached partitions, international partitions allowing accented characters in file and partition names, and finally (with MorphOS and AmigaOS 4) long filenames, up to 108 characters (from 31).

Both AmigaOS 4.x and MorphOS featured a new version of FFS called FastFileSystem 2. FFS2 incorporated all of the features of the original FFS including, as its author put it, "some minor changes". In order to preserve backwards compatibility, there were no major structural changes. (However, FF2 on AmigaOS 4.1 differs in that it can expand its features and capabilities with the aid of plug-ins). As with FFS2, the AmigaOS 4 and MorphOS version of Smart FileSystem is a fork of original SFS and are not 100% compatible with it.

Other filesystems like FAT12, FAT16, FAT32 from Windows or ext2 from Linux are available through easily installable (drag and drop) system libraries or third party modules such as FAT95 [8] (features read/write support), which can be found on the Aminet software repository. MorphOS 2 has built-in support for FAT filesystems.

AmigaOS 4.1 adopted a new filesystem called JXFS capable to support partitions over a terabyte of size.

Alternate filesystems from third-party manufacturers include Professional FileSystem, which is a filesystem with an easy structure, based on metadata, allowing high internal coherence, capable of defragmenting itself on the fly, and does not require to be unmounted before being mounted again; and Smart FileSystem which is a journaling filesystem which performs journaled activities during system inactivities, and has been chosen by MorphOS as its standard filesystem.

Official variants of Amiga filesystems (more information in chapter "Amiga Filesystems")

- Old File System/Fast File System
- OFS (DOS0)
- FFS (DOS1)
- OFS International (DOS2)

9: Amiga Operation System

- FFS International (DOS3)
- OFS Directory Caching (DOS4)
- FFS Directory Caching (DOS5)
- Fast File System 2 (AmigaOS4.x/MorphOS)
- OFS Long filenames (DOS6)
- FFS Long filenames (DOS7)

Both DOS6 and DOS7 feature International filenames featured in DOS2 and DO3, but not Directory Caching, which was abandoned due to bugs in the original implementation. DOS4 and DOS5 are not recommended for use for this reason.

Dostypes are backwards compatible with each other, but not forward compatible. A DOS7 formatted disk cannot be read on original Amiga FFS, and a DOS3 disk cannot be read on a KS1.3 Amiga. However, any disk formatted with DOS0 using FFS or FFS2 can be read by any version of the Amiga operating system. For this reason, DOS0 tended to be the format of choice of software developers distributing on floppy, except where a custom filesystem and bootblock was used – a common practice in Amiga games. Where software needed AmigaOS 2 anyway, DOS3 was generally used.

FastFileSystem2 plug-ins

With the July 2007 Update of AmigaOS 4.0 in 2007, the first two plug-ins for FFS2 were

fs_plugin_cache: increases performance of FFS2 by introducing a new method of data buffering.

fs_plugin_encrypt: data encryption plug-in for partitions using the Blowfish algorithm.3

9.10: Guru Meditation

See also: "4.1.1.5: LEDs & Blink codes" on page 36

Guru Meditation

Similar to the "Blue Screen of Death" which shows a system crash on Windows, there is the Guru Meditation Screen on the Amiga. This evolved from the Joyboard, an early by-product of Amiga Inc. when they made game Controllers, actually more for camouflage. This was intended for surfing and skiing games and required a steady posture. Amiga programmers used it to regain composure after an annoying system crash, and sat cross-legged on it, thus creating the metaphor. The decision to keep this little gag was made because the developers wanted to sell people a pleasant, friendly product. A programmer working with the Amiga should be able to laugh better about lost time and efforts instead of just getting frustrated. This was easier with a wink, which became cult with time, than with the "Software Failure" message Commodore actually wanted. Already AmigaOS 0.9 had WACK, a constantly running debugger that could point out the place in the code where an error had occurred.

```
Software Failure.   Press left mouse button to continue.
         Guru Meditation #00000004.0000AAC0
```

Also it is very unlikely that you will ever see a Guru Meditation on THEA500 Mini, here is a short list of what means what:

The first byte specifies the area of the system affected. The top bit will be set if the error is a dead end alert.

9.11: Open-Source Amiga Operation Systems

MorphOS: Is an AmigaOS-like Computer operating system (OS). It is a mixed proprietary and open source OS produced for the Pegasos PowerPC (PPC) processor based Computer, PowerUP accelerator equipped Amiga Computers, and a series of Freescale development boards that use the Genesi firmware, including the Efika and mobileGT. Since MorphOS 2.4, Apple's Mac mini G4 is supported as well, and with the release of MorphOS 2.5 and MorphOS 2.6 the eMac and Power Mac G4 models are respectively supported. The release of MorphOS 3.2 added limited support for Power Mac G5. The core, based on the Quark microkernel, is proprietary, although several libraries and other parts are open source, such as the Ambient desktop.

https://morphos-team.net/

AROS: A free and open-source multi media centric implementation of the AmigaOS 3.1 application programming interface (API). Designed to be portable and flexible. As of 2021, Ports are available for x86-based and PowerPC-based personal Computers (PCs) in native and hosted flavors, with other architectures in development. In a show of full circle development, AROS was also ported to the Motorola 68000 series (m68k) based Amiga 1200, and there is also an ARM port for the Raspberry Pi series.

http://www.aros.org/

Yes, it is absolutely possible to run Aros on THEA500 mini. But unfortunately, not with the build in ROM. You need to download the ROMs (the second on is the extended ROM for better compatibility).

http://www.aros-platform.de/download.html

And the HDF from the same page. Start the Emulator-Gui a described on page change all CPU settings to highest and turn on JIT, insert the HDF-File and set the ROMs, off you go.

10: THEDemoscene & Demos

For all you sceners out there – Yes most demos are running :)

As long as they fit to the specs of THEA500 Mini, meaning a 68030 at most.

For all the others, here are some examples of technical demonstrations that are computed, rendered, calculated and drawn in real time:

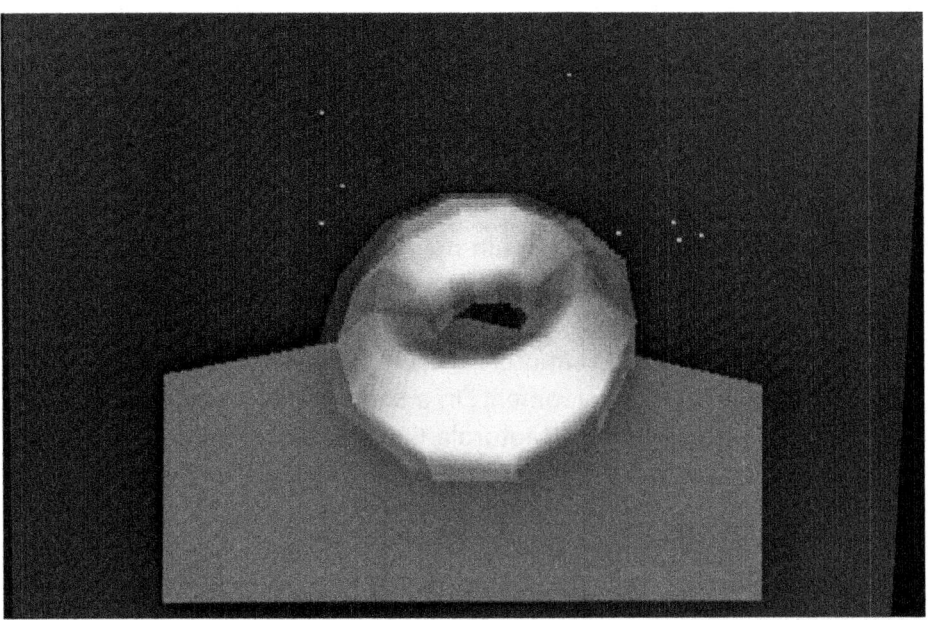

10: THEDemoscene & Demos

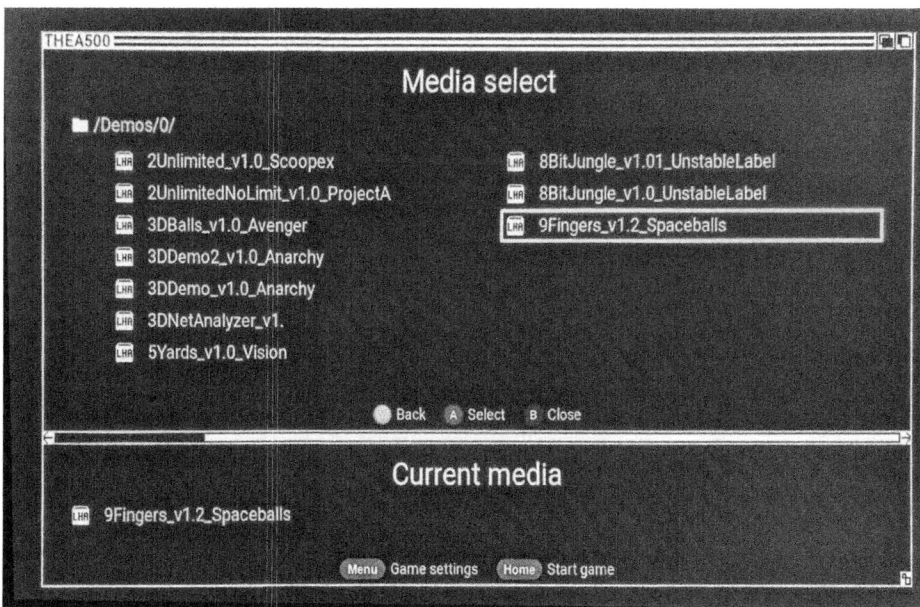

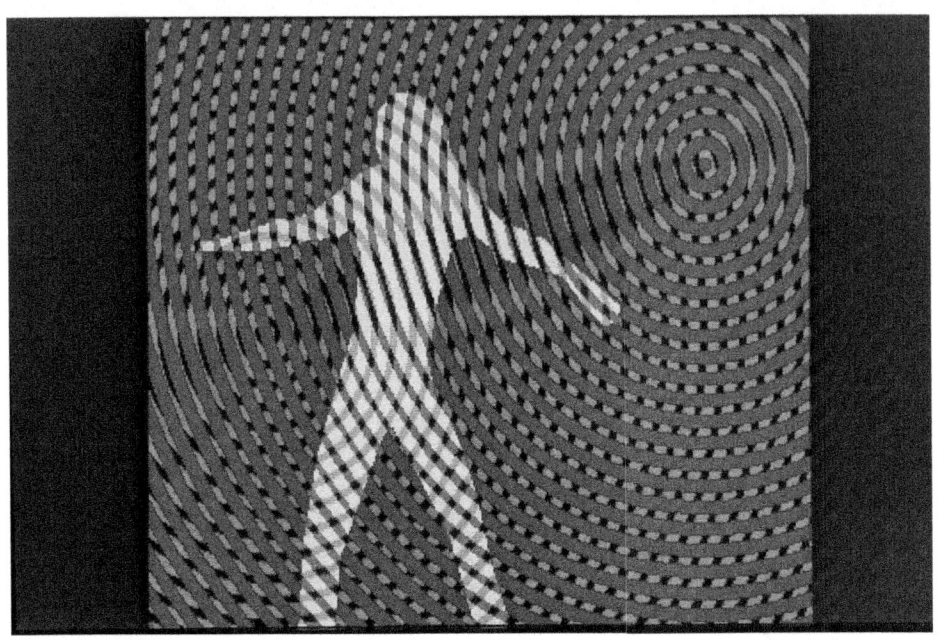

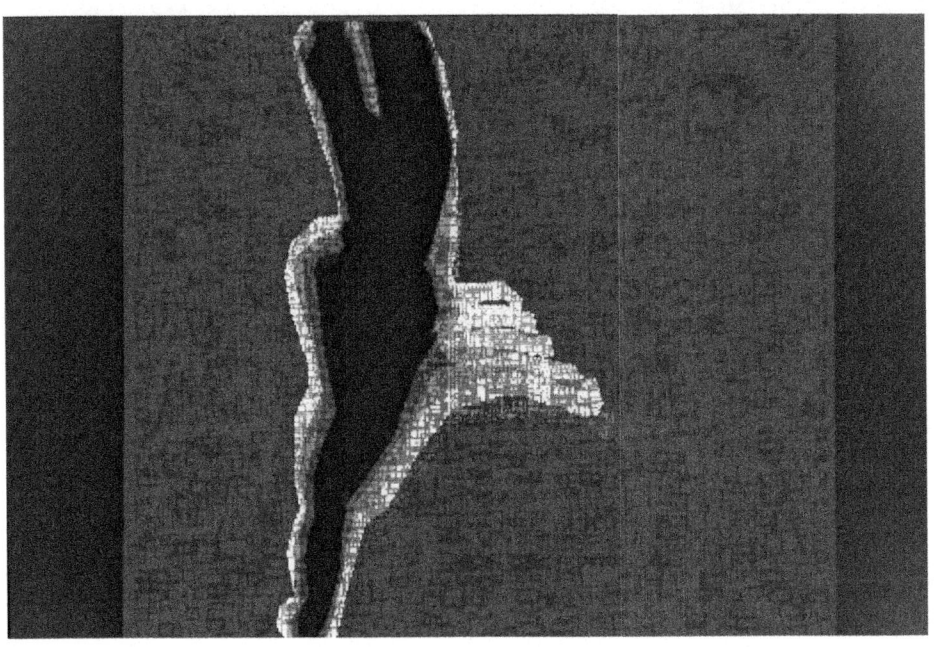

10: THEDemoscene & Demos

This is a wonderful very new demo that shows what a demo can present even if it is just on a PC ;-)

Boing Ball So Crazy: a tribute to the classic Amiga tech demo!

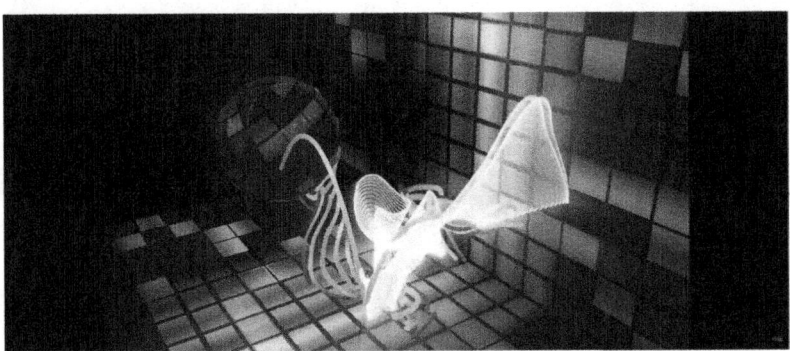

10: THE Demoscene & Demos

The demoscene is a group of people, mainly programmers, graphic artists and musicians, who create digital art on a variety of old and new Computer platforms. Thanks to its multimedia capabilities, the Amiga Computer was immediately embraced by the demoscene, which in turn gave the scene and its culture a high profile. If you're not familiar with demo scene productions, you can think of a demo as compact, self-contained software that combines and demonstrates art and technical excellence. To better understand a demo, remember that everything you see and hear in a demo is generated in real time by Computer code (there is no pre-rendered animation) and that the code itself is relatively compact (which is part of the challenge). Unlike a game, there is no interaction in a demo: just start the demo and sit back and enjoy. All demos are available for download and via YouTube for direct viewing!

1984-1986

In the beginning there was the C64, and it didn't take long until the first cracker groups formed, like "German Cracking Service", "Dynamic Duo" or "Triad". This was at a time when it was just current to switch from datasette to 5.25" discs, and cartridges had long been "out" again. The demoscene was also emerging, and when the Amiga appeared, a whole flood of scene programmers migrated to this new "wonder machine", especially a lot of cracker groups, such as "HQC", or "Red Sector". At that time, even according to many groups, there was a "fair" competition – everyone respected each other, and everything was blissful.

Other groups active on the Commodore 64 at that time were for example "Teeside Cracking Service", "Fairlight", "DCS", "Scottish Cracking Crew", "1001-Crew", "Future Projects", "FSW", "Danish Gold", "Hotline", "Radwar", "ECA", "Jabba", "Commando Frontiers", "Headbanger", "Ultraforce", "Eagle Soft Incorporated" and last but not least "Red Sector (inc.)", which should belong once to the quite big ones in the scene. Finally, the famous "Demomaker" was created in cooperation with "Data Becker".

1987-1989

Well, the time of copy-parties and mailing was over, if you wanted to be a real "scener", you got a modem to offer your "warez" and "cracks" on several boards at once. The scene on the Amiga flourished, the most important groups at that time were "Bamiga Sector One", "Skyline", "Kent Team", "Bitstoppers", "Defjam", "The Star Frontiers", "The Jungle Command", "Trilogy", and not to forget the really big ones of that time, "Quartex", "Paranoimia", "Fairlight" and "Vision Factory".

10: THEDemoscene & Demos

Besides, "normal" cracking was out – those who thought something of themselves and wanted to offer better "customer service" provided their cracks with "trainers". It all started with the C64, back then you could crack programs with "PEEK" and "POKE", especially the freezer modules were very popular at that time: Once you had the address where the number of lives was stored, you could freeze the program at any time and change this value at will. Of course, not everyone has a freezer and the cumbersome input of numbers is not exactly the real thing – so you build a trainer into your intro. There you can set infinite life or energy at the touch of a button – and the once so difficult game no longer caused any problems or headaches.

Among the demos we should mention: The "Star Frontiers" and the "Silents" started with their first intros and scrollers on the Amiga, slowly real demos developed out of it: The groups "Northstar" and "Fairlight" presented their "Megademos", as well as "Alcatraz", and "Phenomena". Mostly, however, they were "only" intros again. It became really interesting only in 1989: Again it was "Phenomena", the "Pure Metal Coders", "Scoopex", and the

"Silents" who coded most of the demos, legendary has become the "RSI-Megademo".

While on the C64 the scene threatened to die several times, it developed splendidly on the Amiga. "Red Sector" and "Tristar" merge to "TRSi", new groups like "Skid Row", "Paradox" and "Crystal" emerge and a turning point occurs for the first time: The scene becomes tougher, meaning it becomes more difficult for individuals to hold their own. Many groups join forces to have a better international presence (e.g. "Skid Row and Valhalla", "Genesis and Angels", "DefJam and CCS", etc.). The 14,400 modems are becoming widespread thanks to price drops, and some groups are already starting to buy members from others – welcome to the market economy.

A further development in the field of game cracks was initiated by the group "Subway": The Mega Trainers. Via comfortable menus you could not only set infinite continues, but also change the configuration of the starting weapons, "Subway" even went so far as to add new weapons (e.g. in "Midnight Resistance") and furthermore the trainers were always given numbers, depending on how many trainer options you could select. The famous "key functions" also came from Subway, so you could jump from level to level in the game by pressing a button, or just quickly change the armament, and much more. The record for the variety of options was held for a long time by "Midnight Resistance +38", to be replaced later by "Xenon2 +281".

Nevertheless, the crackers became increasingly lazy and if they didn't steal each other's scroll routines and sounds, they stole them from commercial games – "Oracle" built the music of "Unreal" into its intros, in the "Rock-n-Roll" crack of "Subway" you can clearly hear the in-game music of "Battle Squadron". New groups emerged for the first time, like "Horizon" or the "Black Monks", "Quartex" didn't quite make it back, then there were "Anthrax", the "Accumulators", "Venture", "Alpha Flight", "Genesis", and so many others I'd rather not list.

Demoscene parties are a combination of friendship, beer, programming contest – even live ones, seminars, a lot of music, graphics (did I mention beer already?), realtime Computer animations, and most of all at lot of fun.

Here are some impression if the biggest European Party called Revision held in Saarbrücken Germany in the famous E-Werk:

10: THEDemoscene & Demos

10: THEDemoscene & Demos

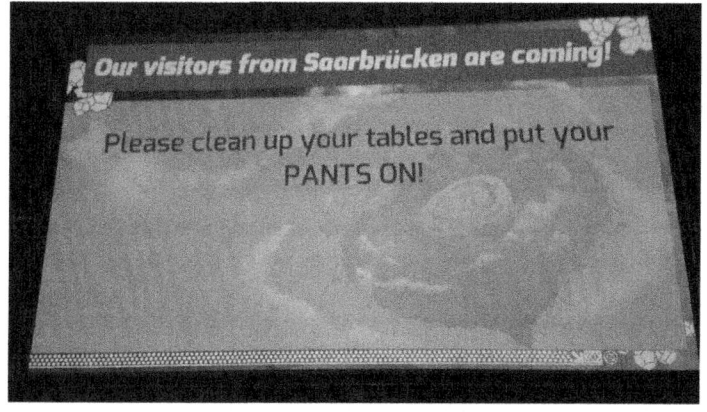

1995-1997

Furthermore, at that time, the "CDTV" and the "LaserDisc" system were just coming out – but both flopped, despite promising forecasts. At that time, people didn't know what to do with the term "multimedia". At least they were spared from the crackers, quite the opposite to the consoles, where the first "game doctors" were soon imported from the Far East. With this you could suck the content of a cartridge onto a floppy disk and thus almost nothing stood in the way of a crack, because who would have thought that a cartridge would need copy protection?

In the demoscene there were the "Pure Metal Coders", who had the most releases around the year 1990, the "Kefrens" with their graphically outstanding "Guardian Dragon". And finally the "Silents", an absolute top group, known for demos like "Hardwired" (in co-production with the also quite well known "Crionics") or "Xpose", the groups "Sanity" or "Melon-Design", the well-known "Razor 1911", not to forget Eric Schwartz with his "Flip The Frog" – demos, although he can't really be counted to the scene. Alcatraz" took the cake with their "Odyssey" demo, which was released on 5 disks and lasted 45 minutes (!), telling the story of the space hero Zork, who is looking for a miracle weapon against evil aliens. Understandably, this demo reached the first place on "The Party" in 1991.

The "most successful" cracker group of the past years, "Skid Row", disbanded in 1993. Many groups split or expanded their horizons now. However, the scene somehow fades into the background in 1995, the time of free demos and buggigen betas is approaching. Thanks to the new medium CD-ROM we now get a lot of junk software very quickly. While at the end of 1995 the illegal business with CD-ROMs blossoms at the PC (here for example the Twilight-CDs would be to be called) also still the last remaining disk cracker are smoked out mercilessly, as the following letter to a reader, who had advertised harmlessly in a magazine, clarifies (a photo was naturally also attached to the letter):

My name is Tanja and I am almost 16 years old. I am about 170cm tall and weigh 65 kilos. Tell me, don't you sometimes have the feeling that a Computer takes all your pocket money out of your purse? They want almost 7DM for a few labels, and then there are only 25 of them. At my age, I get less than I'm entitled to anyway, because as a smoker I have to make do with 50.00DM a month, which is pretty steep, isn't it? So much for my person, now for my software list...

Tanja is in reality maybe Hans-Jürgen, wears black horn-rimmed glasses, full beard, broad neck and a search warrant in her pocket. In another letter she is only almost 15, has lost 10 kilos and is still dancing (apart from copying games) – for that she gets 20 Marks less pocket money. Well, what's the use of storming the room of a 12 year old little pirate and looting his beloved 500 including accessories, while somewhere else CDs with tons of pirated soft are burned like on an assembly line? Anyway, let's turn to the demoscene:

Groups like "Andromeda", "Spaceballs" and "Arnarchy" are appearing and the demos are getting nicer and more colorful. Nevertheless, many still run on all Amigas – from 1MB – of course. The many pixelated graphics and the honestly made sounds, a feast for the eyes, a feast for the ears. Especially the demo group "Sanity" creates a good reputation with their really nicely done "Arte" demos, also "TRSi" did very well everywhere. Here for example the demo "Wicked Sensation" should be mentioned, which reached place 1 at the WoC (no joke!), just ahead of "Sanity" with "WoC.". Furthermore "TRSi-Recordz", a music-label, on which the really excellent Cyberlogik-CDs were released, was founded. The "Cryptoburners" release a few versions of the famous "Protracker".

Commodore releases the 4000 and the 1200, ushering in a new era: AGA games and demos follow. Finally the CD32 is released, at that time the most promising video console in the world. 32 bit, MPEG module optional, all common CD formats (from PhotoCD to CD-Video) could be played, a new chip called Akiko, which was responsible for the Chunky To Planar conversion, a CD as a game medium – the then current Sega and Nintendo consoles seemed like children's toys in comparison. Furthermore there was a lot (50 games) of first class software for the good part right from the start, in the first weeks twice as many units were sold as today Sony PlayStations (also in the first weeks) were sold, the price was absolutely competitive, there was even a commercial that appeared "CD32-Gamer", everything was fine, if only there hadn't been this bankruptcy...

The medium Internet gains the upper hand and through Aminet demos now find a very wide distribution. Beside some outstanding groups like "Scoopex", "The Black Lotus", "TRSI", "Fairlight", "Abyss", "Complex", "Parallax", and the "Mellow Chips" there are also unknown pseudo-groups like "After Eights", "Warp9" and others, about whose demos one can really only laugh. Stolen graphics, ripped sounds, old routines – "how good that Aminet exists, because there I can finally get rid of my shit" – that's what some of them surely thought when they uploaded their crap. "Is everything shit now after all?"

Not at all. If you look instead at the works like "Pulse" by "Nerve Axis", "Tint" or "Glow" by "TBL", "Cyberlogic" by "Alcatraz and TRSI", or the current releases by the "Mellow Chips", you should be careful not to drool on the Keyboard out of sheer enthusiasm! A 68030/50, 68040/40 or 68040/25 is fully sufficient. If you haven't heard of any of the groups mentioned in this paragraph, you should take a look at the Aminet, darken the light in your room and start one of these demos...

11: THESources & Acknowledgments

Many thanks goes to:

all the authors who with a lot of effort and even more dedication, have worked out and published cheats, tips, tricks, solutions, walkthroughs, screenshots and so on. And to all content that is available under Creative Commons Attribution-ShareAlike and similar.

Special thanks are going to this guys, who gave their knowledge and work to complete this book:

- Mirko Engelhardt
    - https://amigaland.de/amiga-walker
- Marc Breisinger
    - http://www.medien.ifi.lmu.de
- Mikael Lundin
    - https://blog.mikaellundin.name
- Amiga history guide
    - http://amiga.emugaming.com/amigaos10.html
- Workbench nostalgia
    - http://www.gregdonner.org/workbench/
- Amiga history
    - http://www.amigahistory.plus.com
- Big book of Amiga hardware
    - http://www.bigbookofamigahardware.com
- CBM Museum
    - http://cbmmuseum.kuto.de/amiga_500.html
- Amiga Forever
    - https://www.amigaforever.com
- Amiga Wiki
    - https://www.amigawiki.org

11: THE Sources & Acknowledgments

- Amiga News
  - https://amiga-news.de
- Old AGames
  - https://www.old-games.com
- Mingos Commodorepage
  - https://www.mingos-commodorepage.com

Cheats and game tips:

- https://www.4cheaters.de
- https://gamefaqs.gamespot.com
- http://www.mogelpower.de
- https://cheats.extreme-gaming.de
- https://strategywiki.org
- https://www.mobygames.com
- http://www.cheatbook.de/
- https://www.myabandonware.com
- https://www.amigafuture.de
- https://www.lemonamiga.com
- https://www.chaptercheats.com
- https://necretro.org/
- https://www.planetcheats.com
- https://pixabay.com

This book uses texts and pictures form wikimedia and wikipedia und the rights of the CCASS License agreement:

https://en.wikipedia.org/

This is first and foremost a book by a fan for fans and I hope everyone will support it.

Thank you very much.

Also From Holger Weßling

A HOBBYIST'S GUIDE TO THEC64 MINI

Holger Weßling

Printed in Dunstable, United Kingdom

76792563R00201